WWF™

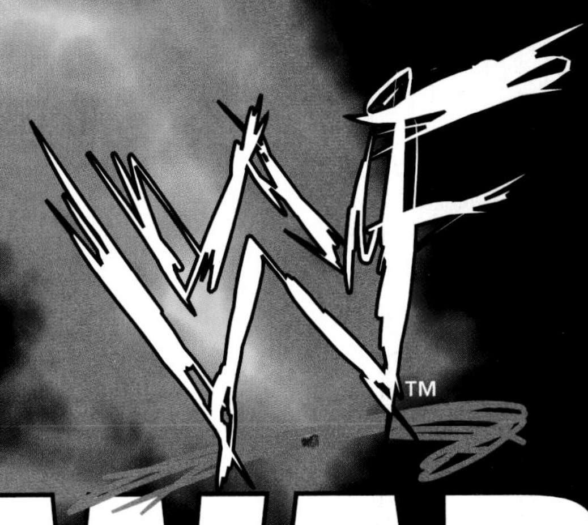

# WAR ZONE™

## OFFICIAL STRATEGY GUIDE

For Nintendo® 64 and PlayStation®

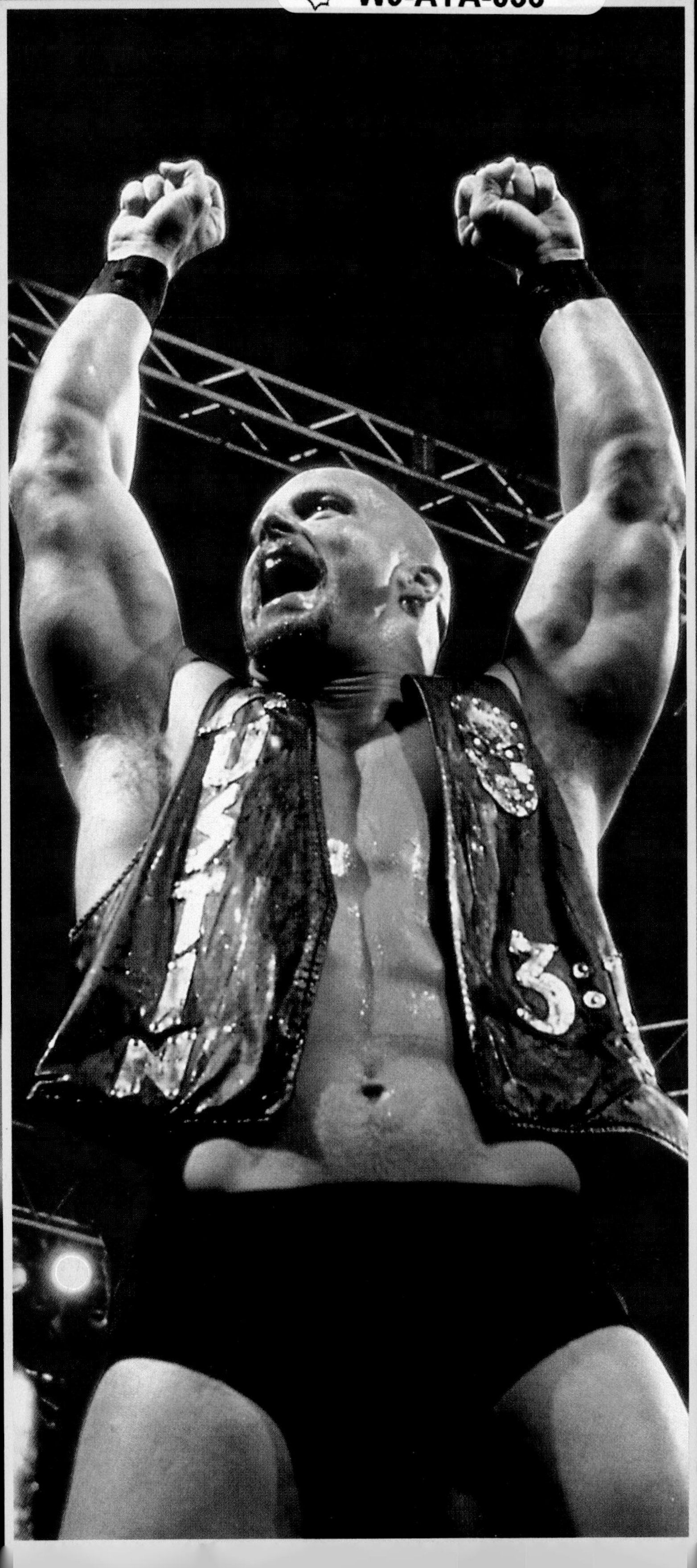

Written by
BILL KUNKEL

Edited by Evan Skolnick

ACCLAIM® SPORTS

# CREDITS

Bill Kunkel
**Writer**

Evan Skolnick
**Editor**

Joe Caponsacco
**Graphic Design**

Kevin Sharkey
**Design Grunt**

Dan Garcia
**Acclaim Marketing**

## Acclaim Publishing

Fabian Nicieza **President/Publisher**
Stacy Lowe **Director of Marketing and Sales**
Alana Zdinak **Director of Manufacturing & Production**
Evan Skolnick **Creative Director**
Joe Caponsacco **Art Director**
Omar Banmally
Michael (Won't borrow money from his friends) Marts **Line Editors**

## WWF War Zone Development Iguana Studios West

**Project Managers:**
Mike Engberg
Vince Bracken

**Associate Manager:**
Clark Westerman

**Project Consultant:**
Rich Reagan

**Designer:**
Tim Huntsman

**Additional Design**
Jeff Robinson
Clark Westerman

**PSX Development :**
John Lund
Justin Towns
Darren Smith
Rob Brannon
Jeremy Howa
Sean Igo

**N64 Development:**
Bruce Gifford
Omar Cannon
Rob Nelson
Scott Pugh
Altair Lane
Chris Braymen

**Lead Artist:**
Jane Bradley

**Artists:**
Paul Boyle
Tom Hudson
Gavin Evertson
Dan Whittington
Chad Lee
Wayne Tyler
Dave Christenson
Lee Phung
Chris Hawkes
Dave Butters
Greg Davis
Jeff Hall

**Motion Editors:**
Jonathan Dansie
Cy Toland
Cameron Burnett
Josh Goodale

**Consultants:**
Bob Tembello
Rod Cousins
Jim Herzner
Jeff Gibson
Mark Schaffer
Jeremy Schwartz

**Game Testing Manager:**
Gary Rowberry

**Game Testers:**
Todd Dowd
Jeff Robinson
Preston Whitney
Ryan McBride
TL Shelton
Greg Murphy

## Acclaim Product Development

**Producer:**
Michael Archer

**Associate Producers:**
Jim Dunn
James Daly
Pete Wanat
Eric Hendrickson

**Marketing Product Manager:**
Michael Jerchower

**Assistant Product Manager:**
Christina Recchio

**Licensing & Packaging Supervisor:**
Maida Lilian

**UK Marketing:**
Frank Sagnier
Theresa Noonan
Ned Browning
Vincent Mercier
Rainer Zipp

**Creative Services:**
Scott Jenkins
Lenny O'Donnell
Terri Ruffino
Beth Pawluk
Jenny Shannon
Sandra Becker

**European Project Supervisor:**
Lisa Koch

**Manager Internet Services:**
Ben Fischbach

**Webmaster:**
Bobby Saha

**Web Graphics Designer:**
Sang-Jin Bae

## Quality Assurance

**Manager:**
Carol Caracciolo

**Supervisors:**
Jeff Rosa
Dale Taylor

**Lead Analysts:**
Eric Hendrickson
Brian Regan

**N64 Game Analysts:**
Bonchi Martinez
Mike Sterzel

**N64 Testers:**
Rich Gomer
Jeremy Pope
Dan Badilla
Ray Yeomans
James Ackermann
Pharoah Sample
Phil Merisier

**PSX Game Analysts:**
Matt McEnerny
John Cyriaque

**PSX Testers:**
Russell Ballenger
Paul DiCarlo
Pharoah Sample
David Campbell
Phil Merisier
Stacy Brickel
Joseph Greene

**Senior Lead Analysts**
James Craddock
Mike Patterson

## Titan Sports:

Jim Bell
Derek Phillips
Michael Foley
Debbie Bonanzio
Vince Russo
Anne Russo
Florence Louis Grand
Tom Pritchard
Peter Pollaco
Jim Ross
Craig Cassenelli

## Special thanks to:

Michael Archer
Tim Huntsman
Derek Phillips
Jeff Rosa
Dale Taylor
JP Carnovale
Brian Regan
Eric Hendrickson
Bonchi Martinez
Mike Sterzel
Matt McEnerney
Rich Gomer
Jeremy Pope
Mark Garone
Peter Ward
Rex Dickson
John Cyriaque

...and, of course,
**Vince McMahon**

# TABLE OF CONTENTS

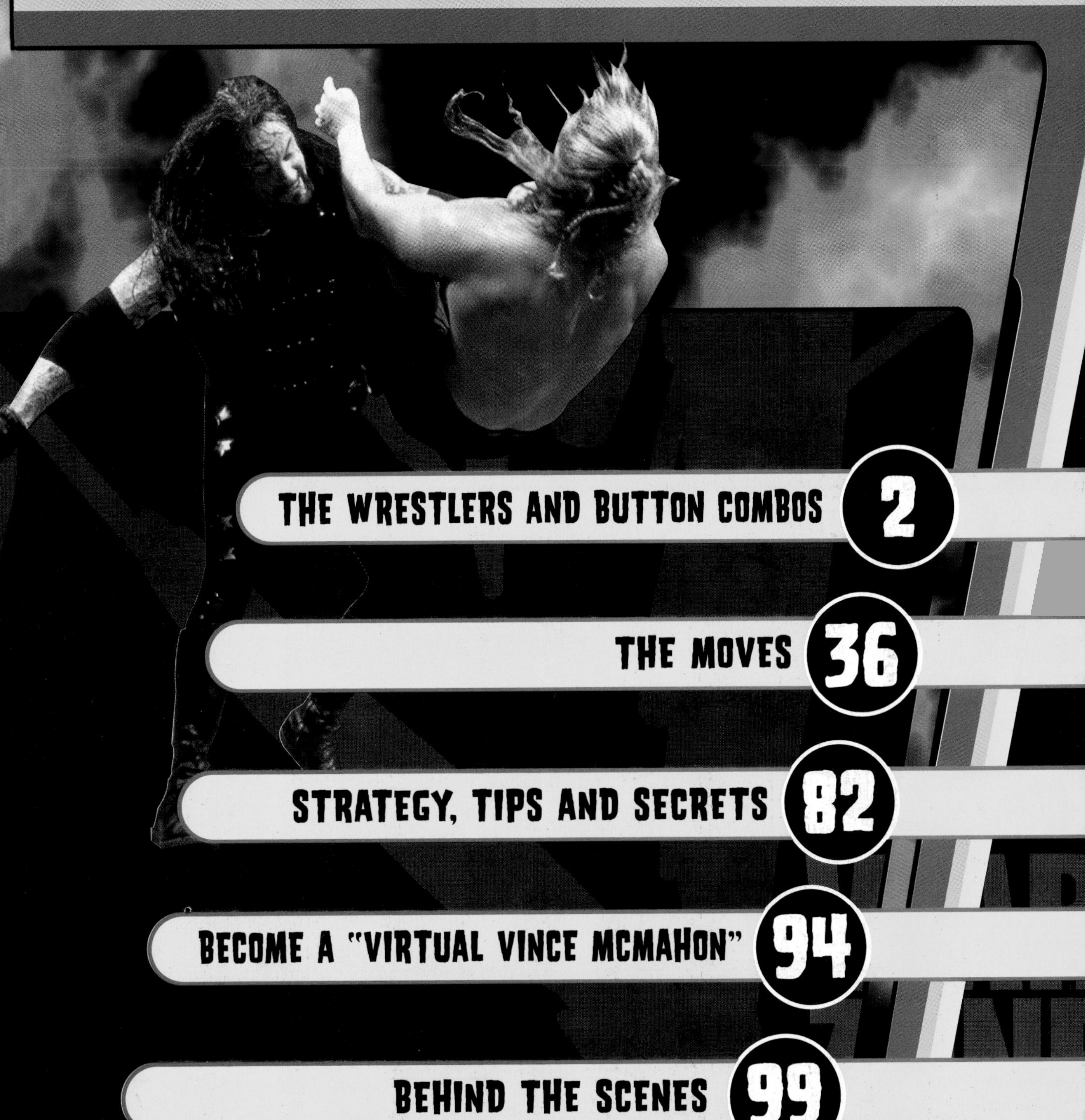

# INTRODUCTION

It was Thanksgiving evening in 1958 that I first discovered the world of professional wrestling. I was eight years old and enjoying the fruits of the earlier day's feast in sandwich form when I looked at the TV and beheld the largest man I'd ever seen. He strode into what looked like a boxing ring wearing a Japanese kimono with long, peroxide blonde hair curling around its silken collar.

The man was Dr. Jerry Graham, just back from the Orient — where he had learned the dreaded Sleeper Hold. I then watched this Sumo-sized man envelop and render unconscious his opponent in a matter of seconds.

I had just had my first taste of the World-Wide Wrestling Federation, the promotion run by Vince McMahon Sr., father of the current kingpin of its enormously popular successor, the World Wrestling Federation. And I was hooked. For decades I watched the likes of Killer Kowalski, Andre the Giant, Bruno Sammartino, Hans Mortier, Haystacks Calhoun, Waldo Von Erich, Freddie Blassie, the Valiant Brothers, Captain Lou, the Grand Wizard, Bobby Davis and a thousand others as they stalked the "squared circle". I even staged wrestling matches in a makeshift ring in the basement with my brothers, sisters and friends.

I was and am, in short, a total sucker for pro wrestling. In the '70s, Arnie Katz and I joined the business, editing and publishing Main Event magazine, which was sold through WWWF arenas from Madison Square Garden to the Philly Spectrum. We also hosted a weekly radio show out of New York, complete with reports on local matches, phone calls from listeners, and interviews with WWWF wrestlers and managers.

Soon, I found myself writing comic books — featuring fantasy wrestlers of a sort — and, in 1978, Arnie and I co-authored the first magazine column to review video and computer games: "Arcade Alley" in Video magazine. By 1981, we had created the original Electronic Games magazine, the world's first newsstand publication devoted to the growing fascination with plugged-in entertainment. Since then, I have never lost my interest in pro wrestling, especially in the World Wrestling Federation. In the mid-'80s, as part of Subway Software, I co-designed the first computer wrestling simulation, MicroLeague WWF Wrestling, and after moving to Las Vegas in 1989, I spent a year co-hosting a local wrestling radio show with Ric "Hotline" Carter and Mike Tenay. And I haven't missed a World Wrestling Federation pay-per-view event since the original Wrestling Classic.

As you might imagine, therefore, the opportunity to write the official Acclaim Strategy Guide for WWF War Zone was as close to a dream project as anything I've ever had the opportunity to do. I've certainly written plenty of strategy guides, but this was wrestling! And what wrestling. WWF War Zone is without doubt the most ambitious, realistic wrestling simulation ever imagined.

So lace up those boots, loosen up your muscles and get ready to step into the ring. And don't forget to hook that leg when you go for a pin!

Bill Kunkel
Las Vegas, NV

Visit the War Zone web site at www.acclaim.net!



**Acclaim Publishing One Acclaim Plaza Glen Cove, NY 11542 Manufactured in the USA ISBN: 1-57840-990-X 2nd printing**

YOU ARE NOW ENTERING THE

WWF™

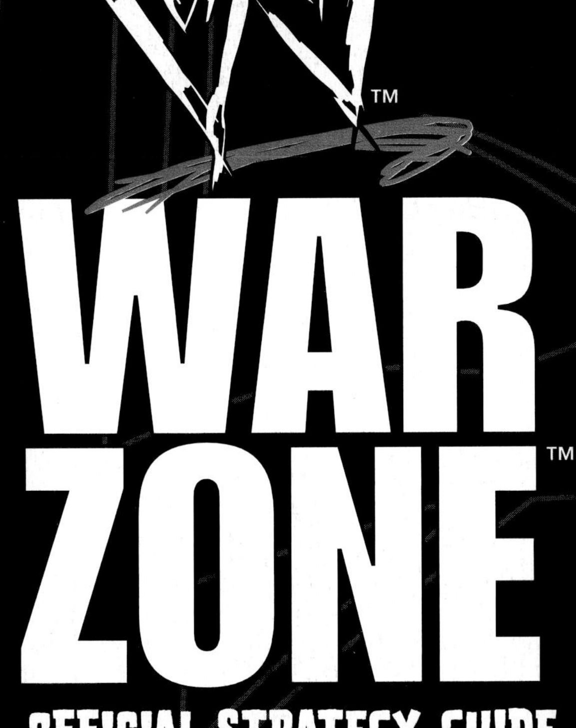

# WAR ZONE™

## OFFICIAL STRATEGY GUIDE

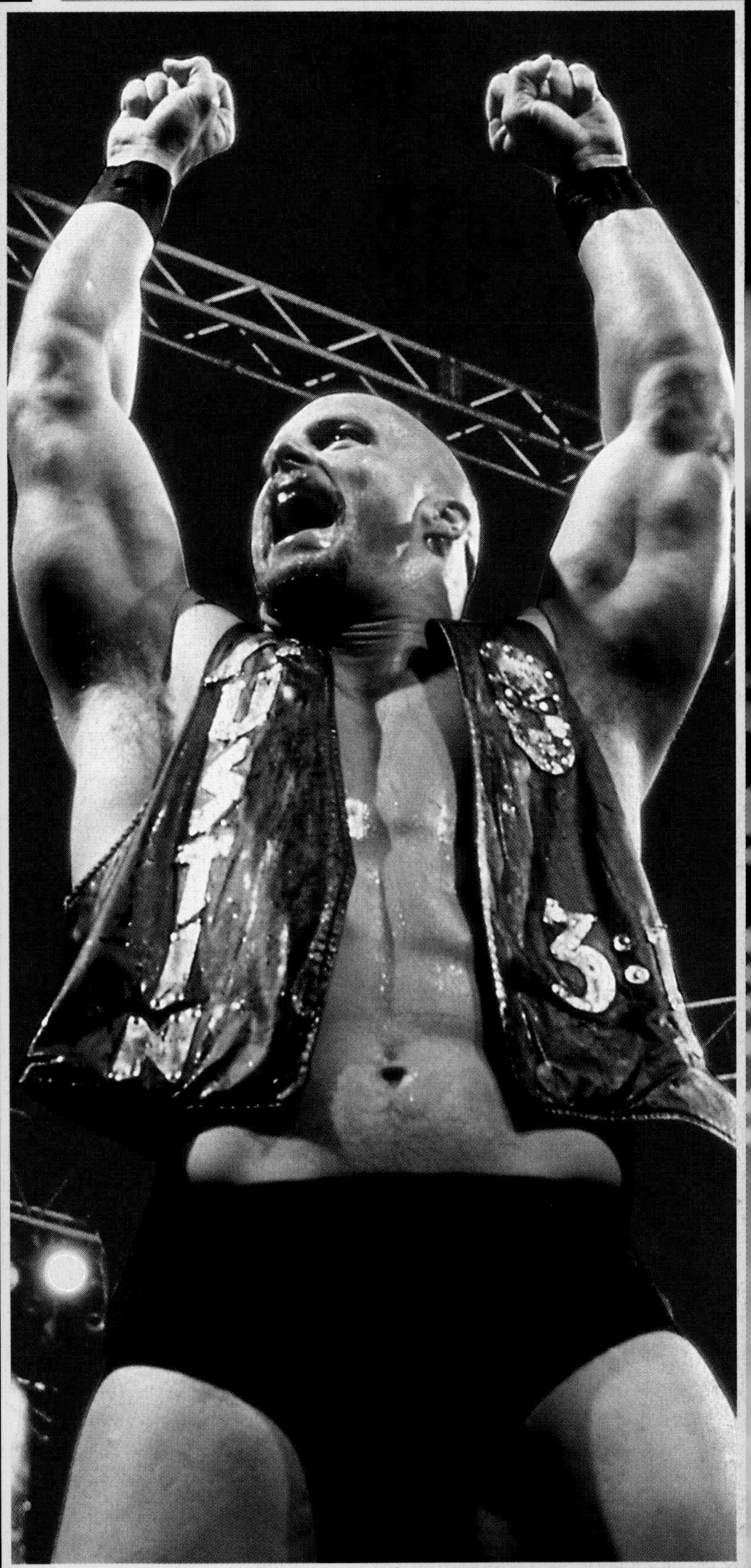

ACCLAIM® SPORTS™

# CHAPTER ONE

# WRESTLERS AND BUTTON COMBOS

This chapter provides a special focus on each of the superstars in WWF War Zone — including how to access the two **"hidden" superstars!**

Each superstar's pages include a biography, general strategy tips and every possible move which that superstar can execute — complete with easy-to-read displays of both the Nintendo64 and PlayStation button combos required to produce those maneuvers. And that includes each supertars's top-secret finishing move!

The object here is to provide you with a blueprint of the superstars you're currently controlling. Keep the appropriate section open while you train with each of the World Wrestling Federation superstars.

# SHARED MOVES LIST (PSX & N64)

## PLAYSTATION

These are moves common to all wrestlers in the game.

### FROM STARTING POSITION

**Punches** Triangle
left,Triangle
**Kicks** Square,
up,Square
**Tie-Up** Circle
**Block** X
**Run** R2
**Whip** left,left,X
**Pose/Flex** Square+Circle
**Taunt** Triangle+X
**Toggle Between Opponents** Tap L2
**Dodge Left** L1
**Dodge Right** R1
**Climb Into/Out of Ring** L2

### FROM A TIE-UP

**Whip** X

### WHEN IN A HOLD

**All Reversals**** X

### GROUND HOLDS -- HEAD

**Pull Opp to feet** Circle

### GROUND HOLDS -- FEET

**Pin Opponent** Circle

### PLAYER IN CORNER

**Climb Turnbuckle** -- Left 2

### OPPONENT IN CORNER

**Turn Opp around in Corner** Circle

### OPPONENT STANDING OUTSIDE RING (WRESTLER INSIDE RING)

**Body Press** Triangle or Circle
**Drop Kick** Square

### OPPONENT ON GROUND OUTSIDE RING (WRESTLER INSIDE RING)

**Splash** Triangle or Circle
**Leg Drop** Square

### OPPONENT CLIMBING TURNBUCKLE/APRON

**Punch Opp on TB/Apron** Triangle
**Pull Opponent off TB/Apron** Circle

### TAG TEAM

**Tag Partner** L2

### WEAPONS

**Pick up/Put down Weapon** Circle
**Hit with Weapon** Triangle

### CAGE MATCH

**Climb Cage** Left 2
**Jump off cage** Triangle
**Jump off cage** Square
**Smash Head into Cage** left,Triangle
**Pull Opponent off Cage** circle

## NINTENDO 64

These are moves common to all wrestlers in the game.

### FROM STARTING POSITION

**Punches** B
left,B
**Kicks** A
up,A
**Tie-Up** Left C
**Block** Down C
**Run** Right C
**Whip** left,left,Down C
**Pose/Flex** A+Left C
**Taunt** B+Down C
**Toggle Between Opponents** Tap Up C
**Dodge** Left Left Shoulder
**Dodge** Right Right Shoulder
**Climb Into/Out of Ring** Up C

### FROM A TIE-UP

**Whip** Down C

### WHEN IN A HOLD

**All Reversals**** Down C

### GROUND HOLDS -- HEAD

**Pull Opp to feet** Left C

### GROUND HOLDS -- FEET

**Pin Opponent** Left C

### IN CORNER

**Climb Turnbuckle** Up C

### OPPONENT IN CORNER

**Turn opp around in Corner** Left C

### OPPONENT STANDING OUTSIDE RING (WRESTLER INSIDE RING)

**Body Press** B or Left C
**Drop Kick** A

### WEAPONS MATCH

**Pick up/Put down Weapon** Left C
**Hit with Weapon** B or A

### OPPONENT ON GROUND OUTSIDE RING (WRESTLER INSIDE RING)

**Splash** B or Left C
**Leg Drop** A

### TAG TEAM MATCH

**Tag Partner** Up C

### OPPONENT CLIMBING TURNBUCKLE/APRON

**Punch Opponent on TB/Apron** B
**Pull Opponent off TB/Apron** Left C

### CAGE MATCH

**Climb Cage** Up C
**Jump off cage** B
**Jump off cage** A
**Smash Head into Cage** left,B
**Pull Opponent off Cage** Left C

***IMPORTANT NOTE:** Button combos which involve directionals (left, right, up, down) are often able to be executed using the opposite directionals, depending on the wrestlers' relative positions. In other words, a move that is accomplished by pressing "left, right, B" would also work with "right, left B". Similarly, "left, left, X" would also work as "right, right, X" and might even work as "up, up, X" or "down, down, X", depending on the move and the wrestlers' positioning at the time. The only exceptions to this rule are moves tagged with an asterisk (*), which will only work exactly as described in this section.

****Only for moves that can be reversed by a particular wrestler. See the Strategy section of the book for details.**

# STONE COLD STEVE AUSTIN™

**Weight:** 252 pounds
**Height:** 6'2"
**From:** Victoria, TX
**Favorite Quote:** "And that's the bottom line, 'cause Stone Cold said so!"
**Finishing Move:** Stone Cold Stunner

## GAME STATS

| | |
|---|---|
| Strength | 7 |
| Toughness | 6 |
| Speed | 5 |
| Recovery | 5 |
| Charisma | 7 |

## WRESTLER BIO

Stone Cold Steve Austin is dripping with nothing but confidence after becoming the World Wrestling Federation Champion. Some peers say the man is a suicide machine with lack of regard for authority and rules — and little hesitation in assaulting World Wrestling Federation owner Vince McMahon. Due to his lack of conformity to Vince's rules, Stone Cold will likely go down as the only champion in history to be arrested by the Federation owner! But you can't deny this superstar is tougher than leather when he steps through the ring ropes. His burning desire to become the greatest champion of all time is a destiny that motivates his cold heart. Without a doubt, there are still plenty of unwritten chapters on Whoop-@$$ in the book of Austin 3:16!

## TIPS

Great striking ability, he's a methodical wrestler with a steady, well-paced attack. Not overpowering, but a great chain wrestler; he can put together combo maneuvers with supreme skill. Average agility but deceptively fast. With a good, balanced attack, Stone Cold even has a fairly good chance of success with his aerial moves.

# BUTTON COMBOS



## PLAYSTATION

### • FROM STARTING POSITION

**Arm Wrench** left,left,Triangle
**Overhead Belly-Belly Suplex** left,right,Circle
**Body Slam** left,down,Triangle
**Clothesline** up,up,Triangle
**Cobra Clutch** left,up,Circle
**DDT** left,down,Square
**Front Backbreaker** left,down,Circle
**Gut Wrench Power Bomb** left,right,Triangle
**Hammerlock** left,left,Circle
**Side Belly-Belly Suplex** up,up,Square
**Samoan Drop** left,up,Triangle
**Short-Arm Clothesline** left,left,Square
**Single-Arm DDT** left,up,Square
**Spinebuster** up,down,Square
**Vertical Suplex** up,down,Circle
**STONE COLD STUNNER** left,left,up,Circle+X

### • FROM THE TIE-UP

**Hammerlock** Square
**Back Breaker** Triangle
**Fisherman's Suplex** Circle
**Inverted Atomic Drop** left,Square
**DDT** left,Triangle
**Overhead Belly-Belly Suplex** left,Circle
**Vertical Suplex** left,up,Square
**Brainbuster** left,right,Triangle
**Power Bomb** left,up,Circle
**STONE COLD STUNNER** left,left,Circle

### • FROM BEHIND

**Cobra Clutch** Square or Triangle or Circle
**Pump Handle Slam** left,left,Square
**Side Slam** left,left,Triangle
**Reverse DDT** left,right,down,Circle

### • RUNNING ATTACK

**Clothesline** Square or Circle
**Vertical Body Press** Triangle

### • ATTACK VS. RUNNING

**Back Body Drop** Square
**Clothesline** Triangle
**Arm Drag** Circle
**Powerslam** up,Circle

### • GROUND HITS- STANDING

**Driving Elbow Smash** down,Triangle
**Fist Drop** Triangle
**Falling Headbutt** down,Square
**Leg Drop** Square
**Stomp** Square
**- RUNNING**
**Leg Drop** Square
**Running Elbow Drop** Square
**Front Elbow** Triangle or Circle

### • GROUND HOLDS

**-STARTING AT LEGS**
**Step-Over Toe Hold** left,left,Square
**Half Crab** left,right,Square
**Texas Cloverleaf** up,down,Square
**STF** up,down,up,Square

**- STARTING AT HEAD**
**Arm Wrench** left,left,Triangle
**Rear Chin Lock** left,right,Triangle
**Reverse Chinlock** up,down,Triangle
**Painkiller** left,up,down,Triangle

### • OPPONENT IN CORNER

**- STANDING, FACING OPPONENT**
**Kick in Corner** Square
**Climb Turnbuckle and Pummel** Triangle
**Repeated Elbows** Circle
**Belly-Belly Suplex** left,left,Square or Triangle
**Top Rope Superplex** left,left, Circle

**- FROM BEHIND OPPONENT**
**Smash Head into Turnbuckle** Square or Triangle or Circle
**Pump Handle Slam** left, Circle

**- RUNNING**
**Clothesline** Square or Triangle or Circle

### • FROM THE TOP TURNBUCKLE

**- OPPONENT LYING ON GROUND**
**Fist Drop** Square or Triangle or Circle
**Double Foot Stomp** Square+X
**Driving Elbow** Triangle+Circle
**Splash** left,left,Triangle+Square

**- OPPONENT STANDING**
**Bionic Elbow** Square or Triangle or Circle
**Clothesline** Triangle+Circle
**Forearm Smash** Square+X
**Shoulder Tackle** left,up,Circle+X

### • FROM THE RING APRON

**- OPPONENT LYING ON GROUND**
**Fist Drop** Square or Triangle or Circle
**Double Foot Stomp** Square+X
**Driving Elbow** Triangle+Circle

**- OPPONENT STANDING**
**Bionic Elbow** Square or Triangle or Circle
**Clothesline Apron** Triangle+Circle
**Forearm Smash** Square+X

## NINTENDO 64

### • FROM STARTING POSITION

**Arm Wrench** left,left,B
**Overhead Belly-Belly Suplex** left,right,Left C
**Body Slam** left,down,B
**Clothesline** up,up,B
**Cobra Clutch** left,up,Left C
**DDT** left,down,A
**Front Backbreaker** left,down,Left C
**Gut Wrench Power Bomb** left,right,B
**Hammerlock** left,left,Left C
**Side Belly-Belly Suplex** up,up,A
**Samoan Drop** left,up,B
**Short-Arm Clothesline** left,left,A
**Single-Arm DDT** left,up,A
**Spinebuster** up,down,A
**Vertical Suplex** up,down,Left C
**STONE COLD STUNNER** left,left,up,Left C+Down C

### • FROM THE TIE-UP

**Hammerlock** A
**Back Breaker** B
**Fisherman's Suplex** Left C
**Inverted Atomic Drop** left,A
**DDT** left,B
**Overhead Belly-Belly Suplex** left,left C
**Vertical Suplex** left,up,A
**Brainbuster** left,right,B
**Power Bomb** left,up,Left C
**STONE COLD STUNNER** left,left,Left C

### • FROM BEHIND

**Cobra Clutch** A or B or Left C
**Pump Handle Slam** left,left,A
**Side Slam** left,left,B
**Reverse DDT** left,right,down,Left C

### • RUNNING ATTACK

**Clothesline** A or Left C
**Vertical Body Press** B

### • ATTACK VS. RUNNING

**Back Body Drop** A
**Clothesline** B
**Arm Drag** Left C
**Powerslam** up,Left C

### • GROUND HITS- STANDING

**Driving Elbow Smash** down,B
**Fist Drop** B
**Falling Headbutt** down,A
**Leg Drop** A
**Stomp** A

**- RUNNING**
**Leg Drop** A
**Running Elbow** Drop A
**Front Elbow** B or Left C

### • GROUND HOLDS

**- STARTING AT LEGS**
**Step-Over Toe Hold** left,left,A
**Half Crab** left,right,A
**Texas Cloverleaf** up,down,A
**STF** up,down,up,A
**- STARTING AT HEAD**
**Arm Wrench** left,left,B
**Rear Chin Lock** left,right,B
**Reverse Chinlock** up,down,B
**Painkiller** left,up,down,B

### • OPPONENT IN CORNER

**- STANDING, FACING OPPONENT**
**Kick in Corner** A
**Climb Turnbuckle and Pummel** B
**Repeated Elbows** Left C
**Belly-Belly Suplex** left,left,A or B
**Top Rope Superplex** left,left,Left C

**- FROM BEHIND OPPONENT**
**Smash Head into Turnbuckle** A or B or Left C
**Pump Handle Slam** left,Left C

**- RUNNING**
**Clothesline** A or B or Left C

### • FROM THE TOP TURNBUCKLE

**- OPPONENT LYING ON GROUND**
**Fist Drop** A or B or Left C
**Double Foot Stomp** A+Down C
**Driving Elbow** B+Left C
**Splash** left,left,B+A

**- OPPONENT STANDING**
**Bionic Elbow** A or B or Left C
**Clothesline** B+Left C
**Forearm Smash** A+Down C
**Shoulder Tackle** left,up,Left C+Down C

### • FROM THE RING APRON

**- OPPONENT LYING ON GROUND**
**Fist Drop** A or B or Left C
**Double Foot Stomp** A+Down C
**Driving Elbow** B+Left C

**- OPPONENT STANDING**
**Bionic Elbow** A or B or Left C
**Clothesline Apron** B+Left C
**Forearm Smash** A+Down C

**Weight:** 227 pounds
**Height:** 6'1"
**From:** San Antonio, TX
**Favorite Quote:** "I'm the 'Showstoppa', the Main Event, the ICON!"
**Finishing Move:** Sweet Chin Music

## GAME STATS

| | |
|---|---|
| Strength | 3 |
| Toughness | 5 |
| Speed | 10 |
| Recovery | 7 |
| Charisma | 5 |

## WRESTLER BIO

Perhaps the most exciting and charismatic superstar ever to grace a World Wrestling Federation ring, Shawn Michaels, the founder of the controversial D-Generation X, is the self-proclaimed ICON of sports-entertainment. Michaels holds the distinction of being the only competitor in history to capture the "Grand Slam" of the Federation (holding the Federation Title, Intercontinental Title, European Title and Tag Team Title).

Whether he utilizes his aerial arsenal or his methodical ground game, the "Showstoppa" promises he will forever outwill his opponents in gaining the victory. And if they can't accept defeat, they can all "SUCK IT!"

## TIPS

Limits are what Shawn Michaels is about — as in smashing, sidestepping and generally exceeding them. Despite numerous serious injuries, he remains the prototype high-risk technician. He's the best flyer in the game, has good striking ability for a wrestler his size and weight, and is, along with Bret Hart, the most agile wrestler in the game. He's occasionally reckless, but his astounding speed — nobody in the game is faster — can compensate for his overenthusiasm.

# BUTTON COMBOS



## PLAYSTATION

### • FROM STARTING POSITION
**Arm Drag*** up,up,Triangle
**Arm Wrench** left,left,Triangle
**Overhead Belly-Belly Suplex** left,right,Triangle
**Body Slam*** left,down,Triangle
**Crucifix** left,left,Square
**DDT*** left,down,Square
**Flying Head Scissors*** up,up,Square
**Drop Toe Hold*** down,down,Square
**Hurricanranna*** left,right,up,Square
**Headlock Takedown*** left,down,Circle
**Japanese Arm Drag*** down,down,Triangle
**Side Belly-Belly Suplex*** left,up,Circle
**Single-Arm DDT*** left,up,Square
**Small Package*** down,down,Circle
**SWEET CHIN MUSIC*** left,down,up,Square+X

### • FROM THE TIE-UP
**Arm Drag** Square
**Side Belly-Belly suplex** Triangle
**DDT** Circle
**Northern Lights Suplex** left,Square
**Samoan Drop** left,Triangle
**Overhead Belly-Belly Suplex** left,Circle
**Double Underhook Suplex** left,right,Square
**Brainbuster** up,down,Triangle
**Piledriver** left,up,Circle

### • FROM BEHIND
**Abdominal Stretch** Square or Triangle or Circle
**Pump Handle Slam** left,left,Square
**Victory Roll** left,left,Triangle
**German Suplex** left,left,up,Circle

### • RUNNING ATTACK
**Cross Body Block** Square
**Clothesline** Triangle
**Crucifix** Circle
**Hurricanranna** Triangle+Circle

### • ATTACK VS. RUNNING
**Drop Kick** Square
**Back Body Drop** Triangle
**Arm Drag** Circle
**Hurricanranna** up,Square

### • GROUND HITS
**- STANDING**
**Elbow Drop** Triangle
**Standing Moonsault*** Down,Triangle
**Stomp** Square
**Knee Drop*** down,Square

**- RUNNING**
**Leg Drop (at side)** Square
**Running Elbow Drop** Square or Triangle or Circle

### • GROUND HOLDS
**- STARTING AT LEGS**
**Knee to Inside Leg** left,left,Square
**Step-Over Toe Hold** left,right,Square
**Elbow to Groin** up,down,Square
**Figure Four Leglock** left,up,left,Square

**- STARTING AT HEAD**
**Arm Wrench** left,left,Triangle
**Reverse Chinlock** left,right,Triangle
**Leg Lock Chokehold** up,down,Triangle

### • OPPONENT IN CORNER
**- STANDING, FACING OPPONENT**
**Chest Chop** Square
**Climb Turnbuckle and Pummel** Triangle
**Splash** Circle
**Flying Head Scissors** left,left,Square
**Monkey Flip** left,left,Triangle
**Swinging DDT** left,left,Circle
**Hurricanranna** left,right,up,Square
**Top Rope Superplex** up,down,up,Circle

**- FROM BEHIND OPPONENT**
**Smash Head into Turnbuckle** Square or Triangle or Circle
**Pump Handle Slam** left,Circle

**- RUNNING**
**Avalanche** Square or Triangle or Circle

### • FROM THE TOP TURNBUCKLE
**- OPPONENT LYING ON GROUND**
**Elbow Drop** Square or Triangle or Circle
**Fist Drop** Square+X
**Splash** Triangle+Circle
**Shooting Star Press*** up,up,Square+Circle
**Moonsault (at side, opp in ring)** X

**- OPPONENT STANDING**
**Drop Kick** Square or Triangle or Circle
**Bionic Elbow** Triangle+Circle
**Sunset Flip (opp in ring)** Square+X
**Drop Kick** Square+X
**Hurricanranna** left,up,Square+Circle
**Moonsault (opp in ring)** X

### • FROM THE RING APRON
**- OPPONENT LYING ON GROUND**
**Elbow Drop** Square or Triangle or Circle
**Fist Drop** Square+X
**Splash** Triangle+Circle

**- OPPONENT STANDING**
**Drop Kick** Square or Triangle or Circle
**Bionic Elbow** Triangle+Circle or Square+X

## NINTENDO 64

### • FROM STARTING POSITION
**Arm Drag*** up,up,B
**Arm Wrench** left,left,B
**Overhead Belly-Belly Suplex** left,right,B
**Body Slam*** left,down,B
**Crucifix** left,left,A
**DDT*** left,down,A
**Flying Head Scissors*** up,up,A
**Drop Toe Hold*** down,down,A
**Hurricanranna*** left,right,up,A
**Headlock Takedown*** left,down,Left C
**Japanese Arm Drag*** down,down,B
**Side Belly-Belly Suplex*** left,up,Left C
**Single-Arm DDT*** left,up,A
**Small Package*** down,down,Left C
**SWEET CHIN MUSIC*** left,down,up,A+Down C

### • FROM THE TIE-UP
**Arm Drag** A
**Side Belly-Belly suplex** B
**DDT** Left C
**Northern Lights Suplex** left,A
**Samoan Drop** left,B
**Overhead Belly-Belly Suplex** left,Left C
**Double Underhook Suplex** left,right,A
**Brainbuster** up,down,B
**Piledriver** left,up,Left C

### • FROM BEHIND
**Abdominal Stretch** A or B or Left C
**Pump Handle Slam** left,left,A
**Victory Roll** left,left,B
**German Suplex** left,left,up,Left C

### • RUNNING ATTACK
**Cross Body Block** A
**Clothesline** B
**Crucifix** Left C
**Hurricanranna** B+Left C

### • ATTACK VS. RUNNING
**Drop Kick** A
**Back Body Drop** B
**Arm Drag** Left C
**Hurricanranna** up,A

### • GROUND HITS
**- Standing**
**Elbow Drop** B
**Standing Moonsault*** down,B
**Stomp** A
**Knee Drop*** down,A

**- RUNNING**
**Leg Drop (at side)** A
**Running Elbow Drop** A or B or Left C

### • GROUND HOLDS
**- STARTING AT LEGS**
**Knee to Inside Leg** left,left,A
**Step-Over Toe Hold** left,right,A
**Elbow to Groin** up,down,A
**Figure Four Leglock** left,up,left,A

**- STARTING AT HEAD**
**Arm Wrench** left,left,B
**Reverse Chinlock** left,right,B
**Leg Lock Chokehold** up,down,B

### • OPPONENT IN CORNER
**- STANDING, FACING OPPONENT**
**Chest Chop** A
**Climb Turnbuckle and Pummel** B
**Splash** Left C
**Flying Head Scissors** left,left,A
**Monkey Flip** left,left,B
**Swinging DDT** left,left,Left C
**Hurricanranna** left,right,up,A
**Top Rope Superplex** up,down,up,Left C

**- FROM BEHIND OPPONENT**
**Smash Head into Turnbuckle** A or B or Left C
**Pump Handle Slam** left,Left C

**- RUNNING**
**Avalanche** A or B or Left C

### • FROM THE TOP TURNBUCKLE
**- OPPONENT LYING ON GROUND**
**Elbow Drop** A or B or Left C
**Fist Drop** A+Down C
**Splash** B+Left C
**Shooting Star Press*** up,up,A+Left C
**Moonsault (at side, opp in ring)** Down C

**- OPPONENT STANDING**
**Drop Kick** A or B or Left C
**Bionic Elbow** B+Left C
**Sunset Flip (opp in ring)** A+Down C
**Drop Kick** A+Down C
**Hurricanranna** left,up,A+Left C
**Moonsault (opp in ring)** Down C

### • FROM THE RING APRON
**- OPPONENT LYING ON GROUND**
**Elbow Drop** A or B or Left C
**Fist Drop** A+Down C
**Splash** B+Left C

**- OPPONENT STANDING**
**Drop Kick** A or B or Left C
**Bionic Elbow** B+Left C or A+Down C

WRESTLERS

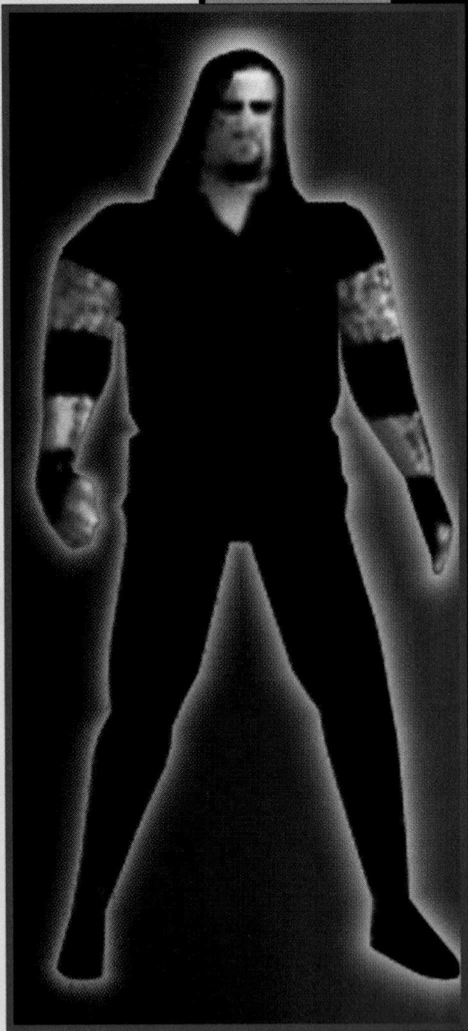

**Weight:** 328 pounds
**Height:** 6'10"
**From:** Death Valley
**Favorite Quote:** "I am the Lord of Darkness!"
**Finishing Move:** Tombstone Piledriver

## GAME STATS

|  |  |
|---|---|
| Strength | 8 |
| Toughness | 7 |
| Speed | 3 |
| Recovery | 8 |
| Charisma | 4 |

## WRESTLER BIO

There is no denying that the Undertaker may be the most awesome presence the World Wrestling Federation has ever seen. The Man from the Dark Side has held the Federation Title on two occasions and has sent some of the biggest monsters in the sport to a hellish fate.

Despite the threat of his demonic younger brother Kane and former manager Paul Bearer, the Lord of Darkness has persevered in the squared circle and remains a constant threat to any titleholder. His finishing maneuver, the Tombstone Piledriver, is one of the most devastating finishers in wrestling history. When the Undertaker applies it, his opponents have no choice but to REST IN PEACE!

## TIPS

The Undertaker is such a dangerous opponent because he blends the most important weapons in a wrestler's arsenal — size, strength and a superb sense of balance. While his rope-walking prowess astounds opponents, his nearly supernatural strength and endurance overwhelms them. The Undertaker's wrestling style is a unique composite of flying moves, high impact slams and a relentlessly aggressive attack. Not a mat wrestler — with his grace and power, the Undertaker is most effective on his feet. He likes to set up his finisher, the Tombstone Piledriver, with a ring-rattling Choke Slam. Not fast, but has explosive, short-range movement and a good striking ability.

# BUTTON COMBOS



## PLAYSTATION

### • FROM STARTING POSITION

**Front Face DDT** left,left,Circle
**Overhead Belly-Belly Suplex*** left,down,Circle
**Choke Slam*** down,down,Triangle
**DDT*** left,down,Square
**Gut Wrench Power Bomb** left,right,Triangle
**Neck Breaker*** left,down,Triangle
**Side Belly-Belly Suplex** left,right,Circle
**Short-Arm Clothesline*** left,up,Circle
**Single-Arm DDT*** left,up,Square
**Snap Mare*** left,up,Triangle
**Throat Toss*** down,up,Circle
**TOMBSTONE PILEDRIVER*** down,down,down,Triangle+Circle
**Vertical Suplex** left,right,Square

### • FROM THE TIE-UP

**Back Breaker** Square
**Atomic Drop** Triangle
**Sidewalk Slam** Circle
**Northern Lights Suplex** left,Square
**DDT** left,Triangle
**Gut Wrench Power Bomb** left,Circle
**Vertical Suplex*** left,down,Square
**Overhead Belly-Belly Suplex*** left,up,Triangle
**Choke Slam** left,right,Circle
**TOMBSTONE PILEDRIVER (F)** up,down,Circle

### • FROM BEHIND

**Neck Breaker** Square or Triangle or Circle
**Reverse DDT** left,left,Square or Triangle
**Reverse DDT** up,up,Triangle
**Side Slam*** left,left,up,Circle

### • RUNNING ATTACK

**Clothesline** Triangle or Square
**Spinning Neck Breaker** Circle

### • ATTACK VS. RUNNING

**Boot to Face** Square
**Clothesline** Triangle
**Powerslam** Circle
**Spinebuster** left,Circle

### • GROUND HITS

**- STANDING**
**Elbow Drop** Triangle
**Knee Drop*** down,Square
**Leg Drop*** down, Triangle
**Stomp** Square

**- RUNNING**
**Leg Drop** Square
**Fist Drop** Triangle
**Falling Headbutt** Circle

### • GROUND HOLDS

**- STARTING AT LEGS**
**Elbow Drop onto Leg** left,left,Square
**Half Crab** left,right,Square
**Surfboard** up,down,Square
**Leg Lock** left,right,left,Square

**- STARTING AT HEAD**
**Arm Wrench** left,left,Triangle
**Squeeze Head** left,right,Triangle
**Painkiller** up,down,Triangle

### • OPPONENT IN CORNER

**- STANDING, FACING OPPONENT**
**Choke with Boot** Square
**Climb Turnbuckle and Pummel** Triangle
**Choke with Boot** Circle
**Overhead Press** left,left,Square
**Belly-Belly Suplex** left,left,Triangle
**Double Underhook Suplex** left,left,Circle
**Top Rope Superplex** up,up,down,Square

**- FROM BEHIND OPPONENT**
**Smash Head into Turnbuckle** Square or Triangle or Circle
**Pump Handle Slam** left,Circle

**- RUNNING**
**Clothesline** Square or Triangle or Circle

### • FROM THE TOP TURNBUCKLE

**- OPPONENT LYING ON GROUND**
**Fist Drop** Square or Triangle or Circle
**Double Foot Stomp** Square+X
**Splash** Triangle+Circle
**Driving Elbow** left,right,Square+Circle

**- OPPONENT STANDING**
**Drop Kick** Square or Triangle or Circle
**Axe Handle Smash** Square+X
**Clothesline** Triangle+Circle
**Forearm Smash** left,right,Square+Circle

### • FROM THE RING APRON

**- OPPONENT LYING ON GROUND**
**Fist Drop** Square or Triangle or Circle
**Double Foot Stomp** Square+X
**Splash** Triangle+Circle

**- OPPONENT STANDING**
**Drop Kick** Square or Triangle or Circle
**Axe Handle Smash** Square+X
**Clothesline** Triangle+Circle

## NINTENDO 64

### • FROM STARTING POSITION

**Front Face DDT** left,left,Left C
**Overhead Belly-Belly Suplex*** left,down,Left C
**Choke Slam*** down,down,B
**DDT*** left,down,A
**Gut Wrench Power Bomb** left,right,B
**Neck Breaker*** left,down,B
**Side Belly-Belly Suplex** left,right,Left C
**Short-Arm Clothesline*** left,up,Left C
**Single-Arm DDT*** left,up,A
**Snap Mare*** left,up,B
**Throat Toss*** down,up,Left C
**TOMBSTONE PILEDRIVER*** down,down,down,B+Left C
**Vertical Suplex** left,right,A

### • FROM THE TIE-UP

**Back Breaker** A
**Atomic Drop** B
**Sidewalk Slam** Left C
**Northern Lights Suplex** left,A
**DDT** left,B
**Gut Wrench Power Bomb** left,Left C
**Vertical Suplex*** left,down,A
**Overhead Belly-Belly Suplex*** left,up,B
**Choke Slam** left,right,Left C
**TOMBSTONE PILEDRIVER (F)** up,down,Left C

### • FROM BEHIND

**Neck Breaker** A or B or Left C
**Reverse DDT** left,left,A or B
**Reverse DDT** up,up,B
**Side Slam*** left,left,up,Left C

### • RUNNING ATTACK

**Clothesline** B or A
**Spinning Neck Breaker** Left C

### • ATTACK VS. RUNNING

**Boot to Face** A
**Clothesline** B
**Powerslam** Left C
**Spinebuster** left,Left C

### • GROUND HITS

**- STANDING**
**Elbow Drop** B
**Knee Drop*** down,A
**Leg Drop*** down, B
**Stomp** A

**- RUNNING**
**Leg Drop** A
**Fist Drop** B
**Falling Headbutt** Left C

### • GROUND HOLDS

**- STARTING AT LEGS**
**Elbow Drop onto Leg** left,left,A
**Half Crab** left,right,A
**Surfboard** up,down,A
**Leg Lock** left,right,left,A

**- STARTING AT HEAD**
**Arm Wrench** left,left,B
**Squeeze Head** left,right,B
**Painkiller** up,down,B

### • OPPONENT IN CORNER

**- STANDING, FACING OPPONENT**
**Choke with Boot** A
**Climb Turnbuckle and Pummel** B
**Choke with Boot** Left C
**Overhead Press** left,left,A
**Belly-Belly Suplex** left,left,B
**Double Underhook Suplex** left,left,Left C
**Top Rope Superplex** up,up,down,A

**- FROM BEHIND OPPONENT**
**Smash Head into Turnbuckle** A or B or Left C
**Pump Handle Slam** left,Left C

**- RUNNING**
**Clothesline** A or B or Left C

### • FROM THE TOP TURNBUCKLE

**- OPPONENT LYING ON GROUND**
**Fist Drop** A or B or Left C
**Double Foot Stomp** A+Down C
**Splash** B+Left C
**Driving Elbow** left,right,A+Left C

**- OPPONENT STANDING**
**Drop Kick** A or B or Left C
**Axe Handle Smash** A+Down C
**Clothesline** B+Left C
**Forearm Smash** left,right,A+Left C

### • FROM THE RING APRON

**- OPPONENT LYING ON GROUND**
**Fist Drop** A or B or Left C
**Double Foot Stomp** A+Down C
**Splash** B+Left C

**- OPPONENT STANDING**
**Drop Kick** A or B or Left C
**Axe Handle Smash** A+Down C
**Clothesline** B+Left C

## NO METERS

Beat the Challenge with the Undertaker, and you'll be able to disable the on-screen health meters! How many hits will it take to topple your opponent? Now you'll have to guess!

WRESTLERS

# KANE™

**Height:** 7′
**Weight:** 325 pounds
**Favorite Quote:** Has never spoken
**Finishing Move:** Tombstone Piledriver

## GAME STATS

| | |
|---|---|
| Strength | 9 |
| Toughness | 9 |
| Speed | 3 |
| Recovery | 6 |
| Charisma | 3 |

## WRESTLER BIO

No superstar in history has made more of an instant impact than Kane. On October 5, 1997, the world met Kane, as the seven-foot monster tore off the door to "Hell in the Cell" in order to get to his brother, the Undertaker. It had been believed that Kane perished in the raging inferno that claimed the lives of the siblings' parents. But miraculously, he survived.

From that time forward, the only person who knew that Kane was alive was the despicable Paul Bearer. For the past 20 years the rotund mortician has been feeding him a version of the fateful day that destroyed his family, portraying the Undertaker as the murderer. Is there any wonder why Kane has gone to extraordinary lengths to obliterate his older brother?

## TIPS

Kane is a classic monster villain. He doesn't fly as much as his brother, but he can leave his feet if he so desires. Kane prefers to battle from a vertical position as long as possible, using his great size and strength to literally man-handle opponents. He finishes up his victims just like his brother, with a Choke Slam and a Tombstone, and he never speaks a word. Big, strong and powerful, Kane's high-impact slams can finish any wrestler in this game.

# BUTTON COMBOS



## PLAYSTATION

### • FROM STARTING POSITION
**Front Face DDT** left,left,Circle
**Overhead Belly-Belly Suplex*** left,down,Circle
**Choke Slam*** down,down,Triangle
**DDT*** left,down,Square
**Gut Wrench Power Bomb** left,right,Triangle
**Neck Breaker*** left,down,Triangle
**Side Belly-Belly Suplex** left,right,Circle
**Short-Arm Clothesline*** left,up,Circle
**Single-Arm DDT*** left,up,Square
**Snap Mare*** left,up,Triangle
**Throat Toss*** down,up,Circle
**TOMBSTONE PILEDRIVER*** down,down,down,Triangle+Circle
**Vertical Suplex** left,right,Square

### • FROM THE TIE-UP
**Back Breaker** Square
**Atomic Drop** Triangle
**Sidewalk Slam** Circle
**Northern Lights Suplex** left,Square
**DDT** left,Triangle
**Gut Wrench Power Bomb** left,Circle
**Vertical Suplex*** left,down,Square
**Overhead Belly-Belly Suplex*** left,up,Triangle
**Choke Slam** left,right,Circle
**TOMBSTONE PILEDRIVER** up,down,Circle

### • FROM BEHIND
**Neck Breaker** Square or Triangle or Circle
**Reverse DDT** left,left,Square or up, up, Square
**Reverse DDT** up,up,Triangle
**Side Slam*** left,left,up,Circle

### • RUNNING ATTACK
**Flying Clothesline** Triangle or Square
**Spinning Neck Breaker** Circle

### • ATTACK VS. RUNNING
**Boot to Face** Square
**Clothesline** Triangle
**Powerslam** Circle
**Spinebuster** left,Circle

### • GROUND HITS
**- STANDING**
**Elbow Drop** Triangle
**Knee Drop*** down,Square
**Leg Drop*** Square
**Stomp** Square

**- RUNNING**
**Leg Drop** Square
**Fist Drop** Triangle or Square
**Falling Headbutt** Circle

### • GROUND HOLDS
**- STARTING AT LEGS**
**Elbow Drop onto Leg** left,left,Square
**Half Crab** left,right,Square
**Surfboard** up,down,Square
**Leg Lock** left,right,left,Square

**- Starting at Head**
**Arm Wrench** left,left,Triangle
**Squeeze Head** left,right,Triangle
**Painkiller** up,down,Triangle

### • OPPONENT IN CORNER
**- STANDING, FACING OPPONENT**
**Choke with Boot** Square
**Climb Turnbuckle and Pummel** Triangle
**Choke with Boot** Circle
**Overhead Press** left,left,Square
**Belly-Belly Suplex** left,left,Triangle
**Double Underhook Suplex** left,left,Circle
**Top Rope Superplex** up,up,down,Square

**- FROM BEHIND OPPONENT**
**Smash Head into Turnbuckle** Square or Triangle or Circle
**Pump Handle Slam** left,Circle

**- RUNNING**
**Clothesline** Square or Triangle or Circle

### • FROM THE TOP TURNBUCKLE
**- OPPONENT LYING ON GROUND**
**Fist Drop** Square or Triangle or Circle
**Double Foot Stomp** Square+X
**Splash** Triangle+Circle
**Driving Elbow** left,right,Square+Circle

**- OPPONENT STANDING**
**Drop Kick** Square or Triangle or Circle
**Axe Handle Smash** Square+X
**Clothesline** Triangle+Circle
**Forearm Smash** left,right,Square+Circle

### • FROM THE RING APRON
**- OPPONENT LYING ON GROUND**
**Fist Drop** Square or Triangle or Circle
**Double Foot Stomp** Square+X
**Splash** Triangle+Circle

**- OPPONENT STANDING**
**Drop Kick** Square or Triangle or Circle
**Axe Handle Smash** Square+X
**Clothesline** Triangle+Circle

## NINTENDO 64

### • FROM STARTING POSITION
**Front Face DDT** left,left,Left C
**Overhead Belly-Belly Suplex*** left,down,Left C
**Choke Slam*** down,down,B
**DDT*** left,down,A
**Gut Wrench Power Bomb** left,right,B
**Neck Breaker*** left,down,B
**Side Belly-Belly Suplex** left,right,Left C
**Short-Arm Clothesline*** left,up,Left C
**Single-Arm DDT*** left,up,A
**Snap Mare*** left,up,B
**Throat Toss*** down,up,Left C
**TOMBSTONE PILEDRIVER*** down,down,down,B+Left C
**Vertical Suplex** left,right,A

### • FROM THE TIE-UP
**Back Breaker** A
**Atomic Drop** B
**Sidewalk Slam** Left C
**Northern Lights Suplex** left,A
**DDT** left,B
**Gut Wrench Power Bomb** left,Left C
**Vertical Suplex*** left,down,A
**Overhead Belly-Belly Suplex*** left,up,B
**Choke Slam** left,right,Left C
**TOMBSTONE PILEDRIVER** up,down,Left C

### • FROM BEHIND
**Neck Breaker** A or B or Left C
**Reverse DDT** left,left,A or B
**Reverse DDT** up,up,B
**Side Slam*** left,left,up,Left C

### • RUNNING ATTACK
**Clothesline** B or A
**Spinning Neck Breaker** Left C

### • ATTACK VS. RUNNING
**Boot to Face** A
**Clothesline** B
**Powerslam** Left C
**Spinebuster** left,Left C

### • GROUND HITS
**- STANDING**
**Elbow Drop** B
**Knee Drop*** down,A
**Leg Drop*** down, B
**Stomp** A

**- RUNNING**
**Leg Drop** A
**Fist Drop** B
**Falling Headbutt** Left C

### • GROUND HOLDS
**- STARTING AT LEGS**
**Elbow Drop onto Leg** left,left,A
**Half Crab** left,right,A
**Surfboard** up,down,A
**Leg Lock** left,right,left,A

**- STARTING AT HEAD**
**Arm Wrench** left,left,B
**Squeeze Head** left,right,B
**Painkiller** up,down,B

### • OPPONENT IN CORNER
**- STANDING, FACING OPPONENT**
**Choke with Boot** A
**Climb Turnbuckle and Pummel** B
**Choke with Boot** Left C
**Overhead Press** left,left,A
**Belly-Belly Suplex** left,left,B
**Double Underhook Suplex** left,left,Left C
**Top Rope Superplex** up,up,down,A

**- FROM BEHIND OPPONENT**
**Smash Head into Turnbuckle** A or B or Left C
**Pump Handle Slam** left,Left C

**- RUNNING**
**Clothesline** A or B or Left C

### • FROM THE TOP TURNBUCKLE
**- OPPONENT LYING ON GROUND**
**Fist Drop** A or B or Left C
**Double Foot Stomp** A+Down C
**Splash** B+Left C
**Driving Elbow** left,right,A+Left C

**- OPPONENT STANDING**
**Drop Kick** A or B or Left C
**Axe Handle Smash** A+Down C
**Clothesline** B+Left C
**Forearm Smash** left,right,A+Left C

### • FROM THE RING APRON
**- OPPONENT LYING ON GROUND**
**Fist Drop** A or B or Left C
**Double Foot Stomp** A+Down C
**Splash** B+Left C

**- OPPONENT STANDING**
**Drop Kick** A or B or Left C
**Axe Handle Smash** A+Down C
**Clothesline** B+Left C

## EXTRA COSTUME OPTIONS

Beat the Challenge with Kane in any difficulty mode, and you'll have access to new pants, masks, shirts, and boots for use with your Custom Wrestler! It's an accessorizing dream!

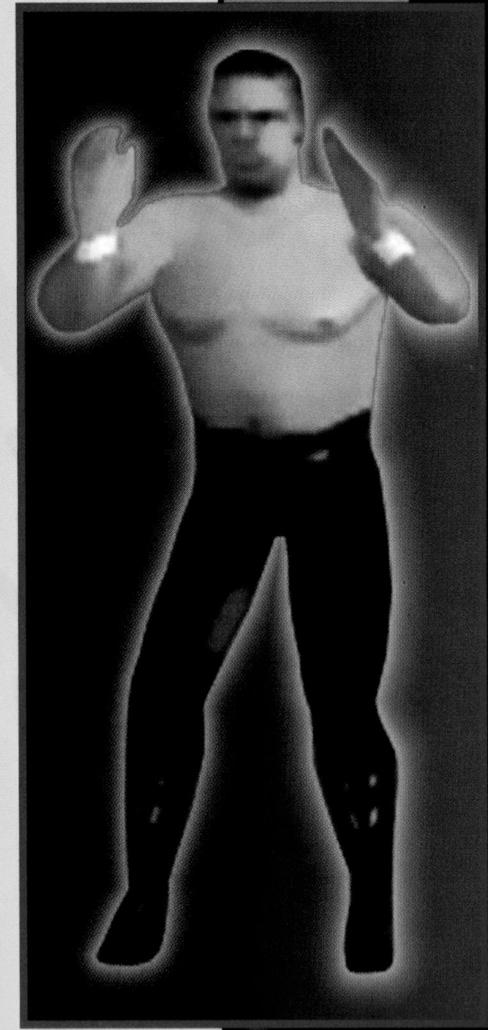

WRESTLERS

# TRIPLE H™

**Height:** 6'4"
**Weight:** 246 pounds
**From:** Greenwich, CT
**Favorite Quote:** "Suck It!"
**Finishing Move:** Pedigree
**Titles Held:** Intercontinental, European (2)

## GAME STATS

| | |
|---|---|
| Strength | 9 |
| Toughness | 7 |
| Speed | 5 |
| Recovery | 5 |
| Charisma | 4 |

## WRESTLER BIO

Citing disciplinary reasons, Federation officials kept Triple H in relative obscurity for more than one year before he captured the 1997 King of the Ring. A few months prior to his royal coronation, Hunter enlisted the services of female bodybuilder Chyna and his career began to take an upward turn. After obtaining a great deal of success over the next few months, Hunter along with close friend Shawn Michaels formed D-Generation X and changed the face of wrestling forever. After Shawn cost the notorious group some embarrassment at WrestleMania XIV, Triple H asserted himself as one of the premier superstars in the sport by taking over leadership of the faction.

Now with Chyna, X-Pac and the New Age Outlaws under his direction, this intelligent individual is responsible for leading the most powerful and influential group in wrestling. There is no doubt that when all is said and done, HHH will be responsible for elevating this sport to heights never before attained.

## TIPS

His language and notorious double entendres have made him the most scandalous character in pro wrestling. But his punishing and often treacherous ring style — and modified Piledriver finisher, known as the Pedigree — have made him one of the most dangerous of all the superstars in the ring. He is well-versed in mat wrestling and tends to smother opponents or keep them otherwise neutralized. He can deliver high-impact maneuvers, or wrestle reactively — waiting for an opponent to commit himself then countering the move instantly. Not much of a flyer. His style is deceptive; he rarely appears to be dominating his opponent, even though he frequently is.

# BUTTON COMBOS



## PLAYSTATION

### • FROM STARTING POSITION

**Arm Wrench** left,left,Triangle
**Overhead Belly-Belly Suplex** left,right,Circle
**Clothesline** left,down,Triangle
**DDT** left,down,Square
**Drop Toe Hold*** down,down,Square
**Hammerlock*** up,up,Triangle
**Japanese Arm Drag*** down,down,Triangle
**Kneebreaker** left,up,Square
**Knee to Face** left,left,Square
**Neck Breaker** left,up,Triangle
**PEDIGREE*** left,down,right,Triangle+Circle
**Fisherman's Suplex** left,up,Circle
**Sleeper** left,left,Circle
**Vertical Suplex** left,down,Circle

### • FROM THE TIE-UP

**Hammerlock** Square
**Neck Breaker** Triangle
**Shoulder Breaker** Circle
**Fisherman's Suplex** left,Square
**Gut Wrench Power Bomb** left,Triangle
**Northern Lights Suplex** left,Circle
**Overhead Belly-Belly Suplex** left,up,Square
**Double Underhook Suplex** up,down,Triangle
**Power Bomb** left,up,Circle

### • FROM BEHIND

**Cobra Clutch** Square or Triangle or Circle
**Atomic Drop** left,left,Square
**Pump Handle Slam** left,left,Triangle
**Neck Breaker** left,up,up,Circle

### • RUNNING ATTACK

**Drop Kick** Square
**Clothesline** Triangle
**Cross Body Block** Circle

### • ATTACK VS. RUNNING

**Drop Toe Hold** Square
**Back Body Drop** Triangle
**Clothesline** Circle
**Powerslam** up,Circle

### • GROUND HITS

**- STANDING**
**Leg Drop (at side)** Square
**Stomp** Square
**Fist Drop** Triangle
**Falling Headbutt** down,Square

**- RUNNING**
**Running Knee Drop** Square
**Fist Drop** Triangle or Circle

### • GROUND HOLDS

**- STARTING AT LEGS**
**Step-Over Toe Hold** left,left,Square
**Half Crab** left,right,Square
**Texas Cloverleaf** up,down,Square
**Figure Four Leglock** left,up,left,Square

**- STARTING AT HEAD**
**Arm Wrench** left,left,Triangle
**Rear Chin Lock** left,right,Triangle
**Knee to Back** up,down,Triangle
**Blatant Choke** left,down,right,Triangle

### • OPPONENT IN CORNER

**- STANDING, FACING OPPONENT**
**Choke with Boot** Square
**Chest Chop** Triangle
**Charging Shoulder** Circle
**Belly-Belly Suplex** left,left,Square
**Superplex** left,left,Triangle
**Top Rope Superplex** left,left,Circle

**- FROM BEHIND OPPONENT**
**Smash Head into Turnbuckle** Square or Triangle or Circle
**Pump Handle Slam** left,Circle

**- RUNNING**
**Avalanche** Square or Triangle or Circle

### • FROM THE TOP TURNBUCKLE

**- OPPONENT LYING ON GROUND**
**Knee Drop** Square or Triangle or Circle
**Double Foot Stomp** Square+X
**Driving Elbow** Triangle+Circle
**Somersault Senton Splash** up,up,Triangle+Square

**- OPPONENT STANDING**
**Axe Handle Smash** Square or Triangle or Circle
**Clothesline** Square+X
**Shoulder Tackle** Triangle+Circle
**Body Press** up,left,Circle+X

### • FROM THE RING APRON

**- OPPONENT LYING ON GROUND**
**Knee Drop** Square or Triangle or Circle
**Double Foot Stomp** Square+X
**Driving Elbow** Triangle+Circle

**- OPPONENT STANDING**
**Axe Handle Smash** Square or Triangle or Circle
**Clothesline** Square+X
**Shoulder Tackle** Triangle+Circle

## NINTENDO 64

### • FROM STARTING POSITION

**Arm Wrench** left,left,B
**Overhead Belly-Belly Suplex** left,right,Left C
**Clothesline** left,down,B
**DDT** left,down,A
**Drop Toe Hold*** down,down,A
**Hammerlock*** up,up,B
**Japanese Arm Drag*** down,down,B
**Kneebreaker** left,up,A
**Knee to Face** left,left,A
**Neck Breaker** left,up,B
**PEDIGREE*** left,down,right,B+Left C
**FISHERMAN'S SUPLEX** left,up,Left C
**SLEEPER** left,left,Left C
**VERTICAL SUPLEX** left,down,Left C

### • FROM THE TIE-UP

**Hammerlock** A
**Neck Breaker** B
**Shoulder Breaker** left C
**Fisherman's Suplex** left,A
**Gut Wrench Power Bomb** left,B
**Northern Lights Suplex** left,Left C
**Overhead Belly-Belly Suplex** left,up,A
**Double Underhook Suplex** up,down,B
**Power Bomb** left,up,Left C

### • FROM BEHIND

**Cobra Clutch** A or B or Left C
**Atomic Drop** left,left,A
**Pump Handle Slam** left,left,B
**Neck Breaker** left,up,up,Left C

### • RUNNING ATTACK

**Drop Kick** A
**Clothesline** B
**Cross Body Block** Left C

### • ATTACK VS. RUNNING

**Drop Toe Hold** A
**Back Body Drop** B
**Flying Back Elbow** Left C
**Powerslam** up,Left C

### • GROUND HITS

**- STANDING**
**Leg Drop (at side)** A
**Stomp** A
**Fist Drop** B
**Falling Headbutt** down,A

**- RUNNING**
**Running Knee Drop** A
**Fist Drop** B or Left C

### • GROUND HOLDS

**- STARTING AT LEGS**
**Step-Over Toe Hold** left,left,A
**Half Crab** left,right,A
**Texas Cloverleaf** up,down,A
**Figure Four Leglock** left,up,left,A

**- STARTING AT HEAD**
**Arm Wrench** left,left,B
**Rear Chin Lock** left,right,B
**Knee to Back** up,down,B
**Blatant Choke** left,down,right,B

### • OPPONENT IN CORNER

**- STANDING, FACING**
**Opponent Choke with Boot** A
**Chest Chop** B
**Charging Shoulder** Left C
**Belly-Belly Suplex** left,left,A
**Superplex** left,left,B
**Top Rope Superplex** left,left,Left C

**- FROM BEHIND OPPONENT**
**Smash Head into Turnbuckle** A or B or Left C
**Pump Handle Slam** left,Left C

**- RUNNING**
**Avalanche** A or B or Left C

### • FROM THE TOP TURNBUCKLE

**- OPPONENT LYING ON GROUND**
**Knee Drop** A or B or Left C
**Double Foot Stomp** A+Down C
**Driving Elbow** B+Left C
**Somersault Senton Splash** up,up,B+A

**- OPPONENT STANDING**
**Axe Handle Smash** A or B or Left C
**Clothesline** A+Down C
**Shoulder Tackle** B+Left C
**Body Press** up,left,Left C+Down C

### • FROM THE RING APRON

**- OPPONENT LYING ON GROUND**
**Knee Drop** A or B or Left C
**Double Foot Stomp** A+Down C
**Driving Elbow** B+Left C

**- OPPONENT STANDING**
**Axe Handle Smash** A or B or Left C
**Clothesline** A+Down C
**Shoulder Tackle** B+Left C

WRESTLERS

# KEN SHAMROCK™

**Height:** 6'1"
**Weight:** 235 pounds
**From:** Sacramento, CA
**Finishing Move:** Shamrock Ankle Lock

## GAME STATS

| | |
|---|---|
| Strength | 6 |
| Toughness | 6 |
| Speed | 8 |
| Recovery | 5 |
| Charisma | 5 |

## WRESTLER BIO

While competing in the Ultimate Fighting Championship (UFC) circuit, ABC-TV called him "The World's Most Dangerous Man." A master of submissions, Ken Shamrock was perhaps the most skilled fighter ever to compete in the Octagon, and quickly became a UFC champion. Once there were no longer any challenges to keep him in the realm of the UFC, Shamrock entered the World Wrestling Federation in February 1997.

Shamrock has astounded many wrestling insiders with his transition from the UFC to the Federation, as the superstar has improved his mat game in perhaps never before seen leaps and bounds. In fact, Ken was voted 1997's "Rookie of the Year" by many of the writers of World Wrestling Federation Magazine. Perhaps his greatest accomplishment thus far was being the sole survivor at the 1997 Survivor Series after dismantling the entire Nation of Domination. No doubt Shamrock will continue to reach new heights in the years to come, as he represents the future of the Federation.

## TIPS

Shamrock's greatest strength is his intensity, his focus. Once he gets In The Zone, as he says, he is a raging engine of destruction. Unfortunately, that focus can become fuzzy if Shamrock's emotions are exploited. He isn't big, but Shamrock is amazingly powerful with excellent striking ability, good speed and even some flying ability. He can wrestle on the mat, where his smaller size is less of a factor. But when Shamrock snaps, look out — he might step out of the TV and give you a Belly-Belly Suplex just for the hell of it.

# BUTTON COMBOS

## PLAYSTATION

### • FROM STARTING POSITION
**Front Face DDT** left,right,Triangle
**Arm Wrench** left,left,Triangle
**Crucifix** left,right,Square
**Hurricanranna** left,right,up,Square
**Japanese Arm Drag*** down,down,Triangle
**Kneebreaker*** left,down,Square
**Leg Drag** left,left,Square
**Reverse Painkiller*** left,down,Triangle
**Samoan Drop*** left,up,Triangle
**Short-Arm Clothesline*** up,up,Triangle
**Sidewalk Slam*** left,down,Circle
**Single-Arm DDT*** left,up,Square
**Small Package** up,down,Circle
**Spinning Neck Breaker** left,left,Circle

### • FROM THE TIE-UP
**Hiptoss** Square
**Top Wristlock** Triangle
**Sidewalk Slam** Circle
**Northern Lights Suplex** left,Square
**Gut Wrench Power Bomb** left,Triangle
**Vertical Suplex** left,Circle
**Overhead Belly-Belly Suplex*** left,up,Square
**Double Underhook Suplex** left,right,Triangle
**Side Belly-Belly Suplex*** left,down,Circle

### • FROM BEHIND
**Russian Leg Sweep** Square or Triangle or Circle
**Pump Handle Slam** left,left,Square
**Reverse DDT** left,left,Triangle
**Victory Roll** left,left,Circle
**Belly-Back Suplex*** left,up,right,Circle

### • RUNNING ATTACK
**Tackle with Punches** Square
**Clothesline** Triangle
**Cross Body Block** Circle
**Hurricanranna** Triangle+Circle

### • ATTACK VS. RUNNING
**Drop Toe Hold** Square
**Clothesline** Triangle
**Belly-Belly Suplex** Circle
**Hurricanranna** up,Square

### • GROUND HITS
**- STANDING**
**Stomp** Square
**Falling Headbutt*** down,Square
**Elbow Drop** Triangle
**Standing Moonsault (at side)*** down,Triangle
**Driving Elbow Smash*** down,Triangle

**- RUNNING**
**Fist Drop** Square or Circle
**Front Elbow** Triangle

### • GROUND HOLDS
**- STARTING AT LEGS**
**Leg Grapevine** left,left,Square
**Texas Cloverleaf** left,right,Square
**STF** up,down,Square
**Inverted STF** up,left,up,Square
**Reverse Fuji Leg Bar** left,up,right,Square
**SHAMROCK ANKLE LOCK** left,right,up,Square+Circle

**- STARTING AT HEAD**
**Leg Lock Chokehold** left,left,Triangle
**Reverse Chinlock** left,right,Triangle
**Short-Arm Scissor** up,down,Triangle
**Painkiller** left,up,down,Triangle
**Fuji Arm Bar** up,left,up,Triangle

### • OPPONENT IN CORNER
**- STANDING, FACING OPPONENT**
**Chest Chop** Square
**Climb Turnbuckle and Pummel** Triangle
**Charging Shoulder Tackle** Circle
**Flying Head Scissors** left,left,Square
**Hurricanranna** left,right,Triangle
**Superplex** left,left,Circle
**Top Rope Superplex** up,down,up,Circle

**- FROM BEHIND OPPONENT**
**Smash Head into Turnbuckle** Square or Triangle or Circle
**Pump Handle Slam** left,Circle

**- RUNNING**
**Avalanche** Square or Triangle or Circle

### • FROM THE TOP TURNBUCKLE
**- OPPONENT LYING ON GROUND**
**Elbow Drop** Square or Triangle or Circle
**Double Foot Stomp** Square+X
**Kamikaze Headbutt** Triangle+Circle
**Splash** left,left,Triangle+Square
**Moonsault** X

**- OPPONENT STANDING**
**Drop Kick** Square or Triangle or Circle
**Body Press** Square+X
**Shoulder Tackle** Triangle+Circle
**Hurricanranna*** left,up,Square+Circle

### • FROM THE RING APRON
**- OPPONENT LYING ON GROUND**
**Elbow Drop** Square or Triangle or Circle
**Double Foot Stomp** Square+X
**Kamikaze Headbutt** Triangle+Circle

**- OPPONENT STANDING**
**Drop Kick** Square or Triangle or Circle
**Body Press** Square+X
**Shoulder Tackle** Triangle+Circle

## NINTENDO 64

### • FROM STARTING POSITION
**Front Face DDT** left,right,B
**Arm Wrench** left,left,B
**Crucifix** left,right,A
**Hurricanranna** left,right,up,A
**Japanese Arm Drag*** down,down,B
**Kneebreaker*** left,down,A
**Leg Drag** left,left,A
**Reverse Painkiller*** left,down,B
**Samoan Drop*** left,up,B
**Short-Arm Clothesline*** up,up,B
**Sidewalk Slam*** left,down,Left C
**Single-Arm DDT*** left,up,A
**Small Package** up,down,Left C
**Spinning Neck Breaker** left,left,Left C

### • FROM THE TIE-UP
**Hiptoss** A
**Top Wristlock** B
**Sidewalk Slam** Left C
**Northern Lights Suplex** left,A
**Gut Wrench Power Bomb** left,B
**Vertical Suplex** left,Left C
**Overhead Belly-Belly Suplex*** left,up,A
**Double Underhook Suplex** left,right,B
**Side Belly-Belly Suplex*** left,down,Left C

### • FROM BEHIND
**Russian Leg Sweep** A or B or Left C
**Pump Handle Slam** left,left,A
**Reverse DDT** left,left,B
**Victory Roll** left,left,Left C
**Belly-Back Suplex*** left,up,right,Left C

### • RUNNING ATTACK
**Tackle with Punches** A
**Clothesline** B
**Cross Body Block** Left C
**Hurricanranna** B+Left C

### • ATTACK VS. RUNNING
**Drop Toe Hold** A
**Clothesline** B
**Belly-Belly Suplex** Left C
**Hurricanranna** up,A

### • GROUND HITS
**- STANDING**
**Stomp** A
**Falling Headbutt*** down,A
**Elbow Drop** B
**Standing Moonsault (at side)*** down,B
**Driving Elbow Smash*** down,B

**- RUNNING**
**Fist Drop** A or Left C
**Front Elbow** B

### • GROUND HOLDS
**- STARTING AT LEGS**
**Leg Grapevine** left,left,A
**Texas Cloverleaf** left,right,A
**STF** up,down,A
**Inverted STF** up,left,up,A
**Reverse Fuji Leg Bar** Left,up,right,A
**SHAMROCK ANKLE LOCK** left,right,up,A+Left C

**- STARTING AT HEAD**
**Leg Lock Chokehold** left,left,B
**Reverse Chinlock** left,right,B
**Short-Arm Scissor** up,down,B
**Painkiller** left,up,down,B
**Fuji Arm Bar** up,left,up,B

### • OPPONENT IN CORNER
**- STANDING, FACING OPPONENT**
**Chest Chop** A
**Climb Turnbuckle and Pummel** B
**Charging Shoulder Tackle** Left C
**Flying Head Scissors** left,left,A
**Hurricanranna** left,right,B
**Superplex** left,left,Left C
**Top Rope Superplex** up,down,up,Left C

**- FROM BEHIND OPPONENT**
**Smash Head into Turnbuckle** A or B or Left C
**Pump Handle Slam** left,Left C

**- RUNNING**
**Avalanche** A or B or Left C

### • FROM THE TOP TURNBUCKLE
**- OPPONENT LYING ON GROUND**
**Elbow Drop** A or B or Left C
**Double Foot Stomp** A+Down C
**Kamikaze Headbutt** B+Left C
**Splash** left,left,B+A
**Moonsault** Down C

**- OPPONENT STANDING**
**Drop Kick** A or B or Left C
**Body Press** A+Down C
**Shoulder Tackle** B+Left C
**Hurricanranna*** left,up,A+Left C

### • FROM THE RING APRON
**- OPPONENT LYING ON GROUND**
**Elbow Drop** A or B or Left C
**Double Foot Stomp** A+Down C
**Kamikaze Headbutt** B+Left C

**- OPPONENT STANDING**
**Drop Kick** A or B or Left C
**Body Press** A+Down C
**Shoulder Tackle** B+Left C

**Weight:** 270 pounds
**Height:** 6'2"
**From:** Warner-Robbins, Georgia
**Favorite Quote:** "I'll put my boot right up your @$$!"
**Finishing Move:** The Dominator

## GAME STATS

| | |
|---|---|
| Strength | 9 |
| Toughness | 8 |
| Speed | 3 |
| Recovery | 7 |
| Charisma | 3 |

## WRESTLER BIO

Faarooq, the former leader of the Nation of Domination, is recognized as the first black World's Heavyweight Champion in the history of the sport of professional wrestling. This superstar, formerly known as Ron Simmons, is a football legend at Florida State University. He is the only player, along with Deion Sanders, to have his jersey retired at the school!

Upon entering the World Wrestling Federation, Faarooq created the Nation and molded it into a powerful faction. Following months of friction between him and fellow member Rocky Maivia, "The Rock" ousted his leadership from the group. With vengeance now his top priority, Faarooq may destroy the very Nation he created!

## TIPS

Faarooq's wrestling style is ground-based, methodical and power-driven; he is an incredibly powerful man with great striking ability. He is also a superb ring general and his tactical and strategic thinking often gives him a major advantage over less-experienced opponents. With a relatively low Charisma rating, however, you'll need to really mix up the moves in order to keep the fans on Faarooq's side. His finisher, the Dominator, is a reverse vertical suplex.

# BUTTON COMBOS



## PLAYSTATION

### • FROM STARTING POSITION
**Bearhug** left,down,Triangle
**DOMINATOR*** up,up,up,Circle+X
**Hiptoss*** up,up,Square
**Japanese Arm Drag*** down,down,Triangle
**Knee to Face** left,down,Square
**Press Slam*** down,down,left,Circle
**Side Belly-Belly Suplex** left,up,Square
**Short-Arm Clothesline** up,down,Triangle
**Shoulder Breaker** left,right,Triangle
**Sidewalk Slam** left,right,Square
**Spinebuster** up,down,Square
**Spinning Neck Breaker** left,right,Circle
**Choke Slam** left,left,up,Triangle
**Vertical Suplex** left,up,Circle

### • FROM THE TIE-UP
**Hiptoss** Square
**Chest Breaker** Triangle
**Side Slam** Circle
**Gut Wrench Power Bomb** left,Square
**Side Belly-Belly Suplex** left,Triangle
**Northern Lights Suplex** left,Circle
**Sidewalk Slam** up,down,Square
**Brainbuster** left,right,Triangle
**Power Bomb** up,left,Circle

### • FROM BEHIND
**Full Nelson** Square or Triangle or Circle
**Atomic Drop** left,left,Square or Triangle
**Belly-Back Suplex*** left,up,right,Circle

### • RUNNING ATTACK
**Shoulder Tackle** Square or Circle
**Clothesline** Triangle

### • ATTACK VS. RUNNING
**Boot to Face** Square
**Clothesline** Triangle
**Power Slam** Circle
**Sidewalk Slam** left,Triangle

### • GROUND HITS
**- STANDING**
**Stomp** Square
**Falling Headbutt*** down,Square
**Axe Handle Smash** Triangle

**- RUNNING**
**Running Knee Drop** Square
**Fist Drop** Triangle
**Falling Headbutt** Circle

### • GROUND HOLDS
**- STARTING AT LEGS**
**Knee to Inside Leg** left,left,Square
**Elbow to Groin** left,right,Square
**Inverted STF** up,down,Square
**Boston Crab*** left,down,right,Square

**- STARTING AT HEAD**
**Arm Wrench** left,left,Triangle
**Knee to Back** left,right,Triangle
**Blatant Choke** up,down,Triangle
**Camel Clutch*** left,up,right,Triangle

### • OPPONENT IN CORNER
**- STANDING, FACING OPPONENT**
**Choke with Boot** Square
**Charging Shoulder** Triangle or Circle
**Overhead Press** left,left,Square
**Superplex** left,left,Triangle
**Top Rope Superplex** left,left,Circle

**- FROM BEHIND OPPONENT**
**Smash Head into Turnbuckle** Square or Triangle or Circle
**Pump Handle Slam** left,Circle

**- RUNNING**
**Clothesline** Square or Triangle or Circle

### • FROM THE TOP TURNBUCKLE
**- OPPONENT LYING ON GROUND**
**Fist Drop** Square or Triangle or Circle
**Knee Drop** Square+X
**Driving Elbow** Triangle+Circle
**Double Foot Stomp** up,left,Triangle+Square

**- OPPONENT STANDING**
**Axe Handle Smash** Square or Triangle or Circle
**Forearm Smash** Square+X
**Clothesline** Triangle+Circle
**Shoulder Tackle** left,up,Circle+X

### • FROM THE RING APRON
**- OPPONENT LYING ON GROUND**
**Fist Drop** Square or Triangle or Circle
**Knee Drop** Square+X
**Driving Elbow** Triangle+Circle

**- OPPONENT STANDING**
**Axe Handle Smash** Square or Triangle or Circle
**Forearm Smash** Square+X
**Clothesline** Triangle+Circle

## NINTENDO 64

### • FROM STARTING POSITION
**Bearhug** left,down,B
**DOMINATOR*** up,up,up,Left C+Down C
**Hiptoss*** up,up,A
**Japanese Arm Drag*** down,down,B
**Knee to Face** left,down,A
**Press Slam*** down,down,left,Left C
**Side Belly-Belly Suplex** left,up,A
**Short-Arm Clothesline** up,down,B
**Shoulder Breaker** left,right,B
**Sidewalk Slam** left,right,A
**Spinebuster** up,down,A
**Spinning Neck Breaker** left,right,Left C
**Choke Slam** left,left,up,B
**Vertical Suplex** left,up,Left C

### • FROM THE TIE-UP
**Hiptoss** A
**Chest Breaker** B
**Side Slam** Left C
**Gut Wrench Power Bomb** left,A
**Side Belly-Belly Suplex** left,B
**Northern Lights Suplex** left,Left C
**Sidewalk Slam** up,down,A
**Brainbuster** left,right,B
**Power Bomb** up,left,Left C

### • FROM BEHIND
**Full Nelson** A or B or Left C
**Atomic Drop** left,left,A or B
**Belly-Back Suplex*** left,up,right,Left C

### • RUNNING ATTACK
**Shoulder Tackle** A or Left C
**Clothesline** B

### • ATTACK VS. RUNNING
**Boot to Face** A
**Clothesline** B
**Power Slam** Left C
**Sidewalk Slam** left,B

### • GROUND HITS
**- STANDING**
**Stomp** A
**Falling Headbutt*** down,A
**Axe Handle Smash** B

**- RUNNING**
**Running Knee Drop** A
**Fist Drop** B
**Falling Headbutt** Left C

### • GROUND HOLDS
**- STARTING AT LEGS**
**Knee to Inside Leg** left,left,A
**Elbow to Groin** left,right,A
**Inverted STF** up,down,A
**Boston Crab*** left,down,right,A

**- STARTING AT HEAD**
**Arm Wrench** left,left,B
**Knee to Back** left,right,B
**Blatant Choke** up,down,B
**Camel Clutch*** left,up,right,B

### • OPPONENT IN CORNER
**- STANDING, FACING OPPONENT**
**Choke with Boot** A
**Charging Shoulder** B or Left C
**Overhead Press** left,left,A
**Superplex** left,left,B
**Top Rope Superplex** left,left,Left C

**- FROM BEHIND OPPONENT**
**Smash Head into Turnbuckle** A or B or Left C
**Pump Handle Slam** left,Left C

**- RUNNING**
**Clothesline** A or B or Left C

### • FROM THE TOP TURNBUCKLE
**- OPPONENT LYING ON GROUND**
**Fist Drop** A or B or Left C
**Knee Drop** A+Down C
**Driving Elbow** B+Left C
**Double Foot Stomp** up,left,B+A

**- OPPONENT STANDING**
**Axe Handle Smash** A or B or Left C
**Forearm Smash** A+Down C
**Clothesline** B+Left C
**Shoulder Tackle** left,up,Left C+Down C

### • FROM THE RING APRON
**- OPPONENT LYING ON GROUND**
**Fist Drop** A or B or Left C
**Knee Drop** A+Down C
**Driving Elbow** B+Left C

**- OPPONENT STANDING**
**Axe Handle Smash** A or B or Left C
**Forearm Smash** A+Down C
**Clothesline** B+Left C

## NO BLOCKING

Beat the War Zone Challenge with Faarooq or Shamrock, and you'll be able to disable the blocking function of the game! Batter up!

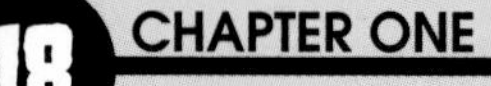

# GOLDUST™

**Height:** 6′ 6″
**Weight:** 260 pounds
**From:** Hollywood, CA
**Titles Held:** Intercontinental Champion
**Finishing Move:** Curtain Call

## GAME STATS

| | |
|---|---|
| Strength | 7 |
| Toughness | 8 |
| Speed | 3 |
| Recovery | 9 |
| Charisma | 3 |

## WRESTLER BIO

The tale of Dustin Runnels, a.k.a. Goldust, is certainly one of the more twisted in the history of the World Wrestling Federation. Goldust first made his mark in the big time at the 1996 Royal Rumble when he defeated Razor Ramon for the Intercontinental Title. Just a few months later, the Golden One introduced Marlena, his director and wife, to the world.

The two enjoyed success in the Federation for quite some time, until a feud with the late Brian Pillman changed their lives forever. After Goldust came out on the losing end of a match with Pillman, Marlena was forced to spend the next 30 days with their foe. When husband and wife were finally reunited, Goldust scorned his love interest and deserted her for "someone new." That someone turned out to be the wicked Luna Vachon, who has twisted Dustin's mind into The Artist Formerly Known As Goldust. Together this new couple gives new meaning to the word "bizarre." Meanwhile, Marlena's status remains a mystery.

## TIPS

While he rarely if ever takes to the air, "The Artist" has a fair chance at success when he does. His ground-based attack is solid and amazingly flexible with one of the highest rated striking ratings in the game. In fact, Goldust is a wrestling chameleon, able to absorb the coloration and style of any opponent — and then turn it against them. His ring psychology is top-notch and his ability to get a "rise" out of an opponent is well-known.

# BUTTON COMBOS

## PLAYSTATION

**• FROM STARTING POSITION**

**Abdominal Stretch** left,right,Circle
**Body Slam** left,down,Circle
**DDT** left,down,Square
**Gut Wrench Power Bomb** left,right,Triangle
**Hiptoss*** down,down,Square
**Japanese Arm Drag*** down,down,Triangle
**Kneebreaker** up,down,Square
**Neck Breaker** left,down,Triangle
**Samoan Drop** left,up,Triangle
**Single-Arm DDT** left,up,Square
**Sleeper** up,down,Triangle
**Snap Mare** left,up,Circle
**Vertical Suplex** up,down,Circle

**• FROM THE TIE-UP**

**Hiptoss** Square
**Atomic Drop** Triangle
**Inverted Atomic Drop** Circle
**DDT** left,Square
**Vertical Suplex** left,Triangle
**Samoan Drop** left,Circle
**Brainbuster** left,down,Square
**Bulldog** left,up,Triangle
**Piledriver** up,down,Circle

**• FROM BEHIND**

**Abdominal Stretch** Square or Triangle or Circle
**Atomic Drop** left,left,Square or Triangle
**Reverse DDT** left,right,down,Circle
**CURTAIN CALL** left,down,down,Circle+X

**• RUNNING ATTACK**

**Drop Kick** Square
**Drop to Knees and Uppercut** Circle
**Clothesline** Triangle

**• ATTACK VS. RUNNING**

**Drop Kick** Square
**Clothesline** Triangle
**Powerslam** Circle
**Back Body Drop** up,Triangle

**• GROUND HITS**

**- STANDING**
**Leg Drop (at side)** Square
**Stomp** Square
**Double Foot Stomp*** down,Square
**Fist Drop** Triangle

**- RUNNING**
**Knee Drop** Square
**Fist Drop** Triangle
**Butt Drop** Circle

**• GROUND HOLDS**

**- STARTING AT LEGS**
**Elbow Drop onto Leg** left,left,Square
**Knee to Inside Leg** left,right,Square
**Spinning Toe Hold** up,down,Square
**Headbutt to Groin*** left,up,right,Square

**- STARTING AT HEAD**
**Arm Wrench** left,left,Triangle
**Rear Chin Lock** left,right,Triangle
**Stump Puller** up,down,Triangle

**• OPPONENT IN CORNER**

**- STANDING, FACING OPPONENT**
**Kick in Corner** Square
**Chest Chop** Triangle
**Repeated Elbows** Circle
**Superplex** left,left,Square or Triangle
**Top Rope Superplex** left,left,Circle

**- FROM BEHIND OPPONENT**
**Smash Head into Turnbuckle** Square or Triangle or Circle
**Pump Handle Slam** left,Circle

**- RUNNING**
**Clothesline** Square or Triangle or Circle

**• FROM THE TOP TURNBUCKLE**

**- OPPONENT LYING ON GROUND**
**Knee Drop** Square or Triangle or Circle
**Butt Drop** Square+X
**Fist Drop** Triangle+Circle
**Somersault Senton Splash** up,up,Triangle+Square

**- OPPONENT STANDING**
**Bionic Elbow** Square or Triangle or Circle
**Forearm Smash** Square+X
**Flying Butt Bump** Triangle+Circle
**Shoulder Tackle** left,up,Circle+X

**• FROM THE RING APRON**

**- OPPONENT LYING ON GROUND**
**Knee Drop** Square or Triangle or Circle
**Butt Drop** Square+X
**Fist Drop** Triangle+Circle

**- OPPONENT STANDING**
**Bionic Elbow** Square or Triangle or Circle
**Forearm Smash** Square+X
**Flying Butt Bump** Triangle+Circle

## NINTENDO 64

**• FROM STARTING POSITION**

**Abdominal Stretch** left,right,Left C
**Body Slam** left,down,Left C
**DDT** left,down,A
**Gut Wrench Power Bomb** left,right,B
**Hiptoss*** down,down,A
**Japanese Arm Drag*** down,down,B
**Kneebreaker** up,down,A
**Neck Breaker** left,down,B
**Samoan Drop** left,up,B
**Single-Arm DDT** left,up,A
**Sleeper** up,down,B
**Snap Mare** left,up,Left C
**Vertical Suplex** up,down,Left C

**• FROM THE TIE-UP**

**Hiptoss** A
**Atomic Drop** B
**Inverted Atomic Drop** Left C
**DDT** left,A
**Vertical Suplex** left,B
**Samoan Drop** left,Left C
**Brainbuster** left,down,A
**Bulldog** left,up,B
**Piledriver** up,down,Left C

**• FROM BEHIND**

**Abdominal Stretch** A or B or Left C
**Atomic Drop** left,left,A or B
**Reverse DDT** left,right,down,Left C
**CURTAIN CALL** left,down,down,Left C+Down C

**• RUNNING ATTACK**

**Drop Kick** A
**Drop to Knees and Uppercut** Left C
**Clothesline** B

**• ATTACK VS. RUNNING**

**Drop Kick** A
**Clothesline** B
**Flying Back Elbow** Left C
**Back Body Drop** up,B

**• GROUND HITS**

**- STANDING**
**Leg Drop (at side)** A
**Stomp** A
**Double Foot Stomp*** down,A
**Fist Drop** B

**- RUNNING**
**Knee Drop** A
**Fist Drop** B
**Butt Drop** Left C

**• GROUND HOLDS**

**- STARTING AT LEGS**
**Elbow Drop onto Leg** left,left,A
**Knee to Inside Leg** left,right,A
**Spinning Toe Hold** up,down,A
**Headbutt to Groin*** left,up,right,A

**- STARTING AT HEAD**
**Arm Wrench** left,left,B
**Rear Chin Lock** left,right,B
**Stump Puller** up,down,B

**• OPPONENT IN CORNER**

**- STANDING, FACING OPPONENT**
**Kick in Corner** A
**Chest Chop** B
**Repeated Elbows** Left C
**Superplex** left,left,A or B
**Top Rope Superplex** left,left,Left C

**- FROM BEHIND OPPONENT**
**Smash Head into Turnbuckle** A or B or Left C
**Pump Handle Slam** left,Left C

**- RUNNING**
**Clothesline** A or B or Left C

**• FROM THE TOP TURNBUCKLE**

**- OPPONENT LYING ON GROUND**
**Knee Drop** A or B or Left C
**Butt Drop** A+Down C
**Fist Drop** B+Left C
**Somersault Senton Splash** up,up,B+A

**- OPPONENT STANDING**
**Bionic Elbow** A or B or Left C
**Forearm Smash** A+Down C
**Flying Butt Bump** B+Left C
**Shoulder Tackle** left,up,Left C+Down C

**• FROM THE RING APRON**

**- OPPONENT LYING ON GROUND**
**Knee Drop** A or B or Left C
**Butt Drop** A+Down C
**Fist Drop** B+Left C

**- OPPONENT STANDING**
**Bionic Elbow** A or B or Left C
**Forearm Smash** A+Down C
**Flying Butt Bump** B+Left C

WRESTLERS

# OWEN HART™

**From:** Calgary, Alberta, Canada
**Height:** 5'11"
**Weight:** 227 pounds
**Finishing Move:** Sharp Shooter
**Title(s) Held:** Federation Tag Team (2), Intercontinental (2), European

## GAME STATS

| | |
|---|---|
| Strength | 4 |
| Toughness | 6 |
| Speed | 9 |
| Recovery | 6 |
| Charisma | 5 |

## WRESTLER BIO

The career of Owen Hart has evolved since he entered the World Wrestling Federation as the "Blue Blazer". Despite earning a great deal of success in the ring, Owen had always been prevented from attaining superstar status in part because of the large shadow cast by his older brother, Bret. After Bret's controversial departure from the World Wrestling Federation, Owen's opportunity to shine in the spotlight has presented itself. Always considered one of the most athletic and charismatic superstars in the Federation, fans around the world will have a chance to see what Owen Hart can do now that the focus will be solely on him.

## TIPS

He isn't large, but Owen is aggressive, with a relentless quality that makes him a dangerous opponent. He can fly, but he isn't a flyer anymore. His ability on the mat is legendary, so it's a good idea for him to use takedowns on larger opponents, then punish them on the canvas with leglocks that can eventually set up the opponent for a Sharp Shooter.

# BUTTON COMBOS

## PLAYSTATION

### • FROM STARTING POSITION

**Abdominal Stretch** left,down,Triangle
**Arm Drag*** up,up,Triangle
**Overrhead Belly-Belly Suplex** left,left,Circle
**Double Underhook Suplex*** down,down,Circle
**Flying Head Scissors** left,left,Square
**Drop Toe Hold*** down,down,Square
**Hurricanranna*** left,right,up,Square
**Gut Wrench Power Bomb** left,right,Triangle
**Japanese Arm Drag*** down,down,Triangle
**Fisherman's Suplex*** up,up,Circle
**Side Belly-Belly Suplex** left,up,Triangle
**Small Package** left,up,Circle
**Snap Mare** left,down,Square

### • FROM THE TIE-UP

**Arm Drag** Square
**Neck Breaker** Triangle
**Side Belly-Belly Suplex** Circle
**Gut Wrench Power Bomb** left,Square
**Samoan Drop** left,Triangle
**Vertical Suplex** left,Circle
**Overhead Belly-Belly Suplex** left,up,Square
**Piledriver** up,down,Triangle
**Double Underhook Suplex** up,down,Circle

### • FROM BEHIND

**Cross Face Chicken Wing** Square or Triangle or Circle
**Atomic Drop** left,left,Square
**Belly-Back Suplex** left,left,Triangle
**Victory Roll** left,left,Circle
**German Suplex*** left,left,up,Circle

### • RUNNING ATTACK

**Spinning Heel Kick** Square
**Clothesline** Triangle
**Flying Forearm** Circle
**Hurricanranna** Square+X

### • ATTACK VS. RUNNING

**Drop Kick** Square
**Back Body Drop** Triangle
**Belly-Belly Suplex** Circle
**Hurricanranna** up,Square

### • GROUND HITS

**- STANDING**
**Stomp** Square
**Falling Headbutt** down,Square
**Elbow Drop** Triangle
**Splash** down,Triangle

**- RUNNING**
**Knee Drop** Square
**Fist Drop** Triangle
**Falling Headbutt** Circle

### • GROUND HOLDS

**- STARTING AT LEGS**
**Surfboard** left,left,Square
**Leg Grapevine** left,right,Square
**Wishbone Leg Splitter** up,down,Square
**Reverse Indian Deathlock** left,right,up,Square
**Inverted STF** up,left,up,Square
**SHARP SHOOTER** left,left,up,Square+X

**- STARTING AT HEAD**
**Arm Wrench** left,left,Triangle
**Rear Chin Lock** left,right,Triangle
**Leg Lock Chokehold** up,down,Triangle

### • OPPONENT IN CORNER

**- STANDING, FACING OPPONENT**
**Repeated Kicks to Ribs** Square
**Climb Turnbuckle and Pummel** Triangle
**Splash** Circle
**Flying Head Scissors** left,left,Square
**Monkey Flip** left,left,Triangle
**Swinging DDT** left,left,Circle
**Hurricanranna** left,right,up,Square
**Superplex** up,left,down,Triangle

**- FROM BEHIND OPPONENT**
**Smash Head into Turnbuckle** Square or Triangle or Circle
**Pump Handle Slam** left,Circle

**- RUNNING**
**Avalanche** Square or Triangle or Circle

### • FROM THE TOP TURNBUCKLE

**- OPPONENT LYING ON GROUND**
**Kamikaze Headbutt** Square or Triangle or Circle
**Somersault Senton Splash** Square+X
**Splash** Triangle+Circle
**Shooting Star Press*** up,up,Square+Circle
**Moonsault** X

**- OPPONENT STANDING**
**Forearm Smash** Square or Triangle or Circle
**Hurricanranna** Square+X
**Torpedo Dropkick** Triangle+Circle
**Wheel Kick** left,left,Square+Circle
**Sunset Flip** Triangle+Square+Circle

### • FROM THE RING APRON

**- OPPONENT LYING ON GROUND**
**Kamikaze Headbutt** Square or Triangle or Circle
**Somersault Senton Splash** Square+X
**Splash** Triangle+Circle

**- OPPONENT STANDING**
**Forearm Smash** Square or Triangle or Circle
**Hurricanranna** Square+X
**Torpedo Dropkick** Triangle+Circle

## NINTENDO 64

### • FROM STARTING POSITION

**Abdominal Stretch** left,down,B
**Arm Drag*** up,up,B
**Overhead Belly-Belly Suplex** left,left,Left C
**Double Underhook Suplex*** down,down,Left C
**Flying Head Scissors** left,left,A
**Drop Toe Hold*** down,down,A
**Hurricanranna*** left,right,up,A
**Gut Wrench Power Bomb** left,right,B
**Japanese Arm Drag*** down,down,B
**Fisherman's Suplex*** up,up,Left C
**Side Belly-Belly Suplex** left,up,B
**Small Package** left,up,Left C
**Snap Mare** left,down,A

### • FROM THE TIE-UP

**Arm Drag** A
**Neck Breaker** B
**Side Belly-Belly Suplex** Left C
**Gut Wrench Power Bomb** left,A
**Samoan Drop** left,B
**Vertical Suplex** left,Left C
**Overhead Belly-Belly Suplex** left,up,A
**Piledriver** up,down,B
**Double Underhook Suplex** up,down,Left C

### • FROM BEHIND

**Cross Face Chicken Wing** A or B or Left C
**Atomic Drop** left,left,A
**Belly-Back Suplex** left,left,B
**Victory Roll** left,left,Left C
**German Suplex*** left,left,up,Left C

### • RUNNING ATTACK

**Spinning Heel Kick** A
**Clothesline** B
**Flying Forearm** Left C
**Hurricanranna** A+Down C

### • ATTACK VS. RUNNING

**Drop Kick** A
**Back Body Drop** B
**Belly-Belly Suplex** Left C
**Hurricanranna** up,A

### • GROUND HITS

**- STANDING**
**Stomp** A
**Falling Headbutt** down,A
**Elbow Drop** B
**Splash** down,B

**- RUNNING**
**Knee Drop** A
**Fist Drop** B
**Falling Headbutt** Left C

### • GROUND HOLDS

**- STARTING AT LEGS**
**Surfboard** left,left,A
**Leg Grapevine** left,right,A
**Wishbone Leg Splitter** up,down,A
**Reverse Indian Deathlock** left,right,up,A
**Inverted STF** up,left,up,A
**SHARP SHOOTER** left,left,up,A+Down C

**- STARTING AT HEAD**
**Arm Wrench** left,left,B
**Rear Chin Lock** left,right,B
**Leg Lock Chokehold** up,down,B

### • OPPONENT IN CORNER

**- STANDING, FACING OPPONENT**
**Repeated Kicks to Ribs** A
**Climb Turnbuckle and Pummel** B
**Splash** Left C
**Flying Head Scissors** left,left,A
**Monkey Flip** left,left,B
**Swinging DDT** left,left,Left C
**Hurricanranna** left,right,up,A
**Superplex** up,left,down,B

**- FROM BEHIND OPPONENT**
**Smash Head into Turnbuckle** A or B or Left C
**Pump Handle Slam** left,Left C

**- RUNNING**
**Avalanche** A or B or Left C

### • FROM THE TOP TURNBUCKLE

**- OPPONENT LYING ON GROUND**
**Kamikaze Headbutt** A or B or Left C
**Somersault Senton Splash** A+Down C
**Splash** B+Left C
**Shooting Star Press*** up,up,A+Left C
**Moonsault** Down C

**- OPPONENT STANDING**
**Forearm Smash** A or B or Left C
**Hurricanranna** A+Down C
**Torpedo Dropkick** B+Left C
**Wheel Kick** left,left,A+Left C
**Sunset Flip** B+A+Left C

### • FROM THE RING APRON

**- OPPONENT LYING ON GROUND**
**Kamikaze Headbutt** A or B or Left C
**Somersault Senton Splash** A+Down C
**Splash** B+Left C

**- OPPONENT STANDING**
**Forearm Smash** A or B or Left C
**Hurricanranna** A+Down C
**Torpedo Dropkick** B+Left C

™

**Weight:** 275 pounds
**Height:** 6′5″
**From:** The South Pacific
**Favorite Quote:** "Know Your Role!"
**Finishing Move:** The Rock Bottom

## GAME STATS

| | |
|---|---|
| Strength | 7 |
| Toughness | 8 |
| Speed | 6 |
| Recovery | 6 |
| Charisma | 3 |

## WRESTLER BIO

Rocky Maivia, the self-proclaimed "Ruler of the Nation of Domination", is a third-generation superstar with immeasurable athleticism — and cockiness to boot! After graduating as an All-American football star from the University of Miami, Maivia entered the World Wrestling Federation and quickly became the Intercontinental Champion.

After fans' opinion of Rocky soured, Maivia turned his back on the masses and joined the Nation of Domination. However, egos would soon clash when "The Rock" began to undermine Faarooq's leadership of the faction. Following months of friction between the two superstars, Maivia ordered the rest of the Nation to brutally attack their former leader! Now, the Nation takes orders from "The Rock"!

## TIPS

In the ring, the Rock is a model athlete. His conditioning is superb and he only admits new maneuvers to his repertoire after he has mastered them. He works a basic ground game but should liberally mix in a blend of Drop Kicks and air attacks, since he has a high likelihood of success. The Rock, despite his fondness for throwing punches, has a below-average striking ability, but he's fast, his Shoulderbreaker is "rock" solid and his head-and-arm suplex, known as The Rock Bottom, has buried many opponents. Use it wisely.

# BUTTON COMBOS



## PLAYSTATION

### • FROM STARTING POSITION

**Front Face DDT** left,right,Triangle
**Arm Drag*** up,up,Triangle
**Drop Toe Hold*** down,down,Square
**Hurricanranna** left,right,up,Square
**Headlock Takedown** left,left,Circle
**Japanese Arm Drag*** down,down,Triangle
**Overhead Belly-Belly Suplex** left,up,Circle
**Samoan Drop*** left,up,Triangle
**Side Belly-Belly Suplex*** left,down,Square
**Short-Arm Clothesline** up,up,Circle
**Shoulder Breaker*** left,down,Triangle
**Spinebuster** up,down,Triangle
**Laying the Smack Down*** left,right,up,Triangle
**ROCK BOTTOM*** left,left,up,Triangle+Circle

### • FROM THE TIE-UP

**Arm Drag** Square
**Shoulder Breaker** Triangle
**DDT** Circle
**Side Belly-Belly Suplex** left,Square
**Inverted Atomic Drop** left,Triangle
**Sidewalk Slam** left,Circle
**Double Underhook Suplex** left,down,Square
**Brainbuster** left,right,Triangle
**Piledriver** up,down,Circle

### • FROM BEHIND

**Cross Face Chicken Wing** Square or Triangle or Circle
**Pump Handle Slam** left,left,Square
**Reverse DDT** left,left,Triangle
**Victory Roll** left,left,Circle
**Belly-Back Suplex** left,up,right,Circle

### • RUNNING ATTACK

**Drop Kick** Square
**Clothesline** Triangle
**Crucifix** Circle
**Hurricanranna** Triangle+Circle

### • ATTACK VS. RUNNING

**Drop Kick** Square
**Back Body Drop** Triangle
**Power Slam** Circle
**Hurricanranna** up,Square

### • GROUND HITS

**- STANDING**
**Leg Drop (at side)** Square
**Stomp** Square
**Falling Headbutt** down,Square
**Splash** down,Triangle
**Fist Drop** Triangle

**- RUNNING**
**Leg Drop (at side)** Square
**Knee Drop** Square or Triangle
**Splash** Circle

### • GROUND HOLDS

**- STARTING AT LEGS**
**Elbow Drop onto Leg** left,left,Square
**Spinning Toe Hold** left,right,Square
**Inverted STF** up,down,Square
**STF** up,down,up,Square

**- STARTING AT HEAD**
**Arm Wrench** left,left,Triangle
**Reverse Chinlock** left,right,Triangle
**Short Arm Scissor** up,down,Triangle

### • OPPONENT IN CORNER

**- STANDING, FACING OPPONENT**
**Choke with Boot** Square
**Climb Turnbuckle and Pummel** Triangle
**Splash** Circle
**Flying Head Scissors** left,left,Square
**Swinging DDT** left,left,Triangle
**Belly-Belly Suplex** left,left,Circle
**Hurricanranna** left,right,up,Square
**Top Rope Superplex** left,up,right,Triangle

**- FROM BEHIND OPPONENT**
**Smash Head into Turnbuckle** Square or Triangle or Circle
**Pump Handle Slam** left,Circle

**- RUNNING**
**Avalanche** Square or Triangle or Circle

### • FROM THE TOP TURNBUCKLE

**- OPPONENT LYING ON GROUND**
**Elbow Drop** Square or Triangle or Circle
**Fist Drop** Triangle+Circle
**Knee Drop** Square+X
**Splash** left,left,Triangle+Square

**- OPPONENT STANDING**
**Drop Kick** Square or Triangle or Circle
**Clothesline** Square+X
**Shoulder Tackle** Triangle+Circle
**Body Press*** up,left,Circle+X

### • FROM THE RING APRON

**- OPPONENT LYING ON GROUND**
**Elbow Drop** Square or Triangle or Circle
**Knee Drop** Square+X
**Fist Drop** Triangle+Circle

**- OPPONENT STANDING**
**Drop Kick** Square or Triangle or Circle
**Clothesline** Square+X
**Shoulder Tackle** Triangle+Circle

## NINTENDO 64

### • FROM STARTING POSITION

**Front Face DDT** left,right,B
**Arm Drag*** up,up,B
**Drop Toe Hold*** down,down,A
**Hurricanranna** left,right,up,A
**Headlock Takedown** left,left,Left C
**Japanese Arm Drag*** down,down,B
**Overhead Belly-Belly Suplex** left,up,Left C
**Samoan Drop*** left,up,B
**Side Belly-Belly Suplex*** left,down,A
**Short-Arm Clothesline** up,up,Left C
**Shoulder Breaker*** left,down,B
**Spinebuster** up,down,B
**Laying the Smack Down*** left,right,up,B
**ROCK BOTTOM*** left,left,up,B+Left C

### • FROM THE TIE-UP

**Arm Drag** A
**Shoulder Breaker** B
**DDT** Left C
**Side Belly-Belly Suplex** left,A
**Inverted Atomic Drop** left,B
**Sidewalk Slam** left,Left C
**Double Underhook Suplex** left,down,A
**Brainbuster** left,right,B
**Piledriver** up,down,Left C

### • FROM BEHIND

**Cross Face Chicken Wing** A or B or Left C
**Pump Handle Slam** left,left,A
**Reverse DDT** left,left,B
**Victory Roll** left,left,Left C
**Belly-Back Suplex** left,up,right,Left C

### • RUNNING ATTACK

**Drop Kick** A
**Clothesline** B
**Crucifix** Left C
**Hurricanranna** B+Left C

### • ATTACK VS. RUNNING

**Drop Kick** A
**Back Body Drop** B
**Power Slam** Left C
**Hurricanranna** up,A

### • GROUND HITS

**- STANDING**
**Leg Drop (at side)** A
**Stomp** A
**Falling Headbutt** down,A
**Splash** down,B
**Fist Drop** B

**- RUNNING**
**Leg Drop** (at side) A
**Knee Drop** A or B
**Splash** Left C

### • GROUND HOLDS

**- STARTING AT LEGS**
**Elbow Drop onto Leg** left,left,A
**Spinning Toe Hold** left,right,A
**Inverted STF** up,down,A
**STF** up,down,up,A
**- STARTING AT HEAD**
**Arm Wrench** left,left,B
**Reverse Chinlock** left,right,B
**Short Arm Scissor** up,down,B

### • OPPONENT IN CORNER

**- STANDING, FACING OPPONENT**
**Choke with Boot** A
**Climb Turnbuckle and Pummel** B
**Splash** Left C
**Flying Head Scissors** left,left,A
**Swinging DDT** left,left,B
**Belly-Belly Suplex** left,left,Left C
**Hurricanranna** left,right,up,A
**Top Rope Superplex** left,up,right,B

**- FROM BEHIND OPPONENT**
**Smash Head into Turnbuckle** A or B or Left C
**Pump Handle Slam** left,Left C

**- RUNNING**
**Avalanche** A or B or Left C

### • FROM THE TOP TURNBUCKLE

**- OPPONENT LYING ON GROUND**
**Elbow Drop** A or B or Left C
**Fist Drop** B+Left C
**Knee Drop** A+Down C
**Splash** left,left,B+A

**- OPPONENT STANDING**
**Drop Kick** A or B or Left C
**Clothesline** A+Down C
**Shoulder Tackle** B+Left C
**Body Press*** up,left,Left C+Down C

### • FROM THE RING APRON

**- OPPONENT LYING ON GROUND**
**Elbow Drop** A or B or Left C
**Knee Drop** A+Down C
**Fist Drop** B+Left C

**- OPPONENT STANDING**
**Drop Kick** A or B or Left C
**Clothesline** A+Down C
**Shoulder Tackle** B+Left C

WRESTLERS

MANKIND

HIDDEN WRESTLER CACTUS JACK

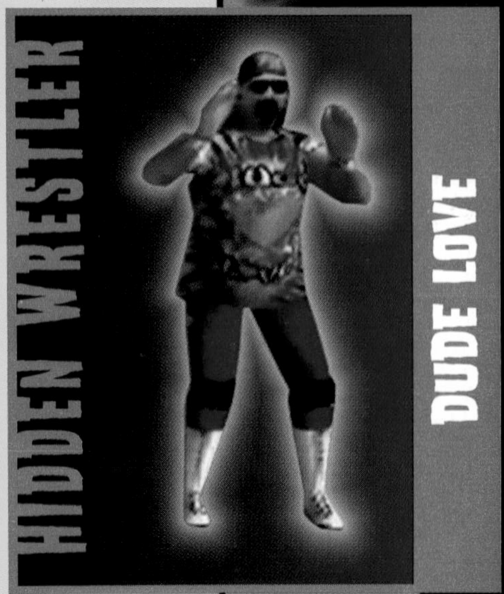

HIDDEN WRESTLER DUDE LOVE

**Height:** 6′2″
**Weight:** 287 lbs.
**From:** The Boiler Room, Truth or Consequences, NM, etc.
**Finishing Move:** Mandible Claw (Mankind), Double-Arm DDT (Dude Love and Cactus Jack)
**Famous Words:** "Have a nice day!" "Bang-bang!"

## GAME STATS

| | |
|---|---|
| Strength | 5 |
| Toughness | 9 |
| Speed | 4 |
| Recovery | 7 |
| Charisma | 5 |

## WRESTLER BIO

Although he ranks right up there with the Undertaker as one of the most bizarre characters in the annals of pro wrestling, Mankind turned out to be a turning point for the man behind the mask. Mick Foley grew up in the New York area as a maniacal World Wrestling Federation fan and wanted to be a wrestler ever since he discovered the sport. He started out in the business under his own name, but took the ring name "Cactus Jack" and, through the late '80s and early '90s, made himself a hardcore legend. He fought in explosive barbed-wire matches, took insane bumps and falls and mutilated his body terribly over the years. The hardcore legend of Cactus Jack grew until it reached critical mass with Foley's arrival at the Big Show. Mankind suggested a man driven by demons of his own creation and tormented by desires which could never be attained.

Foley has now wrestled in the World Wrestling Federation as Mankind, Dude Love and Cactus Jack. The latest stage in the ongoing metamorphosis of Mick Foley has been a return to his Dude Love persona. But we're certain Mankind is always lurking in the boiler room of Mick Foley's overcrowded mind.

Mankind's finisher, the Mandible Claw, was actually invented back in the '50s by Dr. Sam Shephard. In the real-life case that inspired the TV series and film The Fugitive, Shephard was accused of murdering his wife but was found innocent. He then briefly became a pro wrestler and based the Mandible Claw on his knowledge that the softest tissue in the human body is found just beneath the tongue.

## TIPS

He's no flyer, but Mankind will take incredible risks. He has above average striking ability, is extremely aggressive and strong. His many injuries have greatly reduced his agility, however, and he was never fast. But his ability — some might say his desire — to absorb punishment makes him a formidable adversary, and his Mandible Claw is among the most feared finishers in pro wrestling.

# BUTTON COMBOS

## PLAYSTATION

### • FROM STARTING POSITION
**Body Slam** left,up,Circle
**Clothesline** up,up,Triangle
**Cobra Clutch** up,up,Circle
**DDT** left,down,Square
**Front Backbreaker** left,right,Circle
**Gut Wrench Power Bomb** left,right,Triangle
**Hiptoss** up,down,Square
**Kneebreaker** left,down,Circle
**Leg Drag** up,up,Square
**MANDIBLE CLAW (F — MANKIND)** left,right,up,Circle+X
**DOUBLE-ARM DDT (F — CACTUS JACK, DUDE LOVE)** left,right,up,Circle+X
**Neck Breaker** left,down,Triangle
**Samoan Drop** left,up,Triangle
**Side Belly-Belly Suplex** up,down,Circle
**Single-Arm DDT** left,up,Square

### • FROM THE TIE-UP
**Hiptoss** Square
**DDT** Triangle
**Side Belly-Belly Suplex** Circle
**Samoan Drop** left,Square
**Inverted Atomic Drop** left,Triangle
**Vertical Suplex** left,Circle
**Brainbuster** left,right,Square
**Power Bomb** left,down,Triangle
**Piledriver** left,up,Circle
**MANDIBLE CLAW (F — MANKIND)** left,right,Circle

### • FROM BEHIND
**Nerve Hold** Square or Triangle or Circle
**Cross-Face Chicken Wing** left,left,Square
**Reverse DDT** left,left,Triangle
**Side Slam** left,left,up,Circle

### • RUNNING ATTACK
**Clothesline** Triangle
**Spinning Neck Breaker** Square
**Tackle with Punches** Circle

### • ATTACK VS. RUNNING
**Drop Toe Hold** Square
**Back Body Drop** Triangle
**Arm Drag** Circle
**Powerslam** up,Circle

### • GROUND HITS
**- Standing**
**Leg Drop (at side)** Square
**Stomp** Square
**Elbow Drop** Triangle
**Knee Drop*** down,Square

**- RUNNING**
**Knee Drop** Square
**Fist Drop** Triangle
**Falling Headbutt** Circle

### • GROUND HOLDS
**- STARTING AT LEGS**
**Elbow Drop onto Leg** left,left,Square
**Leg Grapevine** left,right,Square
**Headbutt to Groin** up,down,Square
**Reverse Indian Deathlock** left,right,up,Square

**- STARTING AT HEAD**
**Arm Wrench** left,left,Triangle
**Knee to Back** left,right,Triangle
**Painkiller** up,down,Triangle
**MANDIBLE CLAW (F — MANKIND)** left,right,up,Circle+X

### • OPPONENT IN CORNER
**- STANDING, FACING OPPONENT**
**Kick in Corner** Square
**Forearm Smashes** Triangle
**Charging Shoulder** Circle
**Swinging DDT** left,left,Square
**Tree of Woe** left,left,Triangle
**Top Rope Superplex** left,left,Circle

**- FROM BEHIND OPPONENT**
**Smash Head into Turnbuckle** Square or Triangle or Circle
**Pump Handle Slam** left,Circle

**- RUNNING**
**Clothesline** Square or Triangle or Circle

### • FROM THE TOP TURNBUCKLE
**- OPPONENT LYING ON GROUND**
**Elbow Drop** Square or Triangle or Circle
**Splash** Triangle+Circle or Square+X
**Somersault Senton Splash*** up,up,Triangle+Square

**- OPPONENT STANDING**
**Axe Handle Smash** Square or Triangle or Circle
**Bionic Elbow** Square+X
**Clothesline** Triangle+Circle
**Forearm Smash*** up,up,Circle+X

### • FROM THE RING APRON
**- OPPONENT LYING ON GROUND**
**Elbow Drop** Square or Triangle or Circle
**Driving Elbow** Square+X
**Splash** Triangle+Circle

**- OPPONENT STANDING**
**Axe Handle Smash** Square or Triangle or Circle
**Bionic Elbow** Square+X
**Clothesline** Triangle+Circle

## NINTENDO 64

### • FROM STARTING POSITION
**Body Slam** left,up,Left C
**Clothesline** up,up,B
**Cobra Clutch** up,up,Left C
**DDT** left,down,A
**Front Backbreaker** left,right,Left C
**Gut Wrench Power Bomb** left,right,B
**Hiptoss** up,down,A
**Kneebreaker** left,down,Left C
**Leg Drag** up,up,A
**MANDIBLE CLAW (F — MANKIND)** left,right,up,Left C+Down C
**DOUBLE-ARM DDT (F — CACTUS JACK, DUDE LOVE)** left,right,up,Left C+Down C
**Neck Breaker** left,down,B
**Samoan Drop** left,up,B
**Side Belly-Belly Suplex** up,down,Left C
**Single-Arm DDT** left,up,A

### • FROM THE TIE-UP
**Hiptoss** A
**DDT** B
**Side Belly-Belly Suplex** Left C
**Samoan Drop** left,A
**Inverted Atomic Drop** left,B
**Vertical Suplex** left,Left C
**Brainbuster** left,right,A
**Power Bomb** left,down,B
**Piledriver** left,up,Left C
**MANDIBLE CLAW (F — MANKIND)** left,right,Left C

### • FROM BEHIND
**Nerve Hold** A or B or Left C
**Cross-Face Chicken Wing** left,left,A
**Reverse DDT** left,left,B
**Side Slam** left,left,up,Left C

### • RUNNING ATTACK
**Clothesline** B
**Spinning Neck Breaker** A
**Tackle with Punches** Left C

### • ATTACK VS. RUNNING
**Flying Back Elbow** A
**Back Body Drop** B
**Arm Drag** Left C
**Powerslam** up,Left C

### • GROUND HITS
**- STANDING**
**Leg Drop (at side)** A
**Stomp** A
**Elbow Drop** B
**Knee Drop*** down,A

**- RUNNING**
**Knee Drop** A
**Fist Drop** B
**Falling Headbutt** Left C

### • GROUND HOLDS
**- STARTING AT LEGS**
**Elbow Drop onto Leg** left,left,A
**Leg Grapevine** left,right,A
**Headbutt to Groin** up,down,A
**Reverse Indian Deathlock** left,right,up,A

**- STARTING AT HEAD**
**Arm Wrench** left,left,B
**Knee to Back** left,right,B
**Painkiller** up,down,B
**MANDIBLE CLAW (F — MANKIND)** left,right,up,Left C+Down C

### • OPPONENT IN CORNER
**- STANDING, FACING OPPONENT**
**Kick in Corner** A
**Forearm Smashes** B
**Charging Shoulder** Left C
**Swinging DDT** left,left,A
**Tree of Woe** left,left,B
**Top Rope Superplex** left,left,Left C

**- FROM BEHIND OPPONENT**
**Smash Head into Turnbuckle** A or B or Left C
**Pump Handle Slam** left,Left C

**- RUNNING**
**Clothesline** A or B or Left C

### • FROM THE TOP TURNBUCKLE
**- OPPONENT LYING ON GROUND**
**Elbow Drop** A or B or Left C
**Splash** B+Left C or A+Down C
**Somersault Senton Splash*** up,up,B+A

**- OPPONENT STANDING**
**Axe Handle Smash** A or B or Left C
**Bionic Elbow** A+Down C
**Clothesline** B+Left C
**Forearm Smash*** up,up,Left C+Down C

### • FROM THE RING APRON
**- OPPONENT LYING ON GROUND**
**Elbow Drop** A or B or Left C
**Driving Elbow** A+Down C
**Splash** B+Left C

**- OPPONENT STANDING**
**Axe Handle Smash** A or B or Left C
**Bionic Elbow** A+Down C
**Clothesline** B+Left C

**When you win the WWF War Zone Challenge playing Mankind on Normal Difficulty, his alter egos — Dude Love and Cactus Jack — will appear in the player select box and in the Bio Room! Holy Multiple Personalities!**

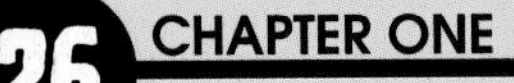

WRESTLERS

TM

**Ht:** 6'1"
**Wt:** 246 lbs.
**From:** Mosh pits across America
**Favorite Quote:** "Pierce This!"
**Finishing Move:** The Mosh Pit

## GAME STATS

| | |
|---|---|
| Strength | 5 |
| Toughness | 6 |
| Speed | 8 |
| Recovery | 5 |
| Charisma | 6 |

## WRESTLER BIO

Mosh and Thrasher, the Headbangers, spend their days breaking bones in the ring, and moshing in the pits of heavy metal concerts in the evening. After attending more Pantera, Sepultura and Marilyn Manson concerts than humanly necessary, this duo incorporated slam dancing into their matches. And thus far it's worked wonders for them! Their former reign as the World Wrestling Federation Tag Team Champions is a testament to that fact.

This team may look small in comparison to the other monsters walking the Federation, but don't let their looks fool you for a moment! Mosh and Thrasher have proven themselves in the Federation by taking its best to the limit.

## TIPS

They aren't big and they don't have tremendous power to back them up, but the Headbangers are relentless, aggressive and fearless. They can fly, they're agile and they're fast, a combination that has allowed to work well both individually and as a team.

# BUTTON COMBOS

## PLAYSTATION

### • FROM STARTING POSITION

**Front-Face DDT** left,right,Triangle
**Arm Drag** up,up,Triangle
**Crucifix** left,up,Circle
**Double Underhook Suplex** left,right,Circle
**Flying Head Scissors** left,up,Square
**Drop Toe Hold** down,down,Square
**Gut Wrench** left,up,Triangle
**Hiptoss** up,down,Circle
**Japanese Arm Drag** down,down,Triangle
**Knee to Face** up,down,Square
**Kneebreaker** left,down,Circle
**Leg Drag** left,left,Square
**Neck Breaker** up,up,Circle
**Reverse Pain Killer** left,down,Square
**Vertical Suplex** left,left,Triangle

### • FROM THE TIE-UP

**Hiptoss** Square
**Neck Breaker** Triangle
**Gut Wrench Power Bomb** Circle
**Sidewalk Slam** left,Square
**Samoan Drop** left,Triangle
**Vertical Suplex** left,Circle
**Brainbuster*** left,up,Square
**Double Underhook Suplex** left,right,Triangle
**Power Bomb*** left,down,Circle

### • FROM BEHIND

**Neck Breaker** Square or Triangle or Circle
**Pump Handle Slam** left,left,Square
**Reverse DDT** left,left,Triangle
**Victory Roll** left,left,Circle
**German Suplex*** left,left,up,Circle

### • RUNNING ATTACK

**Spinning Neck Breaker** Square
**Clothesline** Triangle
**Tackle with Punches** Circle

### • ATTACK VS. RUNNING

**Drop Kick** Square
**Back Body Drop** Triangle
**Powerslam** Circle
**Sidewalk Slam** left,Triangle

### • GROUND HITS

**- STANDING**
**Knee Drop*** down,Square
**Stomp** Square
**Standing Moonsault (at side)*** down,Triangle
**Elbow Drop** Triangle

**- RUNNING**
**Knee Drop** Square
**Fist Drop** Triangle
**Splash** Circle

### • GROUND HOLDS

**- STARTING AT LEGS**
**Elbow Drop onto Leg** left,left,Square
**Leg Grapevine** left,right,Square
**Elbow to Groin** up,down,Square
**Wishbone Leg Splitter** left,up,down,Square

**- STARTING AT HEAD**
**Rear Chin Lock** left,left,Triangle
**Leg Lock Chokehold** left,right,Triangle
**Painkiller** up,down,Triangle

### • OPPONENT IN CORNER

**- STANDING, FACING OPPONENT**
**Chest chop** Square or Triangle
**Splash** Circle
**Monkey Flip** left,left,Square
**Belly-Belly Suplex** left,left,Triangle
**Top Rope Superplex** left,left,Circle
**Hurricanranna*** left,right,down,Square

**- FROM BEHIND OPPONENT**
**Smash Head into Turnbuckle** Square or Triangle or Circle
**Pump Handle Slam** left,Circle

**- RUNNING**
**Charging Butt Bump** Square or Triangle or Circle

### • FROM THE TOP TURNBUCKLE

**- OPPONENT LYING ON GROUND**
**Kamikaze Headbutt** Square or Triangle or Circle
**Driving Elbow** Square+X
**Splash** Triangle+Circle
**Somersault Senton Splash** up,up,Triangle+Square

**- OPPONENT STANDING**
**Drop Kick** Square or Triangle or Circle
**Body Press (in front of opponent)** Square+X
**Shoulder Tackle** Triangle+Circle
**Hurricanranna** left,right,Square+Circle
**THE MOSH PIT*** left,right,up,Circle+X
**Moonsault** X

### • FROM THE RING APRON

**- OPPONENT LYING ON GROUND**
**Kamikaze Headbutt** Square or Triangle or Circle
**Driving Elbow** Square+X
**Splash** Triangle+Circle

**- OPPONENT STANDING**
**Drop Kick** Square or Triangle or Circle
**Body Press** Square+X
**Shoulder Tackle** Triangle+Circle

## NINTENDO 64

### • FROM STARTING POSITION

**Front-Face DDT** left,right,B
**Arm Drag** up,up,B
**Crucifix** left,up,Left C
**Double Underhook Suplex** left,right,Left C
**Flying Head Scissors** left,up,A
**Drop Toe Hold** down,down,A
**Gut Wrench** left,up,B
**Hiptoss** up,down,Left C
**Japanese Arm Drag** down,down,B
**Knee to Face** up,down,A
**Kneebreaker** left,down,Left C
**Leg Drag** left,left,A
**Neck Breaker** up,up,Left C
**Reverse Pain Killer** left,down,A
**Vertical Suplex** left,left,B

### • FROM THE TIE-UP

**Hiptoss** A
**Neck Breaker** B
**Gut Wrench Power Bomb** Left C
**Sidewalk Slam** left,A
**Samoan Drop** left,B
**Vertical Suplex** left,Left C
**Brainbuster*** left,up,A
**Double Underhook Suplex** left,right,B
**Power Bomb*** left,down,Left C

### • FROM BEHIND

**Neck Breaker** A or B or Left C
**Pump Handle Slam** left,left,A
**Reverse DDT** left,left,B
**Victory Roll** left,left,Left C
**German Suplex*** left,left,up,Left C

### • RUNNING ATTACK

**Spinning Neck Breaker** A
**Clothesline** B
**Tackle with Punches** Left C

### • ATTACK VS. RUNNING

**Drop Kick** A
**Back Body Drop** B
**Powerslam** Left C
**Sidewalk Slam** left,B

### • GROUND HITS

**- STANDING**
**Knee Drop*** down,A
**Stomp** A
**Standing Moonsault (at side)*** down,B
**Elbow Drop** B

**- RUNNING**
**Knee Drop** A
**Fist Drop** B
**Splash** Left C

### • GROUND HOLDS

**- STARTING AT LEGS**
**Elbow Drop onto Leg** left,left,A
**Leg Grapevine** left,right,A
**Elbow to Groin** up,down,A
**Wishbone Leg Splitter** left,up,down,A

**- STARTING AT HEAD**
**Rear Chin Lock** left,left,B
**Leg Lock Chokehold** left,right,B
**Painkiller** up,down,B

### • OPPONENT IN CORNER

**- STANDING, FACING OPPONENT**
**Chest chop** A or B
**Splash** Left C
**Monkey Flip** left,left,A
**Belly-Belly Suplex** left,left,B
**Top Rope Superplex** left,left,Left C
**Hurricanranna*** left,right,down,A

**- FROM BEHIND OPPONENT**
**Smash Head into Turnbuckle** A or B or Left C
**Pump Handle Slam** left,Left C

**- RUNNING**
**Charging Butt Bump** A or B or Left C

### • FROM THE TOP TURNBUCKLE

**- OPPONENT LYING ON GROUND**
**Kamikaze Headbutt** A or B or Left C
**Driving Elbow** A+Down C
**Splash** B+Left C
**Somersault Senton Splash** up,up,B+A

**- OPPONENT STANDING**
**Drop Kick** A or B or Left C
**Body Press (in front of opponent)** A+Down C
**Shoulder Tackle** B+Left C
**Hurricanranna** left,right,A+Left C
**THE MOSH PIT*** left,right,up,Left C+Down C
**Moonsault** Down C

### • FROM THE RING APRON

**- OPPONENT LYING ON GROUND**
**Kamikaze Headbutt** A or B or Left C
**Driving Elbow** A+Down C
**Splash** B+Left C

**- OPPONENT STANDING**
**Drop Kick** A or B or Left C
**Body Press** A+Down C
**Shoulder Tackle** B+Left C

WRESTLERS

# THRASHER™

**Ht:** 6′2″
**Wt:** 246 lbs.
**From:** Mosh pits across America
**Favorite Quote:** "Pierce This!"
**Finishing Move:** Somersault Leg Drop

## GAME STATS

|  |  |
|---|---|
| Strength | 4 |
| Toughness | 5 |
| Speed | 9 |
| Recovery | 5 |
| Charisma | 7 |

## WRESTLER BIO

Mosh and Thrasher, the Headbangers, spend their days breaking bones in the ring, and moshing in the pits of heavy metal concerts in the evening. After attending more Pantera, Sepultura and Marilyn Manson concerts than humanly necessary, this duo incorporated slam dancing into their matches. And thus far it's worked wonders for them! Their former reign as the World Wrestling Federation Tag Team Champions is a testament to that fact.

This team may look small in comparison to the other monsters walking the Federation, but don't let their looks fool you for a moment! Mosh and Thrasher have proven themselves in the Federation by taking its best to the limit.

## TIPS

They aren't big and they don't have tremendous power to back them up, but the Headbangers are relentless, aggressive and fearless. They can fly, they're agile and they're fast, a combination that has allowed to work well both individually and as a team.

# BUTTON COMBOS



## PLAYSTATION

### • FROM STARTING POSITION

**Front Face DDT** left,right,Triangle
**Arm Wrench** left,up,Triangle
**Crucifix*** left,up,Circle
**Drop Toe Hold*** down,down,Square
**Fireman's Carry** left,right,Square
**Hurricanranna*** left,right,up,Square
**Headlock Takedown*** left,down,Triangle
**Japanese Arm Drag*** down,down,Triangle
**Overhead Belly-Belly Suplex** up,down,Circle
**Reverse Painkiller*** left,down,Square
**Sidewalk Slam*** left,down,Circle
**Single-Arm DDT*** left,up,Square
**Spinebuster** left,right,Circle

### • FROM THE TIE-UP

**Hiptoss** Square
**Neck Breaker** Triangle
**Inverted Atomic Drop** Circle
**Fisherman's Suplex** left,Square
**Side Slam** left,Triangle
**Samoan Drop** left,Circle
**Northern Lights Suplex*** left,down,Square
**Sidewalk Slam** left,up,Triangle
**Brainbuster** left,up,Circle

### • FROM BEHIND

**Russian Leg Sweep** Square or Triangle or Circle
**Neck Breaker** left,left,Square
**Reverse DDT** left,left,Triangle
**Side Slam** left,left,Circle
**Belly-Back Suplex** left,up,right,Circle

### • RUNNING ATTACK

**Clothesline** Circle or Triangle
**Flying Forearm** Square
**Spinning Neck Breaker** Circle

### • ATTACK VS. RUNNING

**Drop Kick** Square
**Powerslam** Triangle
**Spinebuster** Circle
**Hurricanranna** up,Square

### • GROUND HITS

**- STANDING**
**Leg Drop (at side)** Square
**Stomp** Square
**Fist Drop** Triangle
**Standing Moonsault (at side)*** down,Triangle
**Knee Drop*** down,Triangle

**- RUNNING**
**Leg Drop (at side)** Square
**Knee Drop** Square or Triangle or Circle

### • GROUND HOLDS

**- STARTING AT LEGS**
**Elbow to Groin** left,left,Square
**Reverse Indian Deathlock** left,right,Square
**STF** up,down,Square
**Boston Crab** left,down,right,Square

**- STARTING AT HEAD**
**Arm Wrench** left,left,Triangle
**Leg Lock Chokehold** left,right,Triangle
**Short-Arm Scissor** up,down,Triangle

### • OPPONENT IN CORNER

**- STANDING, FACING OPPONENT**
**Chest Chop** Square or Triangle
**Splash** Circle
**Flying Head Scissors** left,left,Square
**Hurricanranna** left,left,Triangle
**Swinging DDT** left,left,Circle
**Superplex*** left,down,right,Triangle

**- FROM BEHIND OPPONENT**
**Smash Head into Turnbuckle** Square or Triangle or Circle
**Pump Handle Slam** left,Circle

**- RUNNING**
**Charging Butt Bump** Square or Triangle or Circle

### • FROM THE TOP TURNBUCKLE

**- OPPONENT LYING ON GROUND**
**Elbow Drop** Square or Triangle or Circle
**Leg Drop** Square+X
**Somersault Senton Splash** Triangle+Circle
**SOMERSAULT LEG DROP*** left,up,up,Triangle+Square
**Shooting Star Press*** up,up,Square+Circle

**- OPPONENT STANDING**
**Axe Handle Smash** Square or Triangle or Circle
**Body Press** Square+X
**Torpedo Dropkick** Square+X
**Sunset Flip** Triangle+Circle
**Hurricanranna*** left,up,Square+Circle

### • FROM THE RING APRON

**- OPPONENT LYING ON GROUND**
**Elbow Drop** Square or Triangle or Circle
**Leg Drop** Square+X
**Somersault Senton Splash** Triangle+Circle

**- OPPONENT STANDING**
**Axe Handle Smash** Square or Triangle or Circle
**Body Press** Square+X
**Torpedo Dropkick** Triangle+Circle

## NINTENDO 64

### • FROM STARTING POSITION

**Front Face DDT** left,right,B
**Arm Wrench** left,up,B
**Crucifix*** left,up,Left C
**Drop Toe Hold*** down,down,A
**Fireman's Carry** left,right,A
**Hurricanranna*** left,right,up,A
**Headlock Takedown*** left,down,B
**Japanese Arm Drag*** down,down,B
**Overhead Belly-Belly Suplex** up,down,Left C
**Reverse Painkiller*** left,down,A
**Sidewalk Slam*** left,down,Left C
**Single-Arm DDT*** left,up,A
**Spinebuster** left,right,Left C

### • FROM THE TIE-UP

**Hiptoss** A
**Neck Breaker** B
**Inverted Atomic Drop** Left C
**Fisherman's Suplex** left,A
**Side Slam left,B**
**Samoan Drop** left,Left C
**Northern Lights Suplex*** left,down,A
**Sidewalk Slam** left,up,B
**Brainbuster** left,up,Left C

### • FROM BEHIND

**Russian Leg Sweep** A or B or Left C
**Neck Breaker** left,left,A
**Reverse DDT** left,left,B
**Side Slam** left,left,Left C
**Belly-Back Suplex** left,up,right,Left C

### • RUNNING ATTACK

**Clothesline** Left C or B
**Flying forearm** A
**Spinning Neck Breaker** Left C

### • ATTACK VS. RUNNING

**Drop Kick** A
**Powerslam** B
**Spinebuster** Left C
**Hurricanranna** up,A

### • GROUND HITS

**- STANDING**
**Leg Drop (at side)** A
**Stomp** A
**Fist Drop** B
**Standing Moonsault (at side)*** down,B
**Knee Drop*** down,B

**- RUNNING**
**Leg Drop (at side)** A
**Knee Drop** A or B or Left C

### • GROUND HOLDS

**- STARTING AT LEGS**
**Elbow to Groin** left,left,A
**Reverse Indian Deathlock** left,right,A
**STF** up,down,A
**Boston Crab** left,down,right,A

**- STARTING AT HEAD**
**Arm Wrench** left,left,B
**Leg Lock Chokehold** left,right,B
**Short-Arm Scissor** up,down,B

### • OPPONENT IN CORNER

**- STANDING, FACING OPPONENT**
**Chest Chop** A or B
**Splash** Left C
**Flying Head Scissors** left,left,A
**Hurricanranna** left,left,B
**Swinging DDT** left,left,Left C
**Superplex*** left,down,right,B

**- FROM BEHIND OPPONENT**
**Smash Head into Turnbuckle** A or B or Left C
**Pump Handle Slam** left,Left C

**- RUNNING**
**Charging Butt Bump** A or B or Left C

### • FROM THE TOP TURNBUCKLE

**- OPPONENT LYING ON GROUND**
**Elbow Drop** A or B or Left C
**Leg Drop** A+Down C
**Somersault Senton Splash** B+Left C
**SOMERSAULT LEG DROP*** left,up,up,B+A
**Shooting Star Press*** up,up,A+Left C

**- OPPONENT STANDING**
**Axe Handle Smash** A or B or Left C
**Body Press** A+Down C
**Torpedo Dropkick** A+Down C
**Sunset Flip** B+Left C
**Hurricanranna*** left,up,A+Left C

### • FROM THE RING APRON

**- OPPONENT LYING ON GROUND**
**Elbow Drop** A or B or Left C
**Leg Drop** A+Down C
**Somersault Senton Splash** B+Left C

**- OPPONENT STANDING**
**Axe Handle Smash** A or B or Left C
**Body Press** A+Down C
**Torpedo Dropkick** B+Left C

WAR ZONE

™

**From:** Calgary, Alberta, Canada
**Finishing Move:** Sharp Shooter
**Current Status:** No longer with the WWF
**Famous Words:** "I'm the best there is, the best there was, and the best there ever will be!"

## GAME STATS

| | |
|---|---|
| Strength | 4 |
| Toughness | 6 |
| Speed | 7 |
| Recovery | 5 |
| Charisma | 8 |

## WRESTLER BIO

There is no pro wrestler with more in-ring credibility than the Hit man Bret Hart. Son of the legendary Stu Hart, Bret learned the ropes in his dad's Calgary basement, known as "the Dungeon" (also the training ground for everyone from Owen Hart to the British Bulldogs).

Bret first came to the attention of the fans as one half of the original Hart Foundation with brother-in-law Jim "The Anvil" Neidhart and manager Jimmy "The Mouth of the South" Hart (who was no relation). The tag team was one of the dominant forces during the World Wrestling Federation's international breakthrough in the mid to late-'80s. But when the tandem decided to opt for solo careers, it was Bret whose star rose farthest and fastest.

Hart is one of the soundest, most well-versed technicians in the history of the sport. His mat work, transitions, and chain wrestling is textbook and the Sharp Shooter is a sureshot submission move.

## TIPS

While slightly below average in size, Bret has a well-balanced attack that serves him well. He can take to the air on occasion and is a master at stringing moves together. He is the most agile wrestler in the game — along with Shawn Michaels — and one of the fastest. Not tremendously powerful, he is a wrestler rather than a strongman and must rely on wrestling to win his matches.

# BUTTON COMBOS



## PLAYSTATION

### • FROM STARTING POSITION

**Body Slam** left,down,Circle
**Clothesline** left,up,Square
**Crucifix** left,left,Square
**Fireman's Carry*** down,down,Square
**Drop Toe Hold*** down,down,Triangle
**Hiptoss*** up,up,Square
**Kneebreaker** left,right,Circle
**Leg Drag** left,down,Square
**Overhead Belly-Belly Suplex** left,left,Triangle
**Samoan Drop** left,up,Triangle
**Small Package*** down,down,Circle
**Spinebuster** up,down,Circle
**Vertical Suplex** up,down,Triangle

### • FROM THE TIE-UP

**Hiptoss** Square
**Top Wristlock** Triangle
**Atomic Drop** Circle
**Neck Breaker** left,Square
**Inverted Atomic Drop** left,Triangle
**Northern Lights Suplex** left,Circle
**Samoan Drop** left,right,Square
**Piledriver** left,up,Triangle
**Side Back Breaker** left,left,Circle
**Whip** left,left,X

### • FROM BEHIND

**Cross-Face Chicken Wing** Square or Triangle or Circle
**Russian Leg Sweep** left,left,Square
**Atomic Drop** left,left,Triangle
**German Suplex** left,left,up,Circle

### • RUNNING ATTACK

**Crucifix** Triangle+Circle
**Drop Kick** Square
**Hart Attack** Triangle
**Spinning Neck Breaker** Circle

### • ATTACK VS. RUNNING

**Drop Kick** Square
**Clothesline** Triangle
**Drop Toe Hold** Circle
**Powerslam** up,Circle

### • GROUND HITS

**- STANDING**
**Driving Elbow Smash*** down,Triangle
**Fist Drop** Triangle
**Knee Drop*** down,Square
**Leg Drop** Square
**Stomp** Square

**- RUNNING**
**Fist Drop** Square or Triangle
**Splash** Circle

### • GROUND HOLDS

**- STARTING AT LEGS**
**Elbow Drop onto Leg** left,left,Square
**Half Crab** left,right,Square
**Headbutt to Groin** up,down,Square
**Sharp Shooter** left,left,up,Square+X

**- STARTING AT HEAD**
**Leg Lock Chokehold** left,left,Triangle
**Rear Chin Lock** left,right,Triangle
**Short-Arm Scissor** up,down,Triangle
**Painkiller** left,up,down,Triangle

### • OPPONENT IN CORNER

**- STANDING, FACING OPPONENT**
**Forearm Smashes** Square
**Climb Turnbuckle and Pummel** Triangle
**Forearm Smashes** Circle
**Monkey Flip** left,left,Square
**Swinging DDT** left,left,Triangle
**Belly-Belly Suplex** left,left,Circle
**Top Rope Superplex** left,right,left,Square

**- FROM BEHIND OPPONENT**
**Smash Head into Turnbuckle** Square or Triangle or Circle
**Pump Handle Slam** left,Circle

**- RUNNING**
**Charging Clothesline** Square or Triangle or Circle

### • FROM THE TOP TURNBUCKLE

**- OPPONENT LYING ON GROUND**
**Knee Drop** Square or Triangle or Circle
**Driving Elbow** Square+X
**Elbow Drop** Triangle+Circle
**Kamikaze Headbutt** left,right,Triangle+Square

**- OPPONENT STANDING**
**Drop Kick** Square or Triangle or Circle
**Bionic Elbow** Square+X
**Sunset Flip** Triangle+Circle
**Body Press** up,left,Circle+X

### • FROM THE RING APRON

**- OPPONENT LYING ON GROUND**
**Knee Drop** Square or Triangle or Circle
**Driving Elbow** Square+X
**Elbow Drop** Triangle+Circle

**- OPPONENT STANDING**
**Drop Kick** Square or Triangle or Circle
**Bionic Elbow** Square+X
**Clothesline** Triangle+Circle

## NINTENDO 64

### • FROM STARTING POSITION

**Body Slam** left,down,Left C
**Clothesline** left,up,A
**Crucifix** left,left,A
**Fireman's Carry*** down,down,A
**Drop Toe Hold*** down,down,B
**Hiptoss*** up,up,A
**Kneebreaker** left,right,Left C
**Leg Drag** left,down,A
**Overhead Belly-Belly Suplex** left,left,B
**Samoan Drop** left,up,B
**Small Package*** down,down,Left C
**Spinebuster** up,down,Left C
**Vertical Suplex** up,down,B

### • FROM THE TIE-UP

**Hiptoss** A
**Top Wristlock** B
**Atomic Drop** Left C
**Neck Breaker** left,A
**Inverted Atomic Drop** left,B
**Northern Lights Suplex** left,Left C
**Samoan Drop** left,right,A
**Piledriver** left,up,B
**Side Back Breaker** left,left,Left C
**Whip** left,left,Down C

### • FROM BEHIND

**Cross-Face Chicken Wing** A or B or Left C
**Russian Leg Sweep** left,left,A
**Atomic Drop** left,left,B
**German Suplex** left,left,up,Left C

### • RUNNING ATTACK

**Crucifix** B+Left C
**Drop Kick** A
**Hart Attack** B
**Spinning Neck Breaker** Left C

### • ATTACK VS. RUNNING

**Drop Kick** A
**Clothesline** B
**Drop Toe Hold** Left C
**Powerslam** up,Left C

### • GROUND HITS

**- STANDING**
**Driving Elbow Smash*** down,B
**Fist Drop** B
**Knee Drop*** down,A
**Leg Drop** A
**Stomp** A

**- RUNNING**
**Fist Drop** A or B
**Splash** Left C

### • GROUND HOLDS

**- STARTING AT LEGS**
**Elbow Drop onto Leg** left,left,A
**Half Crab** left,right,A
**Headbutt to Groin** up,down,A
**SHARP SHOOTER** left,left,up,A+Down C

**- STARTING AT HEAD**
**Leg Lock Chokehold** left,left,B
**Rear Chin Lock** left,right,B
**Short-Arm Scissor** up,down,B
**Painkiller** left,up,down,B

### • OPPONENT IN CORNER

**- STANDING, FACING OPPONENT**
**Forearm Smashes** A
**Climb Turnbuckle and Pummel** B
**Forearm Smashes** Left C
**Monkey Flip** left,left,A
**Swinging DDT** left,left,B
**Belly-Belly Suplex** left,left,Left C
**Top Rope Superplex** left,right,left,A

**- FROM BEHIND OPPONENT**
**Smash Head into Turnbuckle** A or B or Left C
**Pump Handle Slam** left,Left C

**- RUNNING**
**Charging Clothesline** A or B or Left C

### • FROM THE TOP TURNBUCKLE

**- OPPONENT LYING ON GROUND**
**Knee Drop** A or B or Left C
**Driving Elbow** A+Down C
**Elbow Drop** B+Left C
**Kamikaze Headbutt** left,right,B+A

**- OPPONENT STANDING**
**Drop Kick** A or B or Left C
**Bionic Elbow** A+Down C
**Sunset Flip** B+Left C
**Body Press** up,left,Left C+Down C

### • FROM THE RING APRON

**- OPPONENT LYING ON GROUND**
**Knee Drop** A or B or Left C
**Driving Elbow** A+Down C
**Elbow Drop** B+Left C

**- OPPONENT STANDING**
**Drop Kick** A or B or Left C
**Bionic Elbow** A+Down C
**Clothesline** B+Left C

## RING GIRL WRESTLER

Beat the Challenge with Bret Hart or Owen Hart, and you'll be able to select the ring girl as a wrestler! Now there's a distracting opponent!

WRESTLERS

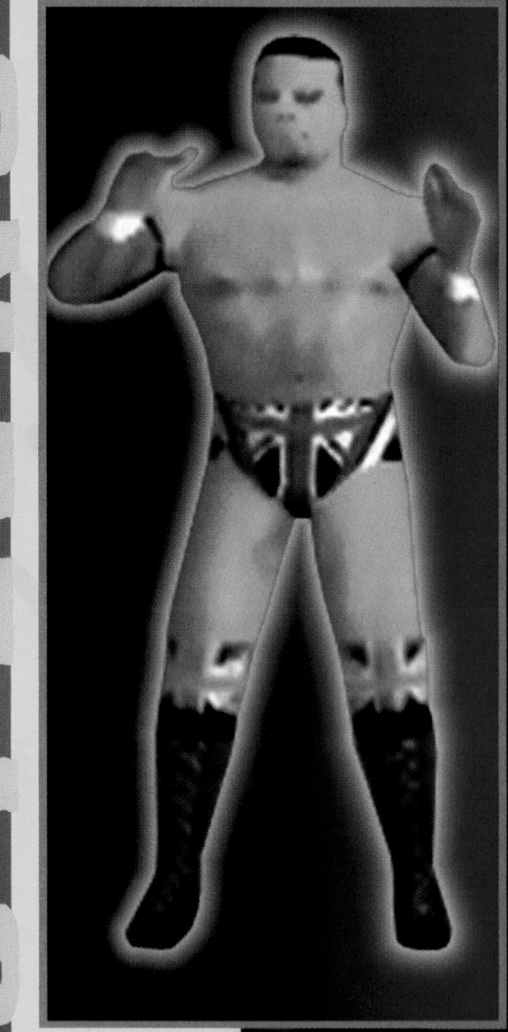

**Height:** 6′0″
**Weight:**253 lbs
**From:** Manchester, England
**Finisher:** Charging Powerslam
**Current Status:** No longer with the WWF
**Famous Words:**
"First I bark — and then I bite!"

## GAME STATS

| | |
|---|---|
| Strength | 9 |
| Toughness | 7 |
| Speed | 6 |
| Recovery | 4 |
| Charisma | 4 |

## WRESTLER BIO

Davey Boy Smith first gained international attention as one half of the legendary British Bulldogs tag team. With his partner, the Dynamite Kid, the tandem was Hall of Fame quality, ruling the World Wrestling Federation for several years in the mid to late '80s, until Dynamite was hobbled with a serious back injury. In the Bulldogs' heydey, however, Smith had handled most of the heavy work and power moves, while Dynamite had stunned the crowd with his daredevil flying maneuvers and incredible technique.

It's not surprising, therefore, that when the Bulldog went solo, he pumped up to work a power-oriented match. His Charging Powerslam finisher is symbolic of the machine-like strength possessed by this former member of the Hart Foundation (he is Bret and Owen's brother-in-law). The Bulldog is a powerhouse with a solid background in mat wrestling, able to deal with opponents whether standing or on the canvas.

## TIPS

Don't think that the Bulldog has totally forsaken some of the more acrobatic moves from his tag team days; he will occasionally surprise an opponent with a Drop Kick to the mush. He also possesses good leaping ability for a man his size and matches up well with any type of opponent. He has average striking ability, is among the strongest wrestlers in the game and, surprisingly, one of the fastest.

# BUTTON COMBOS



## PLAYSTATION

### • FROM STARTING POSITION

**Arm Drag** down,down,Triangle
**Arm Wrench** left,left,Triangle
**Bearhug** up,down,Triangle
**Body Slam** left,down,Circle
**Charging Powerslam** up,down,up,Triangle+Circle
**Overhead Belly-Belly Suplex** left,right,Circle
**Crucifix** left,up,Square
**Fireman's Carry** down,down,Square
**Gorilla Press Slam** up,up,down,Circle
**Hanging Vertical Suplex** down,up,up,Triangle
**Hiptoss*** up,up,Square
**Samoan Drop** left,up,Triangle
**Small Package** up,up,Circle
**Snap Mare** left,down,Square

### • FROM THE TIE-UP

**Hiptoss** Square
**Top Wristlock** Triangle
**Chest Breaker** Circle
**Fisherman's Suplex** left,Square
**Gut Wrench Power Bomb** left,Triangle
**Samoan Drop** left,Circle
**Overhead Belly-Belly Suplex** left,right,Square
**Double Underhook Suplex** left,down,Triangle
**Hanging Vertical Suplex** left,up,Circle
**CHARGING POWERSLAM** up,down,Circle

### • FROM BEHIND

**Russian Leg Sweep** Square or Triangle or Circle
**Atomic Drop** left,left,Square or Triangle
**Victory Roll** left,left,Circle
**Belly-Back Suplex** left,up,right,Circle

### • RUNNING ATTACK

**Clothesline** Triangle
**Crucifix** Triangle+Circle
**Flying Shoulder Tackle** Square
**Spinning Neck Breaker** Circle

### • ATTACK VS. RUNNING

**Drop Kick** Square
**Clothesline** Triangle
**Arm Drag** Circle
**Power Slam** up,Circle

### • GROUND HITS

**- STANDING**
**Elbow Drop** Triangle
**Double Foot Stomp*** down,Square
**Stomp** Square

**- RUNNING**
**Knee Drop** Square or Circle
**Elbow Drop** Triangle

### • GROUND HOLDS

**- STARTING AT LEGS**
**Spinning Toe Hold** left,left,Square
**Leg Grapevine** left,right,Square
**Texas Cloverleaf** up,down,Square
**Boston Crab** left,down,right,Square

**- STARTING AT HEAD**
**Arm Wrench** left,left,Triangle
**Rear Chin Lock** left,right,Triangle
**Stump Puller** up,down,Triangle
**Camel Clutch** left,up,right,Triangle

### • OPPONENT IN CORNER

**- STANDING, FACING OPPONENT**
**Kick to Ribs** Square
**Climb Turnbuckle and Pummel** Triangle
**Slap Face** Circle
**Oklahoma Stampede** left,left,Square
**Belly-Belly Suplex** left,left,Triangle
**Superplex** left,left,Circle
**Top Rope Superplex** up,down,left,Square

**- FROM BEHIND OPPONENT**
**Smash Head into turnbuckle** Square or Triangle or Circle
**Pump Handle Slam** left,Circle

**- RUNNING**
**Clothesline** Square or Triangle or Circle

### • FROM THE TOP TURNBUCKLE

**- OPPONENT LYING ON GROUND**
**Knee Drop** Square or Triangle or Circle
**Kamikaze Headbutt** Triangle+Circle
**Splash** Square+X
**Somersault Senton Splash*** up,up,Triangle+Square

**- OPPONENT STANDING**
**Torpedo Dropkick** Square or Triangle or Circle
**Body Press** Square+X
**Sunset Flip** Triangle+Circle
**Clothesline** left,right,Circle+X

### • FROM THE RING APRON

**- OPPONENT LYING ON GROUND**
**Knee Drop** Square or Triangle or Circle
**Kamikaze Headbutt** Triangle+Circle
**Splash** Square+X

**- OPPONENT STANDING**
**Torpedo Dropkick** Square or Triangle
**Body Press** Square+X or Triangle+Circle

## NINTENDO 64

### • FROM STARTING POSITION

**Arm Drag** down,down,B
**Arm Wrench** left,left,B
**Bearhug** up,down,B
**Body Slam** left,down,Left C
**Charging Powerslam** up,down,up,B+Left C
**Overhead Belly-Belly Suplex** left,right,Left C
**Crucifix** left,up,A
**Fireman's Carry** down,down,A
**Gorilla Press Slam** up,up,down,Left C
**Hanging Vertical Suplex** down,up,up,B
**Hiptoss*** up,up,A
**Samoan Drop** left,up,B
**Small Package** up,up,Left C
**Snap Mare** left,down,A

### • FROM THE TIE-UP

**Hiptoss** A
**Top Wristlock** B
**Chest Breaker** Left C
**Fisherman's Suplex** left,A
**Gut Wrench Power Bomb** left,B
**Samoan Drop** left,Left C
**Overhead Belly-Belly Suplex** left,right,A
**Double Underhook Suplex** left,down,B
**Hanging Vertical Suplex** left,up,Left C
**CHARGING POWERSLAM** up, down,Left C

### • FROM BEHIND

**Russian Leg Sweep** A or B or Left C
**Atomic Drop** left,left,A or B
**Victory Roll** left,left,Left C
**Belly-Back Suplex** left,up,right,Left C

### • RUNNING ATTACK

**Clothesline** B
**Crucifix** B+Left C
**Flying Shoulder Tackle** A
**Spinning Neck Breaker** Left C

### • ATTACK VS. RUNNING

**Drop Kick** A
**Clothesline** B
**Arm Drag** Left C
**Power Slam** up,Left C

### • GROUND HITS

**- STANDING**
**Elbow Drop** B
**Double Foot Stomp*** down,A
**Stomp** A

**- RUNNING**
**Knee Drop** A or Left C
**Elbow Drop** B

### • GROUND HOLDS

**- STARTING AT LEGS**
**Spinning Toe Hold** left,left,A
**Leg Grapevine** left,right,A
**Texas Cloverleaf** up,down,A
**Boston Crab** left,down,right,A

**- STARTING AT HEAD**
**Arm Wrench** left,left,B
**Rear Chin Lock** left,right,B
**Stump Puller** up,down,B
**Camel Clutch** left,up,right,B

### • OPPONENT IN CORNER

**- STANDING, FACING OPPONENT**
**Kick to Ribs** A
**Climb Turnbuckle and Pummel** B
**Slap Face** Left C
**Oklahoma Stampede** left,left,A
**Belly-Belly Suplex** left,left,B
**Superplex** left,left,Left C
**Top Rope Superplex** up,down,left,A

**- FROM BEHIND OPPONENT**
**Smash Head into turnbuckle** A or B or Left C
**Pump Handle Slam** left,Left C

**- RUNNING**
**Clothesline** A or B or Left C

### • FROM THE TOP TURNBUCKLE

**- OPPONENT LYING ON GROUND**
**Knee Drop** A or B or Left C
**Kamikaze Headbutt** B+Left C
**Splash** A+Down C
**Somersault Senton Splash*** up,up,B+A

**- OPPONENT STANDING**
**Torpedo Dropkick** A or B or Left C
**Body Press** A+Down C
**Sunset Flip** B+Left C
**Clothesline** left,right,Left C+Down C

### • FROM THE RING APRON

**- OPPONENT LYING ON GROUND**
**Knee Drop** A or B or Left C
**Kamikaze headbutt** B+Left C
**Splash** A+Down C

**- OPPONENT STANDING**
**Torpedo Dropkick** A or B
**Body Press** A+Down C or B+Left C

Beat the Challenge with British Bulldog or Rocky Maivia on any difficulty level, and everyone's head swells to giant size! Good ol' J.R. should feel right at home!

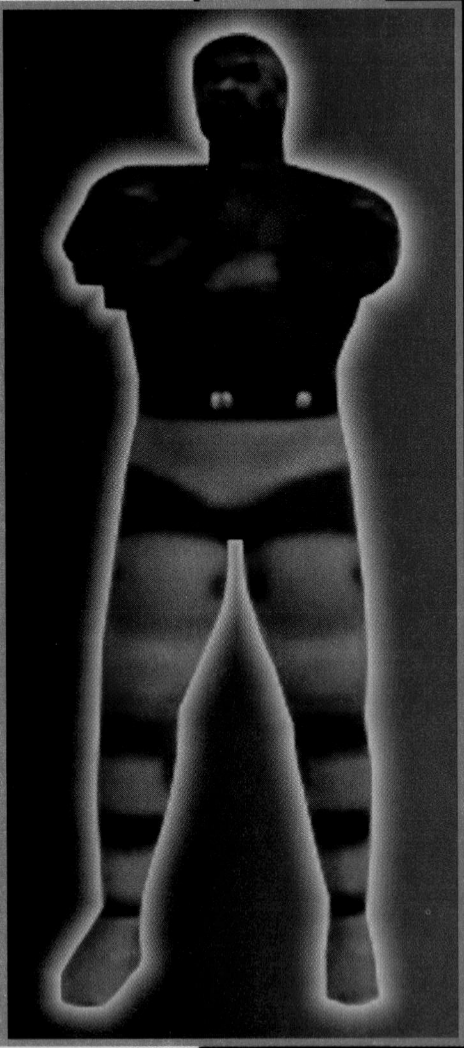

WRESTLERS

# AHMED JOHNSON™

**Height:** 6'2"
**Weight:** 305 lbs.
**From:** Pearl River, MS
**Finisher:** Pearl River Plunge
**Current Status:** No longer with the WWF
**Famous Words:** "You're going down!"

## GAME STATS

| | |
|---|---|
| Strength | 10 |
| Toughness | 8 |
| Speed | 3 |
| Recovery | 4 |
| Charisma | 5 |

## WRESTLER BIO

Ahmed Johnson first came to national attention when he wrestled for a small Texas promotion where he was scouted by the World Wrestling Federation, who brought him to the Big Show as the "Pearl River Powerhouse".

Other than a brief period with the Nation of Domination, Johnson has been a strong fan favorite, with great support from the fans. His Nubian look and heavily-muscled frame got him over from the start and he has mainly played to that strength.

## TIPS

Your basic prototype power wrestler, Ahmed Johnson has surprisingly high aerial ratings. He's not much of a chain wrestler and has a hard time with transitions from one hold to another. He has average striking ability but is as aggressive as any grappler in this game. Despite his size and thick torso, he has superb agility, but beware of injuries — Ahmed has a tendency to get hurt. But he does the most damage with high impact slams, such as the Pearl River Plunge, a variant of the Power Bomb in which the wrestler executing the move rides to the mat with his opponent.

# BUTTON COMBOS



## PLAYSTATION

### • FROM STARTING POSITION

**Bearhug** up,down,Triangle
**Overhead Belly-Belly Suplex** left,right,Circle
**Body Slam** left,down,Triangle
**Gut Wrench Power Bomb** left,right,Triangle
**Hiptoss*** up,up,Square
**Kneebreaker** left,up,Square
**PEARL RIVER PLUNGE** left,right,up,Square+X
**Short-Arm Clothesline** up,up,Triangle
**Sidewalk Slam** left,down,Square
**Snap Mare** left,down,Circle
**Spinebuster** up,down,Square
**Choke Slam** left,left,up,Triangle
**Torture Rack** left,up,Circle
**Vertical Suplex** up,down,Circle

### • FROM THE TIE-UP

**Back Breaker** Square
**Atomic Drop** Triangle
**Gut Wrench Power Bomb** Circle
**Samoan Drop** left,Square
**Bulldog** left,Triangle
**Overhead Belly-Belly Suplex** left,Circle
**Side Slam** left,up,Square
**Brainbuster** left,right,Triangle
**Power Bomb** left,down,Circle

### • FROM BEHIND

**Russian Leg Sweep** Square or Triangle or Circle
**Pump Handle Slam** left,left,Square
**Side Slam** left,left,Triangle
**Belly-Back Suplex** left,up,right,Circle

### • RUNNING ATTACK

**Clothesline** Circle
**Flying Shoulder Tackle** Square
**Tackle with Punches** Triangle

### • ATTACK VS. RUNNING

**Sidewalk Slam** Square
**Back Body Drop** Triangle
**Power Slam** Circle
**Spinebuster** left,Circle

### • GROUND HITS

**- STANDING**
**Splash*** down,Triangle
**Axe Handle Smash** Triangle
**Knee Drop*** down,Square
**Stomp** Square

**- RUNNING**
**Leg Drop** Square
**Fist Drop** Triangle or Circle

### • GROUND HOLDS

**- STARTING AT LEGS**
**Knee to Inside Leg** left,left,Square
**Leg Grapevine** left,right,Square
**Wishbone Leg Splitter** up,down,Square
**Leg Lock** left,right,left,Square

**- STARTING AT HEAD**
**Arm Wrench** left,left,Triangle
**Squeeze Head** left,right,Triangle
**Rear Chin Lock** up,down,Triangle
**Painkiller** left,up,down,Triangle

### • OPPONENT IN CORNER

**- STANDING, FACING OPPONENT**
**Choke with Boot** Square
**Chops** Triangle
**Charging Shoulder Tackle** Circle
**Overhead Press** left,left,Square or Triangle or Circle

**- FROM BEHIND OPPONENT**
**Smash Head into Turnbuckle** Square or Triangle or Circle
**Pump Handle Slam** left,Circle

**- RUNNING**
**Clothesline** Square or Triangle or Circle

### • FROM THE TOP TURNBUCKLE

**- OPPONENT LYING ON GROUND**
**Fist Drop** Square or Triangle or Circle
**Double Foot Stomp** Square+X
**Driving Elbow** Triangle+Circle
**Kamikaze Headbutt** left,right,Triangle+Square

**- OPPONENT STANDING**
**Bionic Elbow** Square or Triangle or Circle
**Clothesline** Triangle+Circle
**Forearm Smash** Square+X
**Shoulder Tackle** left,up,Circle+X

### • FROM THE RING APRON

**- OPPONENT LYING ON GROUND**
**Fist Drop** Square or Triangle or Circle
**Double Foot Stomp** Square+X
**Driving Elbow** Triangle+Circle

**- OPPONENT STANDING**
**Bionic Elbow** Square or Triangle or Circle
**Clothesline** Triangle+Circle
**Bionic Elbow** Triangle+Circle
**Forearm Smash** Square+X

## NINTENDO 64

### • FROM STARTING POSITION

**Bearhug** up,down,B
**Overhead Belly-Belly Suplex** left,right,Left C
**Body Slam** left,down,B
**Gut Wrench Power Bomb** left,right,B
**Hiptoss*** up,up,A
**Kneebreaker** left,up,A
**PEARL RIVER PLUNGE** left,right,up,A+Down C
**Short-Arm Clothesline** up,up,B
**Sidewalk Slam** left,down,A
**Snap Mare** left,down,Left C
**Spinebuster** up,down,A
**Choke Slam** left,left,up,B
**Torture Rack** left,up,Left C
**Vertical Suplex** up,down,Left C

### • FROM THE TIE-UP

**Back Breaker** A
**Atomic Drop** B
**Gut Wrench Power Bomb** Left C
**Samoan Drop** left,A
**Bulldog** left,B
**Overhead Belly-Belly Suplex** left,Left C
**Side Slam** left,up,A
**Brainbuster** left,right,B
**Power Bomb** left,down,Left C

### • FROM BEHIND

**Russian Leg Sweep** A or B or Left C
**Pump Handle Slam** left,left,A
**Side Slam** left,left,B
**Belly-Back Suplex** left,up,right,Left C

### • RUNNING ATTACK

**Clothesline** Left C
**Flying Shoulder Tackle** A
**Tackle with Punches** B

### • ATTACK VS. RUNNING

**Sidewalk Slam** A
**Back Body Drop** B
**Power Slam** Left C
**Spinebuster** left,Left C

### • GROUND HITS

**- STANDING**
**Splash*** down,B
**Axe Handle Smash** B
**Knee Drop*** down,A
**Stomp** A

**- RUNNING**
**Leg Drop** A
**Fist Drop** B or Left C

### • GROUND HOLDS

**- STARTING AT LEGS**
**Knee to Inside Leg** left,left,A
**Leg Grapevine** left,right,A
**Wishbone Leg Splitter** up,down,A
**Leg Lock** left,right,left,A

**- STARTING AT HEAD**
**Arm Wrench** left,left,B
**Squeeze Head** left,right,B
**Rear Chin Lock** up,down,B
**Painkiller** left,up,down,B

### • OPPONENT IN CORNER

**- STANDING, FACING OPPONENT**
**Choke with Boot** A
**Chops** B
**Charging Shoulder Tackle** Left C
**Overhead Press** left,left,A or B or Left C

**- FROM BEHIND OPPONENT**
**Smash Head into Turnbuckle** A or B or Left C
**Pump Handle Slam** left,Left C

**- RUNNING**
**Clothesline** A or B or Left C

### • FROM THE TOP TURNBUCKLE

**- OPPONENT LYING ON GROUND**
**Fist Drop** A or B or Left C
**Double Foot Stomp** A+Down C
**Driving Elbow** B+Left C
**Kamikaze Headbutt** left,right,B+A

**- OPPONENT STANDING**
**Bionic Elbow** A or B or Left C
**Clothesline** B+Left C
**Forearm Smash** A+Down C
**Shoulder Tackle** left,up,Left C+Down C

### • FROM THE RING APRON

**- OPPONENT LYING ON GROUND**
**Fist Drop** A or B or Left C
**Double Foot Stomp** A+Down C
**Driving Elbow** B+Left C

**- OPPONENT STANDING**
**Bionic Elbow** A or B or Left C
**Clothesline** B+Left C
**Bionic Elbow** B+Left C
**Forearm Smash** A+Down C

## SUPER SECRETS

## EGO MODE

Beat the Challenge with Ahmed Johnson, and you'll be able to access Ego Mode, which gives your wrestler a head that grows as he gets support from the fans! So let those cheers go right to your head!

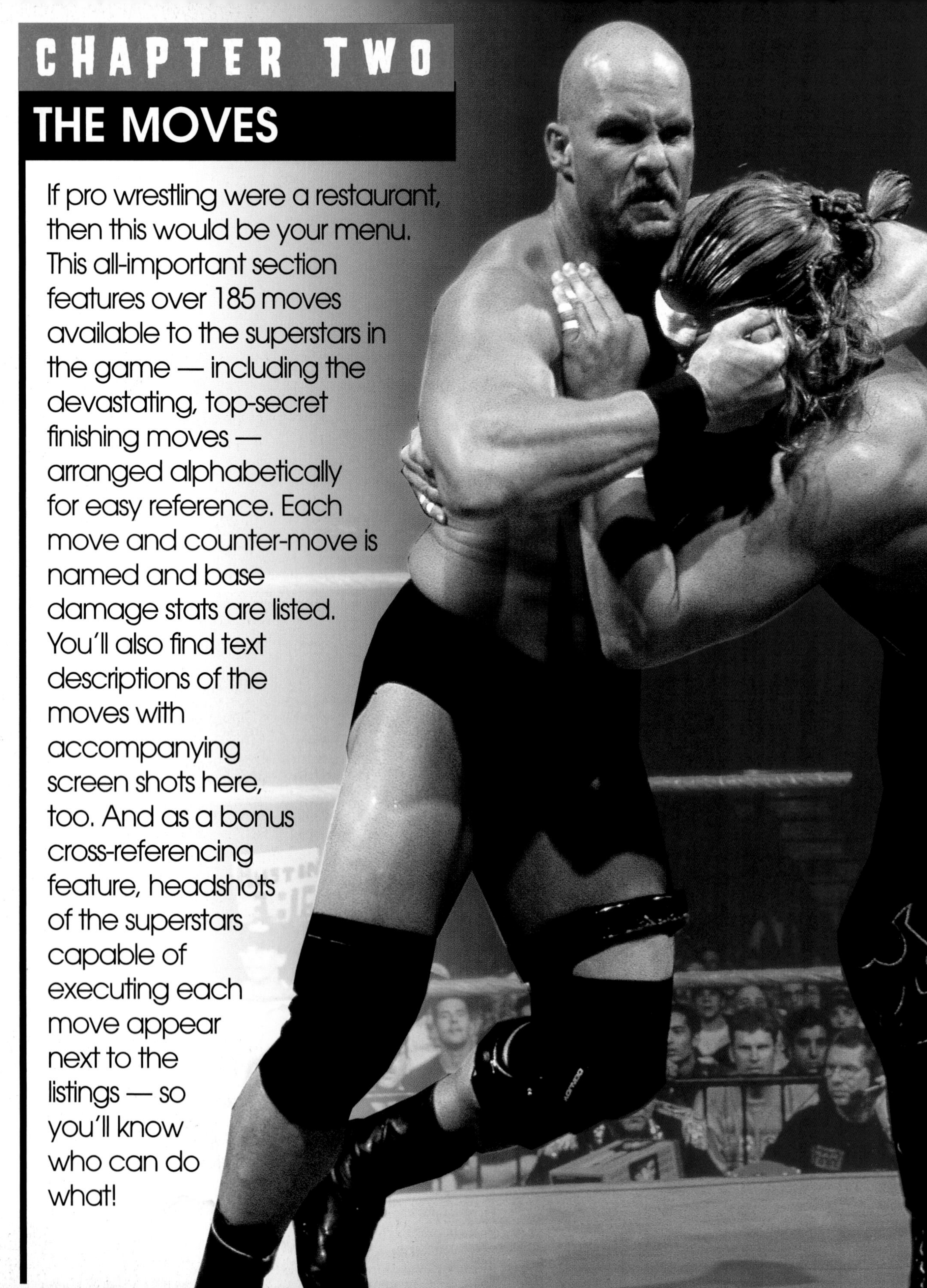

# CHAPTER TWO

## THE MOVES

If pro wrestling were a restaurant, then this would be your menu. This all-important section features over 185 moves available to the superstars in the game — including the devastating, top-secret finishing moves — arranged alphabetically for easy reference. Each move and counter-move is named and base damage stats are listed. You'll also find text descriptions of the moves with accompanying screen shots here, too. And as a bonus cross-referencing feature, headshots of the superstars capable of executing each move appear next to the listings — so you'll know who can do what!

# How to Use this Section

War Zone provides you with so many possible wrestling moves, they could fill a book — in fact, they did! What better way to show you your options than by listing them alphabetically and accompanying the vast majority of them with actual demonstration screen shots?

While flipping through this section, you might notice that Kane is the unfortunate victim of almost all these crippling hits, holds and moves. Why? Well, we could tell you that it's so you can more easily determine who's executing the move and who's on the receiving end.

But the simple truth is, we asked the superstars to speak up if they didn't want this thankless job. Kane was the only one who didn't say anything...

## Wrestler Abbreviations

| | | | |
|---|---|---|---|
| **AJ** | Ahmed Johnson | **MK** | Mankind |
| **BB** | British Bulldog | **MS** | Mosh |
| **BH** | Bret Hart | **OH** | Owen Hart |
| **CJ** | Cactus Jack | **RM** | Rocky Maivia |
| **DL** | Dude Love | **SC** | Steve Austin |
| **FQ** | Faarooq | **SM** | Shawn Michaels |
| **GD** | Goldust | **SR** | Shamrock |
| **HH** | Hunter Hearst- Helmsley | **TH** | Thrasher |
| **KN** | Kane | **UT** | Undertaker |

**Screens illustrating the move**

**Move Name**

**Text describing the move**

### BRAINBUSTER

**This move begins exactly like a Vertical Suplex (see Vertical Suplex), except once the victim is hoisted into the full vertical position, legs and feet aimed at the ceiling, the wrestler executing the move drops directly down, crumpling the victim, who lands hard on the back of his own head and shoulders.**

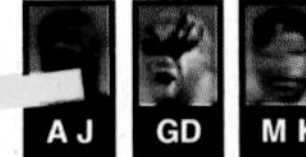
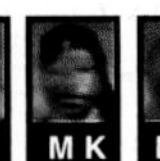

AJ GD MK MS RM SM SC TH

**Headshots of all War Zone wrestlers who can execute the move**

**Reversal:**

**Brainbuster**

**DAMAGE: 8**

**Some moves are reversible — if you have the reverse move in your wrestler's move list, you can try to reverse. Some reversals are "generic", meaning that any wrestler can try to reverse that move.**

**Base damage of the move, not counting any bonuses**

## ABDOMINAL STRETCH

This is administered with the attacking wrestler standing behind his opponent. He then anchors his opponent's leg to the mat by wrapping his leg around it in a "grapevine"-type lock. Finally, the wrestler executing the move entwines his torso around his victim like a serpent, thereby stretching his opponent's abdominal muscles.

GD OH SM

**DAMAGE: 2**

## ARM DRAG

SM OH MS RM BB

Usually delivered, judo-style, to a charging (or standing) opponent. The wrestler making the throw grabs his opponent by the arm and throws him, across his body, to the mat.

**DAMAGE: 3**

## ARM WRENCH

The attacking wrestler grabs his victim's left wrist with both hands and yanks his arm back, then wraps his left arm around his opponent's right elbow. The attacking wrestler then places his right hand on his opponent's shoulder and clasps the inside of his own right elbow with his left hand, locking it up.

AJ BH BB CJ DL FQ GD HH KN MK MS OH RM SR SM SC TH UT

**DAMAGE: 4**

## ATOMIC DROP

**DAMAGE: 3**

AJ BH BB FQ GD HH KN OH UT

The wrestler executing the move steps behind his opponent, secures him around the abdomen, and hoists him up onto his shoulder, as if to make a Belly Back Suplex. Instead of falling backwards, however, the wrestler in command slams his opponent, feet-first, down onto the mat, with the base of the victim's spine crashing into his braced knee.

Reversal:

**Headlock Takedown**

## AVALANCHE

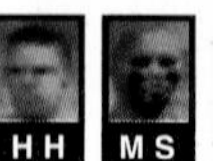

HH MS OH RM SR SM TH

With his opponent helpless in a corner, the wrestler goes to the diagonal corner, then charges. When he is several steps away from the stunned victim, he goes airborne and lands chest-to-chest against the victim.

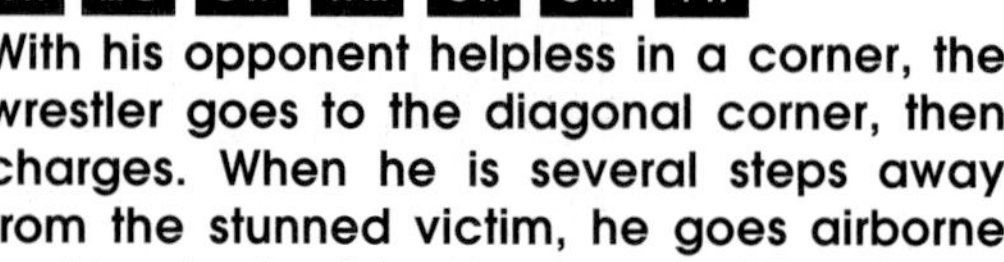

**DAMAGE: 6**

## AXE HANDLE SMASH

A blow delivered by an attacking wrestler with his hands linked together, smashing downward as if chopping wood with an axe.

SM GD OH SM SC TH UT

**DAMAGE: 4**

## BACK BODY DROP DAMAGE: 6

  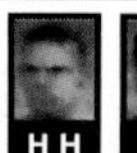     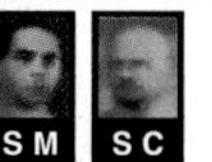

AJ GD HH MK MS OH RM SM SC

The charging wrestler's momentum is used against him as the wrestler executing this move bends forward, causing the charging opponent to fall onto the aggressor's back. The aggressor then straightens up, flipping the victim up and over for a back-first fall.

**Reversal:**

**Piledriver (Generic)**

## BACK BREAKER DAMAGE: 2

AJ KN SC UT

The wrestler making the throw hoists the opponent as if for a Body Slam. But instead of making a throw, he maintains the hold, dropping the victim, back-first, onto his braced knee.

**Reversal:**

**Belly to Belly (Generic)**

## BELLY-BACK SUPLEX

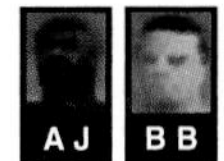 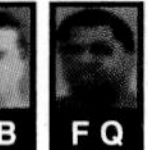      

AJ BB FQ OH MS RM SR SM TH

The move begins with a Gut Wrench from behind, while the Suplex (see Suplex) takes the opponent over the offensive wrestler's shoulder, slamming the back of the victim's head and neck into the mat.

**DAMAGE: 6**

### SUPER SECRETS — EXTRA COSTUME OPTIONS

Beat the Challenge with Kane in any difficulty mode, and you'll have access to new pants, masks, shirts, and boots for use with your Custom Wrestler! It's an accessorizing dream!

## BEARHUG

Two wrestlers face one another and the one executing the move grasps his opponent around the chest or stomach and squeezes, often lifting the victim off his feet.

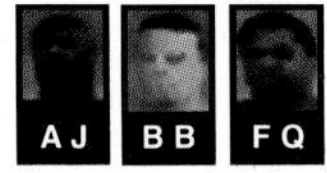


**DAMAGE: 5**

## BELLY-BELLY SUPLEX

When your opponent is in the corner, the wrestler on offense locks his arms around his opponent in a Bearhug, then hoists and throws him, while spinning and falling backward.

**DAMAGE: 5**

## BIONIC ELBOW

With the victim standing, the attacking wrestler leaps from the top turnbuckle with his arms cocked partway back, so that his elbows smash into his opponent's face, neck or chest.

**DAMAGE: 5**

## BOOT TO FACE

As a charging opponent runs toward the wrestler, he lifts his leg so that the opponent runs headlong into the sole of his boot.

**DAMAGE: 4**

## BODY PRESS

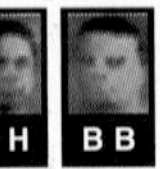
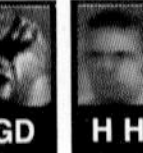
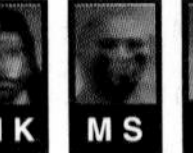

The attacking wrestler leaps from the top turnbuckle, goes parallel with the mat, then slams broadside into his opponent's chest, knocking him down into a pinning situation. Some wrestlers can execute this move from the inside of the ring to a standing opponent who is outside the ring.

**DAMAGE: 6**

## BLATANT CHOKE

FQ HH

Similar to a Choke, but (as you might guess) even more blatant.

**DAMAGE: 3**

## BODY SLAM DAMAGE: 5

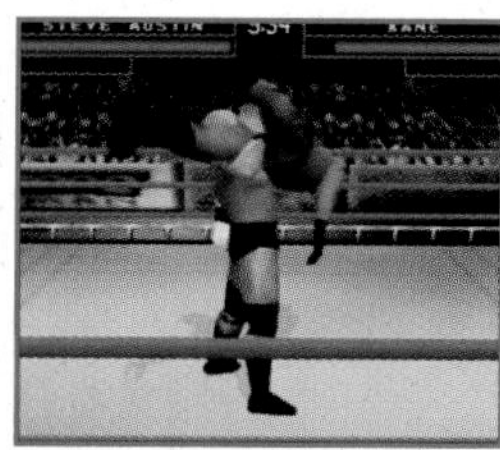

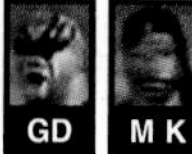

AJ BH BB GD MK SM SC

Hoist opponent with your lifting arm locked under his crotch and the other arm thrown over your opponent's shoulder. Hoist, invert and slam!

Reversal:

**Vertical Suplex reversal (generic)**

## BOSTON CRAB

BB FQ TH

With his opponent on his stomach, the wrestler applying the hold turns away from the victim, but lifts his opponent's feet and ankles, bending them backwards and locking his arms over them. The attacking wrestler then sits back, pulling the victim's feet toward his head and thus bending the victim's spine backward, attempting to get a submission.

**DAMAGE: 4**

## BRAINBUSTER

This move begins exactly like a Vertical Suplex (see Vertical Suplex), except once the victim is hoisted into the full vertical position, legs and feet aimed at the ceiling, the wrestler executing the move drops directly down, crumpling the victim, who lands hard on the back of his own head and shoulders.

AJ GD MK MS RM SM SC TH

Reversal:

**Brainbuster**

**DAMAGE: 8**

## BUTT DROP

Pretty much what it sounds like — the attacker leaps into the air and strikes his opponent with his butt. Sometimes called a Senton or a Senton Splash. Can be delivered from a standing position or off the top rope.

GD

**DAMAGE: 5**

# BULLDOG

## CHARGING POWERSLAM

The Bulldog catches a charging opponent, then pivots and swivels on his planted legs as he twists his — and the victim's — body around for an extra strong Bodyslam.

**FINISHER!**

**DAMAGE: 9**

## BULLDOG

AJ BH FQ GD MK MS SC

This is a running throw delivered from a Side Headlock. With the opponent locked up around the neck, the wrestler executing the move runs forward, pulling his opponent with him. After building some momentum, the wrestler on offense leaps into the air — still maintaining the Side Headlock — and lands on his rump, slamming the victim's head into the mat. NOTE: This maneuver can be initiated from a tie-up, from behind an opponent, or while the opponent is dazed on the turnbuckle, depending on who your wrestler is.

**DAMAGE: 5**

## CAMEL CLUTCH

BB FQ

With the opponent on his stomach, the wrestler applying the move straddles his victim's torso, lifting him to his knees. The attacking wrestler then throws his victim's right arm over his own right thigh and the victim's left arm over his own left thigh. He then locks up his fingers under his opponent's chin (see Chinlock) and assumes a sitting position, leaning back to apply extraordinary pressure to the victim's neck and back.

**DAMAGE: 4**

## CHARGING BUTT BUMP

MS TH

With either the opponent charging, the wrestler on offense charging, or both wrestlers running toward one another, the wrestler executing the move executes a 180 degree turn and leaps into the air, extending his backside so that it strikes the opponent in the chest or midsection.

**DAMAGE: 3**

## CHARGING/FLYING SHOULDER TACKLE

FAAROOQ 9:25 KANE

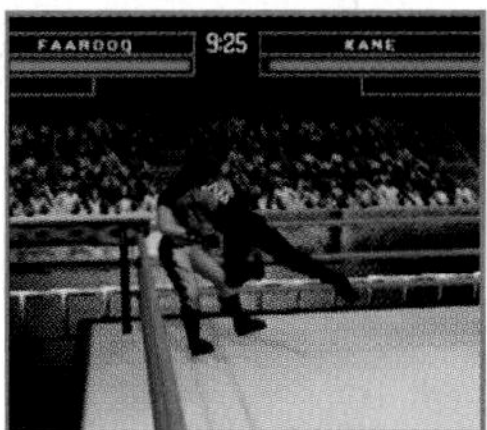

After charging at his opponent, the attacking wrestler delivers a football-style shoulder block to his opponent's chest and shoulder. This is done either in the middle of the ring as a running hit, or against an opponent who is sagging in one of the corners.

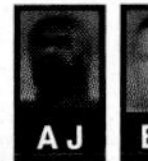

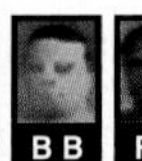

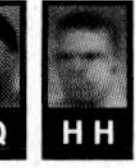

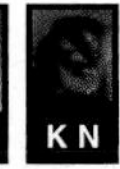

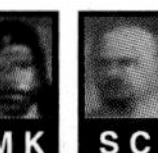

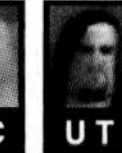

AJ BB FQ HH KN MK SC UT

**DAMAGE: 6**

## CHOKE

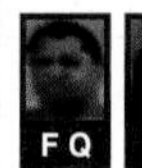

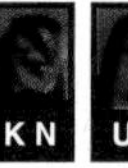

FQ KN UT

Throttling your opponent. Hey, there's no ref in the game, right?

**DAMAGE: 3**

## CHEST CHOP

7:38 KANE

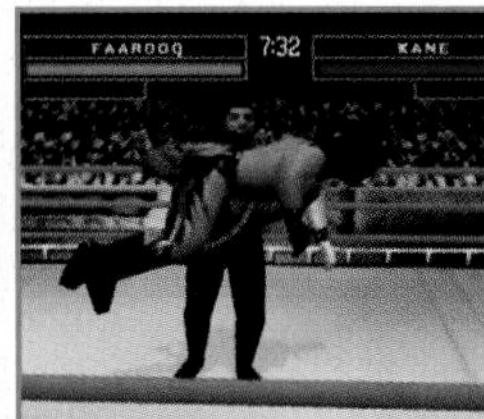

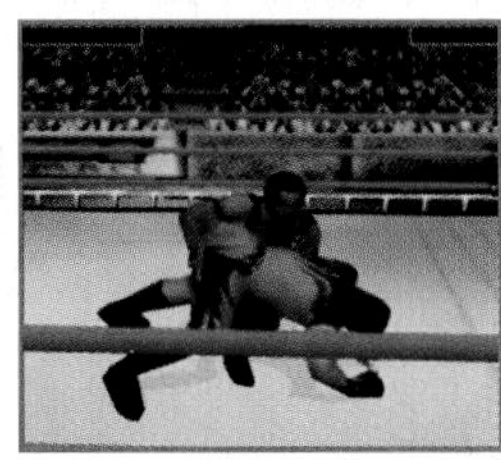

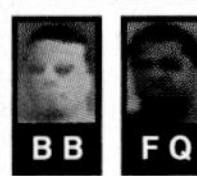

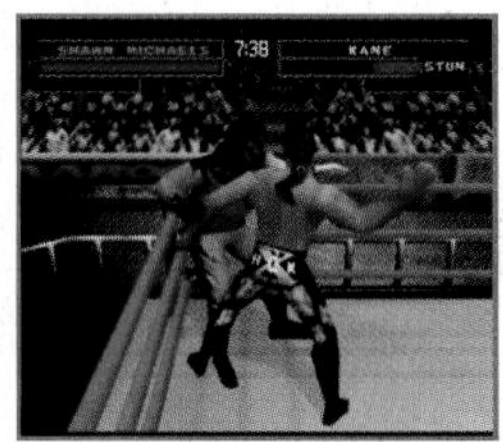

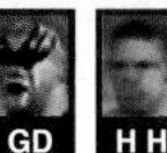

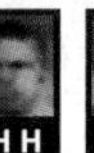

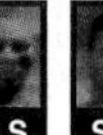

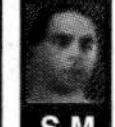

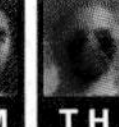

GD HH MS SR SM TH

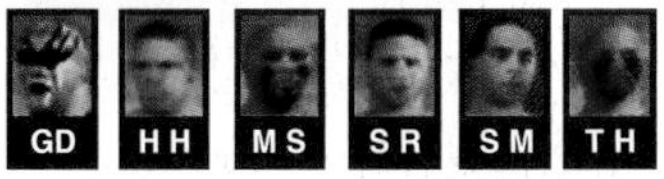

A karate-style, open-handed chop across the victim's chest, while the opponent is helpless in the corner.

**DAMAGE: 2**

## CHEST BREAKER **DAMAGE: 2**

FAAROOQ 7:32 KANE

BB FQ

The attacker hoists victim as if for a Backbreaker, but drops him chest-first onto his own braced knee.

**Reversal:**

**Vertical Suplex reversal (Generic)**

## CHOKE WITH BOOT

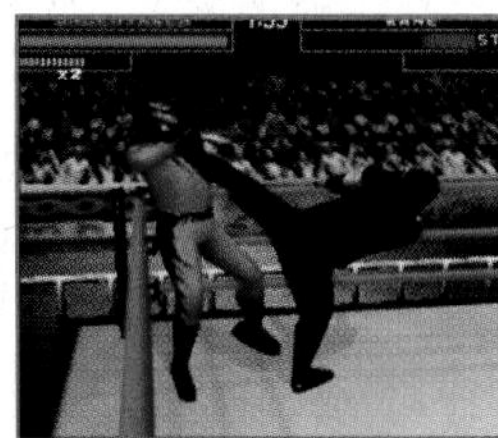

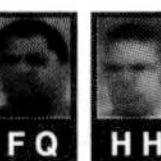

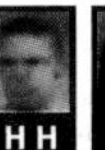

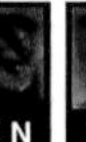

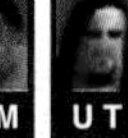

FQ HH KN RM UT

With his opponent helpless in the corner, the attacking wrestler plants one foot on the mat then lifts and wedges his other foot against the victim's throat, choking him.

**DAMAGE: 3**

## CHOKE SLAM

UNDERTAKER 4:26 KANE

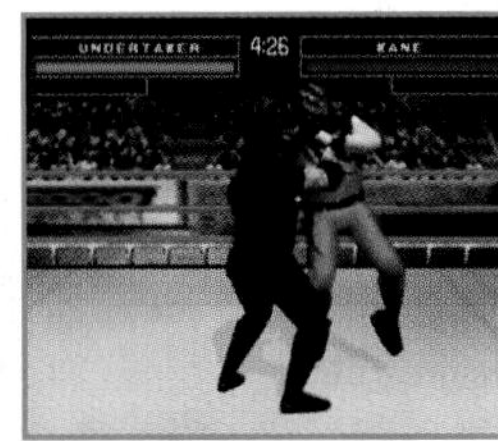

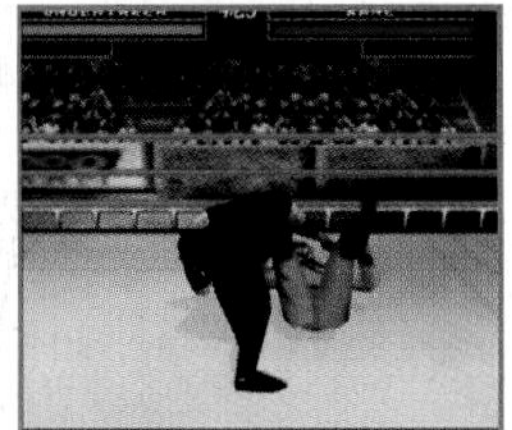

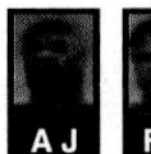

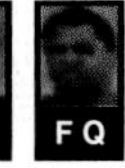

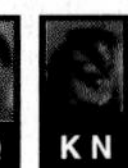

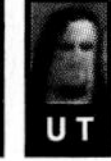

AJ FQ KN UT

The wrestler lifts his opponent by his throat, then slams him down onto his back.

**DAMAGE: 6**

## CLIMB TURNBUCKLE AND PUMMEL

This is the popular move in which one wrestler is collapsed in the corner and his opponent climbs to the second rope and begins throwing punches in bunches.

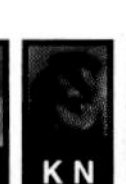

BH BB KN OH RM SR SM SC UT

**DAMAGE: 2**

## CLOTHESLINE

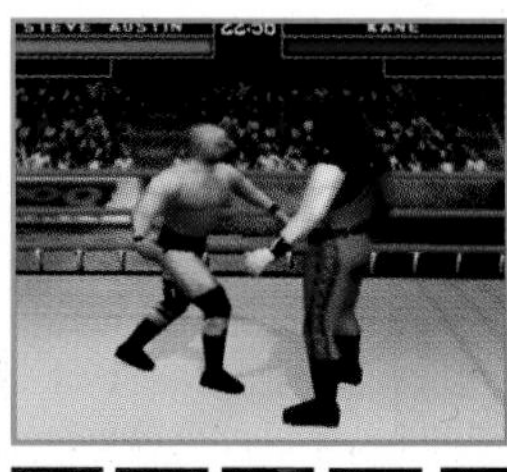

Whether it's executed from a standing position, running at the opponent, against a charging opponent, or even from the top turnbuckle, the results of a Clothesline are similar: the attacking wrestler extends one arm perpendicular to his body and slams the upheld arm into his victim's chest and throat area.

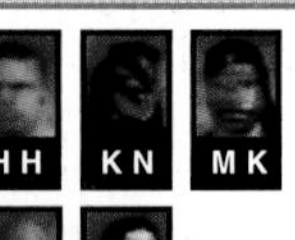

AJ BH BB FQ GD HH KN MK
MS OH RM SR SC TH UT

**DAMAGE: 4-5**

## COBRA CLUTCH

HH MK SC

A form of the Sleeper hold. With both wrestlers standing, the attacker's left arm goes over victim's left shoulder, grabbing his left wrist with his own left hand, forming a "loop". The attacker then slips his own right arm through the "loop" and presses his right palm against the victim's carotid artery, thereby shutting down the blood flow to the victim's brain. The wrestler on offense then cinches the "loop" tight.

**DAMAGE: 5**

## CHOPS

AJ

**DAMAGE: 3**

## COVER PIN

This is how you win the game, kids — hold him down for a three-count! NOTE: Some other moves in the game can also result in a pin.

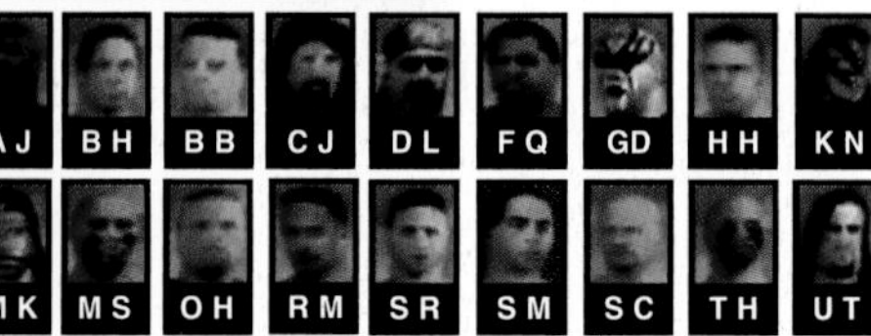

AJ BH BB CJ DL FQ GD HH KN
MK MS OH RM SR SM SC TH UT

**DAMAGE: N/A**

## CROSS BODY BLOCK

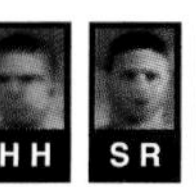


Similar to the Body Press (see Body Press) except it is delivered from the mat rather than the top rope. The attacking wrestler charges his opponent, leaves his feet to go parallel with the mat, then slams broadside into his opponent's chest, knocking him down into a pinning situation.

**DAMAGE: 5**

## COVER PIN KICKOUT

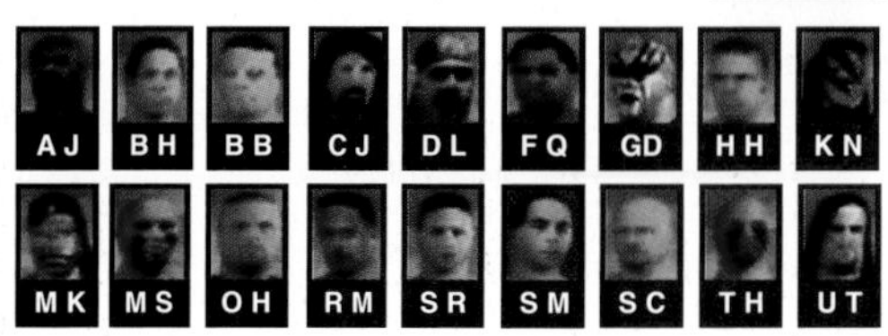


If you've got the strength, you can kick out of a pin before you're counted out. The good news is that if you succeed, your health gets a boost.

**DAMAGE: N/A**

## CROSS FACE CHICKEN WING

With both wrestlers standing and the attacker behind his opponent, he twists the victim's left arm into a Hammerlock. The attacker then slips his own left hand in front of victim's left bicep, and moves up to hold victim's chin. Attacker then releases the Hammerlock, throws his own right hand up to the victim's chin, and locks his own hands. Submission hold.

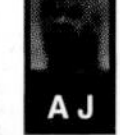

**DAMAGE: 5**

## CRUCIFIX

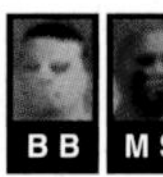

**DAMAGE: 3** (standing) **6** (running)

The attacking wrestler charges his opponent, actually running slightly behind him before wrapping both arms around one of the victim's shoulders and hoisting himself into the air, wrapping his legs around the victim's other shoulder. If the wrestler is already running before this move is executed, the base damage is doubled.

**Reversal:**

**Samoan Drop**

# GOLDUST — CURTAIN CALL

With both men standing, and Goldust in a belly-to-back position, Goldust leans his opponent backwards, wrapping his own right arm around the victim's head. He then grabs the victim by the tights with his own left hand, hoists his opponent up into a Vertical Suplex position — except he falls forward instead of backward.

**FINISHER!**

**TOP SECRET**

**DAMAGE: 9**

## DDT DAMAGE: 7 (from Standing Position) 3 (from a Tie-up)

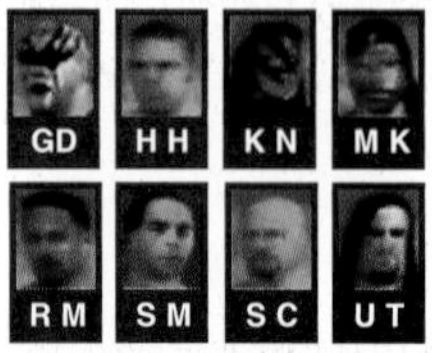

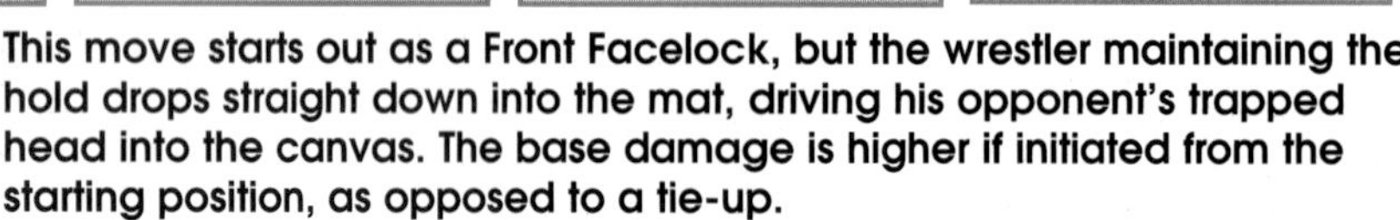


This move starts out as a Front Facelock, but the wrestler maintaining the hold drops straight down into the mat, driving his opponent's trapped head into the canvas. The base damage is higher if initiated from the starting position, as opposed to a tie-up.

**Reversal:**

**Northern Lights Suplex**

## DOUBLE FOOT STOMP

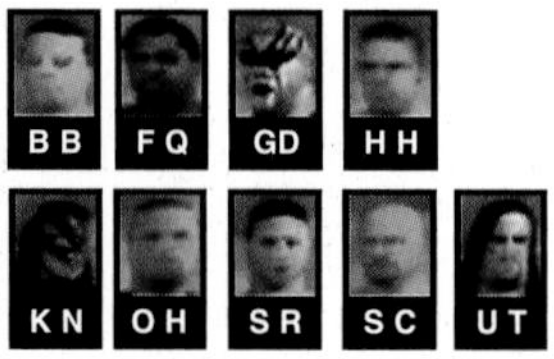

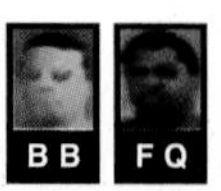

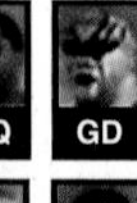

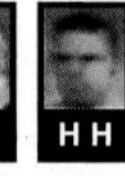

With his opponent lying helplessly on the mat, the attacking wrestler jumps up and stomps on the victim's torso with both feet. This can be executed from the mat or from the top turnbuckle, depending on the wrestler you're playing.

**DAMAGE: 4**

## DOUBLE UNDERHOOK SUPLEX

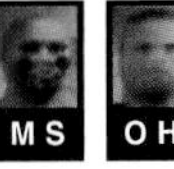


The wrestler on offense faces his opponent then bends him forward and hooks his victim's arms behind victim's back, so that the inside of the attacker's left elbow is touching the inside of victim's right elbow. The attacking wrestler then interlocks his fingers and hoists his victim for an arching, back-first slam onto the mat.

**DAMAGE: 7** (from Standing Position) **9** (from a Tie-Up)

## DRIVING ELBOW SMASH

Similar to an Elbow Drop, but the elbow is tucked closer to the attacking wrestler's own body, to hit with the point of the elbow instead of the tricep.

**DAMAGE: 4**

## DROP TO KNEES AND UPPERCUT

As you'd expect from the name, the wrestler drops to his knees while delivering an uppercut punch to his opponent's jaw.

**DAMAGE: 4**

| CACTUS JACK | DUDE LOVE | DOUBLE-ARM DDT |
|---|---|---|

**FINISHER!** **FINISHER!**

## TOP SECRET

This move starts out much like a Double Underhook Suplex, with the attacking wrestler facing his opponent, bending him forward and hooking his arms behind his own back, in a sort of reverse Full Nelson. Instead of lifting the victim up for a suplex, however, the attacker sits down hard, forcing his opponent's trapped head straight down into the mat.

**DAMAGE: 9**

## FAAROOQ — DOMINATOR

The move begins as if Faarooq is executing a Power Bomb. But instead of slamming the victim on his back, he flips his opponent while falling forward, slamming the victim face-first into the mat.

TOP SECRET

FINISHER!

**DAMAGE: 9**

## DROP KICK

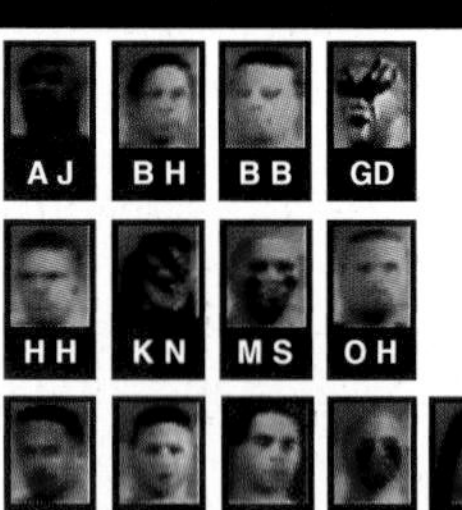


Whether from a standing position, charging at the opponent, against a running opponent, or even from the top turnbuckle, the attacker jumps into the air and lands a double-footed kick to his opponent's head or upper body.

**DAMAGE: 5**

## ELBOW DROP

The victim is on the mat (usually face-up) and the attacking wrestler cocks his dominant arm and falls to the canvas, slamming his tricep into the victim's chest, throat or head. This can be executed from a standing position or with a running start.

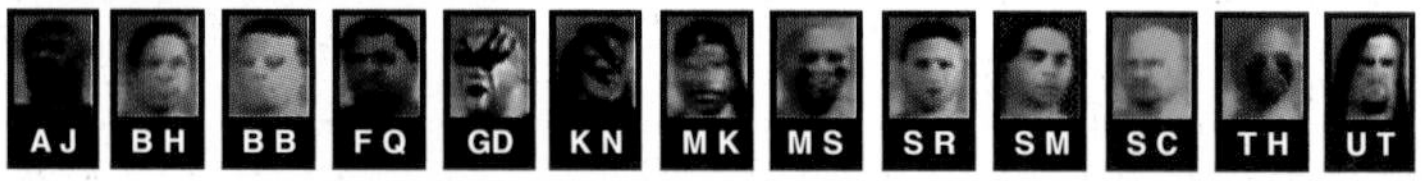

**DAMAGE: 4**

## ELBOW DROP ONTO LEG

See Elbow Drop.

**DAMAGE: 5**

## ELBOW TO GROIN

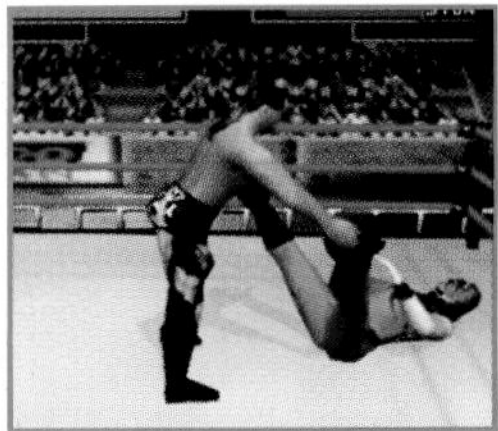

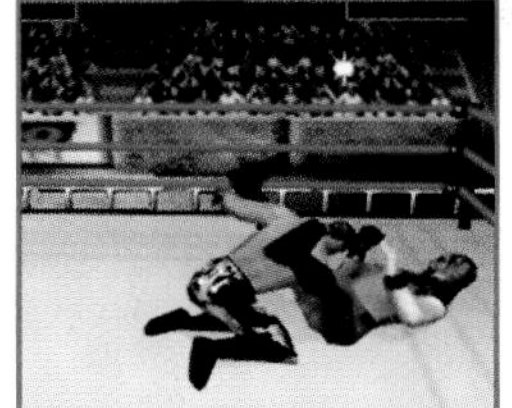

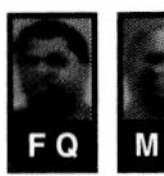

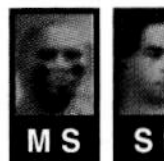

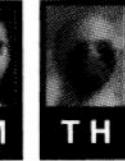

FQ
MS
SM
TH

Similar to the Elbow Drop, except that the target location is a bit more tender.

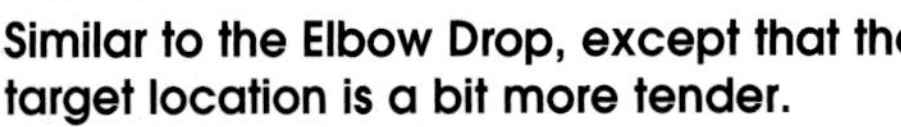

**DAMAGE: 4**

## DROP TOE HOLD

THRASHER
29:31
KANE

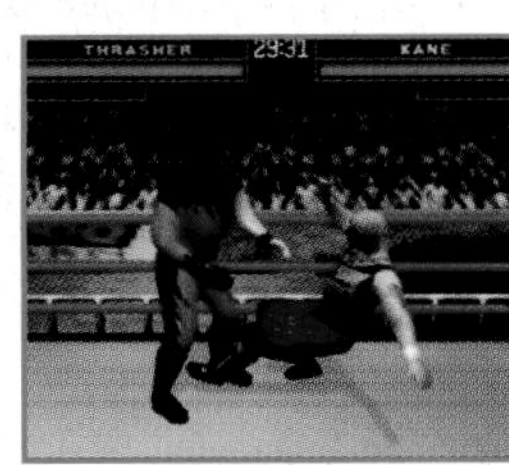

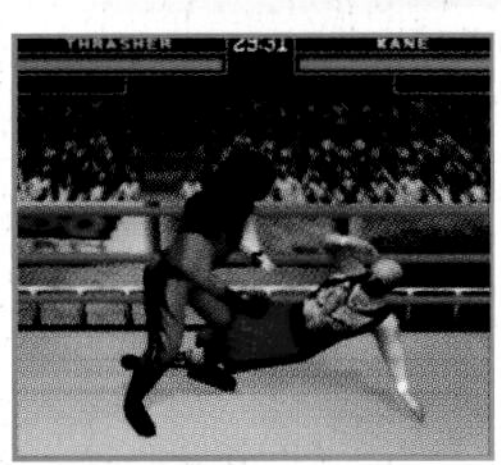

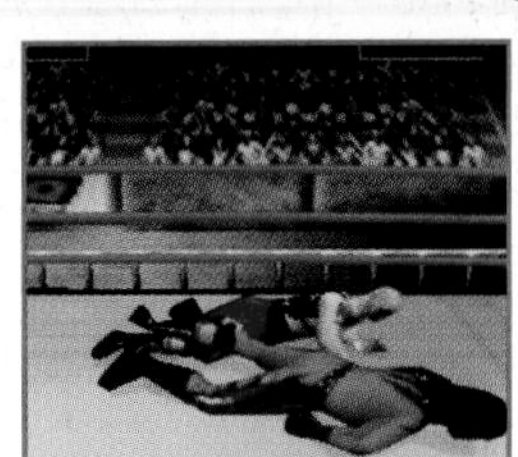

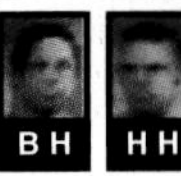

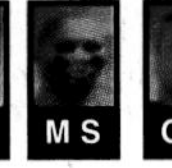

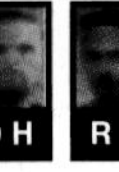

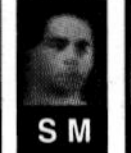

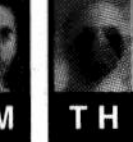

BH
HH
MS
OH
RM
SM
TH

The wrestler executing the move drops to the mat and uses his legs to first trip then lock up his opponent's ankles, causing him to fall forward, remaining trapped in a Toe hold. This can be executed from either the starting position or against a running opponent, depending on the wrestler.

**DAMAGE: 3**

## FALLING HEADBUTT

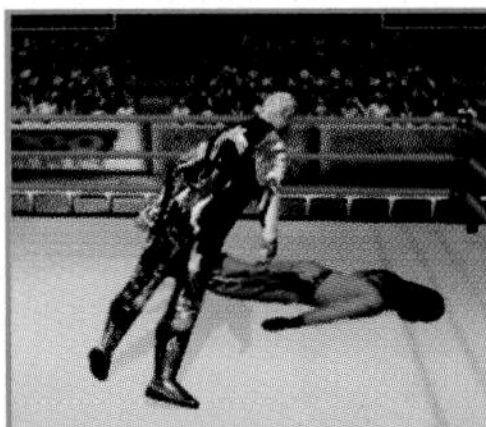

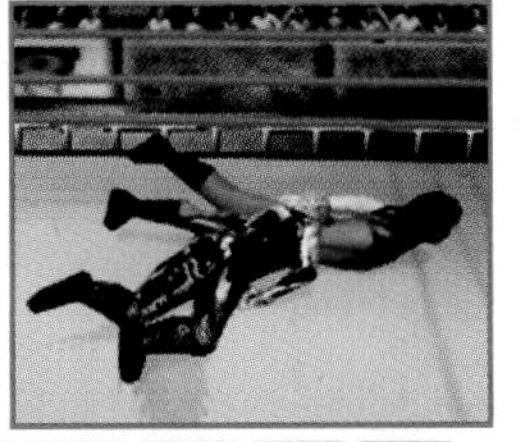

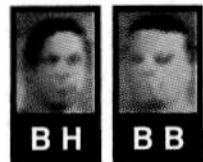

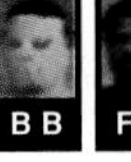

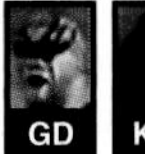

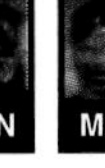

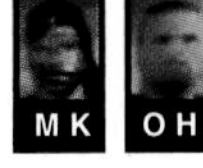

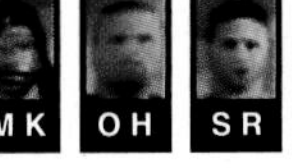

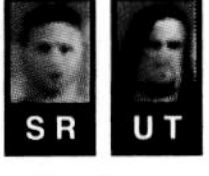

BH
BB
FQ
GD
KN
MK
OH
SR
UT

With his opponent on the mat (usually face-up), the attacking wrestler falls forward to the mat, slamming his head into the victim's body as he lands.

**DAMAGE: 4**

## SUPER SECRETS

## FEMALE CUSTOM WRESTLERS

Beat the War Zone Challenge with Shawn Michaels or Triple H, and the game will allow you to create female custom wrestlers, complete with assorted body types and costumes! Va-va-voom!

CUSTOMIZE
LOWERBODY

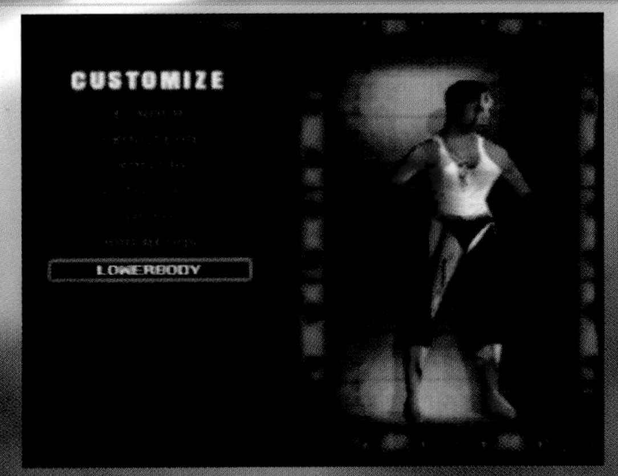

## FLYING BACK ELBOW

The attacker leaps and, after twisting 180 degrees in the air, slams his elbow into his opponent's face.

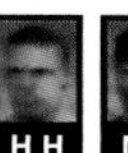

BH GD HH MK TH

**DAMAGE: 5**

## FIGURE FOUR LEGLOCK

With the attacking wrestler facing his prone opponent (who is on his back), he steps into what looks like a Spinning Toehold (see Spinning Toehold). But instead of continuing the spin, the dominant wrestler "folds" the leg under attack over the victim's other leg. The attacking wrestler then inserts his own leg into the tangle of his opponent's limbs, allowing him to sit down and lean back in order to apply incredible pressure to both the victim's locked-up knees.

HH SM

**DAMAGE: 4**

## FIREMAN'S CARRY

BH BB TH

A wrestler throws his opponent across his shoulders to the mat, hoisting him in the style used by firemen when carrying victims from a blaze.

**DAMAGE: 4**

## FISHERMAN'S SUPLEX DAMAGE: 6

Starts out like a standard Vertical Suplex (see Vertical Suplex), except the wrestler making the throw grabs the victim's far leg from behind the knee and hooks it, locking his fingers together to secure the position. Then, instead of releasing the suplex, the wrestler on offense holds onto his opponent throughout the move, and pins opponents shoulders to the mat.

HH OH

Reversal:

**Vertical Suplex**

## FOREARM SMASH

A leaping Forearm delivered from the top turnbuckle or the ring apron against a standing opponent.

AJ FQ GD HH KN MK OH SC UT

**DAMAGE: 8**

## FLYING BUTT BUMP

GD

With the victim dazed, the attacking wrestler leaps off the top rope toward his opponent, but spins his body around so that his rear end slams into the victim, knocking the victim to the mat with the impact.

**DAMAGE: 5**

## FIST DROP

The opponent is down and out, looking up at the rafters as the attacking wrestler stands next to him — or runs toward him, or jumps from the top turnbuckle — and drops to the mat sideways with his dominant fist cocked. As he lands, his fist slams into the victim's head or body.

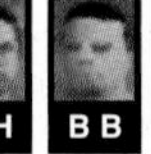

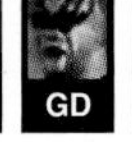

AJ BH BB CJ DL FQ GD HH KN MK MS OH RM SR SM SC TH UT

**DAMAGE: 5**

## FLYING FOREARM

A Forearm delivered from a charging, leaping posture.

OH TH

**DAMAGE: 4**

## FOREARM SMASHES

With his opponent trapped in the corner, the attacking wrestler unleashes a series of Forearms (see Forearm).

BH MK

**DAMAGE: 5**

## FLYING HEAD SCISSORS

OH RM SR SM TH

After running toward his opponent, the wrestler attempting this move leaps into the air, wraps both legs around his opponent's neck and takes him down to the mat, maintaining the lock.

**DAMAGE: 5**

## FOREARM

A blow thrown with the forearm rather than the fist. North American-style forearms are thrown overhand.

**DAMAGE: 2**

## FUJI LEG BAR

A submission-style leg lock in which the attacker interlocks his legs in a scissors-style lock around the victim's leg or arm.

**DAMAGE: 3**

## FRONT-FACE DDT

Very similar to the Stone Cold Stunner, except that it doesn't start with a kick, and that the attacking wrestler drags his victim along for a running start before dropping down to the canvas.

**DAMAGE: 6**

## FRONT BACK BREAKER

The attacker lifts his victim, as if for a Body Slam, but brings his victim's back down across his own braced knee.

**DAMAGE: 6**

## FULL NELSON

The attacker comes up behind his opponent and wraps his arms around the victim's triceps and shoulders, pinning his victim's arms together over his head and maintaining a standing lockup by interlacing his fingers behind the victim's neck — then applying pressure, forcing the head down.

**DAMAGE: 2**

## FRONT ELBOW

With his victim lying stunned on the mat, the running attacker smashes downward with both elbows.

**DAMAGE: 4**

## FUJIWARA ARM BAG

This maneuver is delivered with the attacker standing and the victim on the mat. The wrestler executing the move grabs the victim's arm and falls backwards, trapping it in a leg scissorlock.

**DAMAGE: 5**

## GORILLA PRESS SLAM

The victim is hoisted over the attacking wrestler's head, like a barbell, then slammed to the mat, back-first.

**DAMAGE: 8**

## GERMAN SUPLEX

In this move the wrestler on offense stands belly-to-back against his opponent, whom he grasps around the midsection. He then arches back, suplexing the victim directly backwards and to the mat, where the victim lands on the back of his head and shoulders.

**DAMAGE: 8**

## GRAB AND PUNCH

The attacking wrestler grabs his opponent's head and punches it. Not among the more subtle maneuvers, but effective.

**DAMAGE: 2**

## GUT WRENCH POWER BOMB

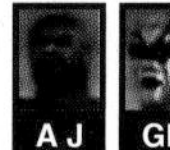

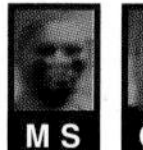
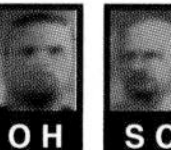

The attacking wrestler bends his opponent toward him, then reaches over and grasps the victim around the back and stomach, locking his hands together. The wrestler on offense then hoists his opponent into the air and throws him to the mat, back-first.

**DAMAGE: 6**

**DAMAGE: 2** (from Standing Position) **1** (from a Tie-Up)

This is the basic move from which most Armlocks (such as the Painkiller) are derived. The wrestler applying the hold takes the opponent's dominant arm and bends it behind him, pushing the forearm up toward the victim's own shoulder blades. This move applies tremendous pressure to the victim's shoulder and can even dislocate it.

Reversal:

**Hammerlock reversal (generic)**

## HALF CRAB

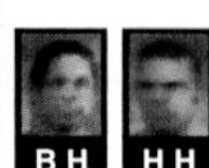

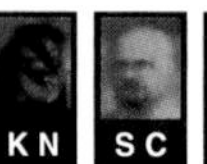

This is a Boston Crab (see Boston Crab) in which the attacking wrestler only attacks one of his opponent's legs.

**DAMAGE: 3**

## HANGING VERTICAL SUPLEX

This is exactly like a Vertical Suplex (see Vertical Suplex), except that when the wrestler on offense gets his victim into a full vertical position, he holds him up there for several seconds, allowing blood to rush to the victim's head, before falling backwards and completing the move.

**DAMAGE: 8** (from Standing Position) **9** (from a Tie-Up)

## HART ATTACK

The attacking wrestler charges at his stunned or otherwise immobilized victim, then leaps into the air, in a sitting position, and hooks his forearm around his opponent's throat, in a form of Clothesline. But instead of releasing the Clothesline, the wrestler executing the move holds his victim and slams him backwards to the canvas.

**DAMAGE: 7**

## HAYMAKER

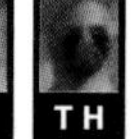

A particularly hard punch.

**DAMAGE: 5**

## HEADBUTT TO GROIN

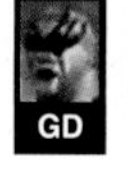


A Falling Headbutt (see Falling Headbutt) onto a prone opponent whose legs have been spread. The attacking wrestler slams his head into the victim's groin area as he lands.

**DAMAGE: 4**

## HEADLOCK TAKEDOWN

**DAMAGE: 3**

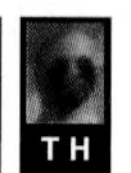


Takedown delivered from a standing headlock.

Reversal:

**Atomic Drop**

## HEADBUTT

As you'd expect, the attacking wrestling uses his own head to butt his opponent's.

**DAMAGE: 2**

## HIPTOSS

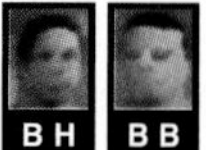
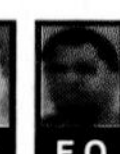
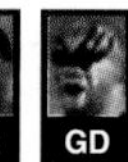

Sometimes called a Cornish Hype, this is a rolling throw in which the wrestler making the throw hoists his hip in order to catch an oncoming wrestler around the arm, and snap the victim into a forward flip.

**DAMAGE: 3**

## HIT (OPPONENT ON TURNBUCKLE)

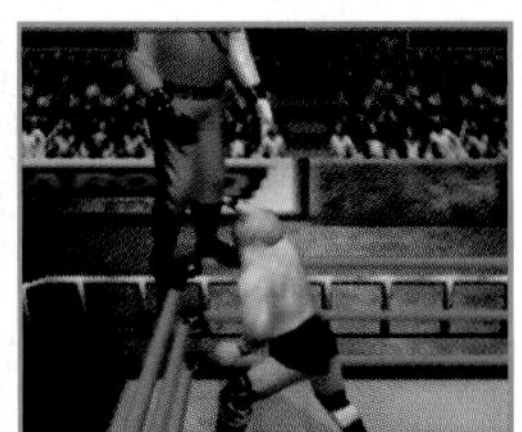

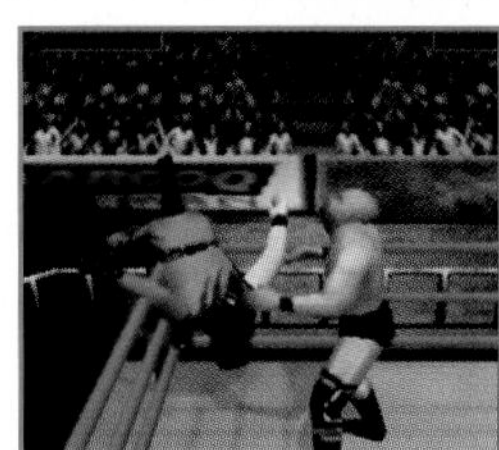

If you're in any condition to punch your opponent while he's up on the top turnbuckle, it's usually a good idea.

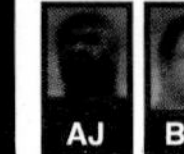

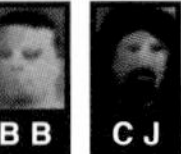

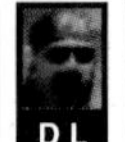

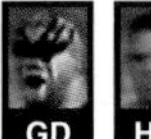

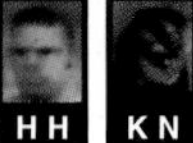

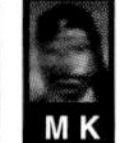

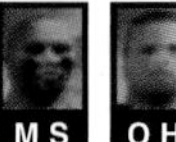

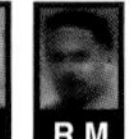

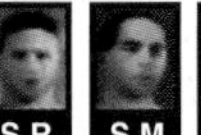

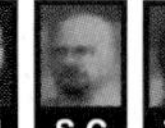

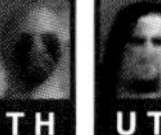

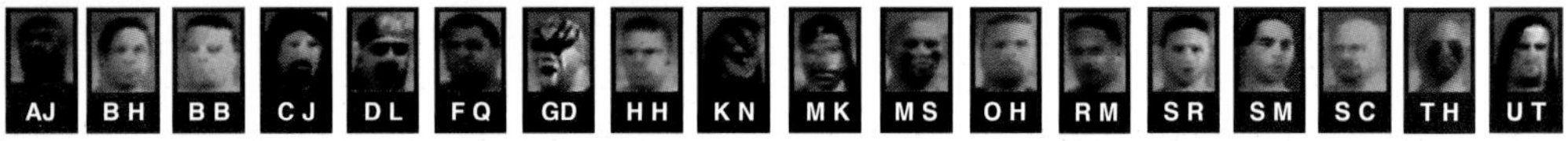

AJ
BH
BB
CJ
DL
FQ
GD
HH
KN
MK
MS
OH
RM
SR
SM
SC
TH
UT

**DAMAGE: 2-3**

## HURRICANRANNA

**DAMAGE: 5** (Opponent in corner) **8** (all others)

SHAWN MICHAELS
13:48
KANE

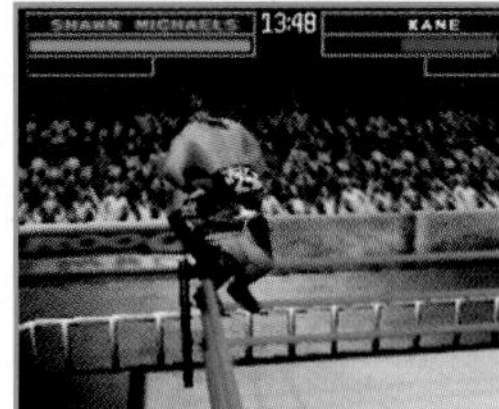

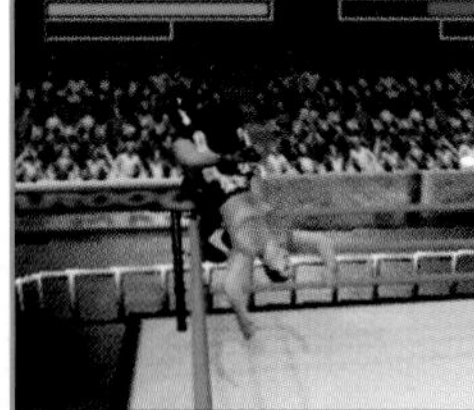

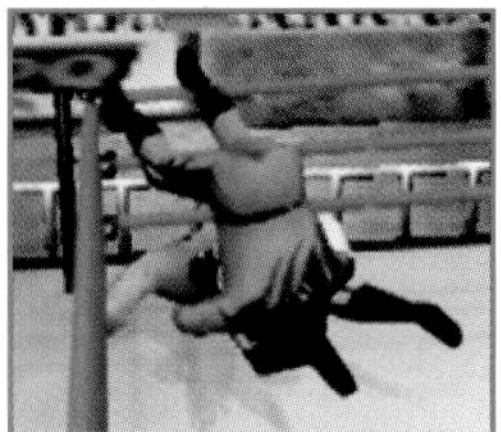

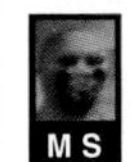

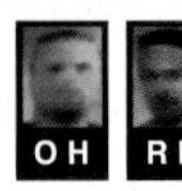

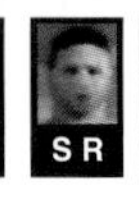

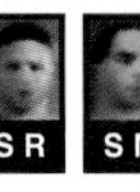

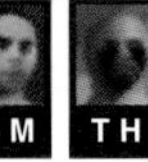

MS
OH
RM
SR
SM
TH

The attacking wrestler jumps onto his opponent's shoulders, where he faces toward him from a sitting position. The wrestler on offense then snaps backward, taking the opponent with him in a forced flip. If delivered correctly, the victim will actually land on his head, DDT-style.

**Reversal:**

**Power Bomb**

## SUPER SECRETS

## WRESTLE THE TRAINER ...FOR REAL

Go into the Training Room and select any move from the menu, and you will get a message telling you that the Trainer is now selectable as a wrestler in the game! Just hope he doesn't take all that abuse you've piled on him personally!

DEFAULT
TRAINER
CUSTOM

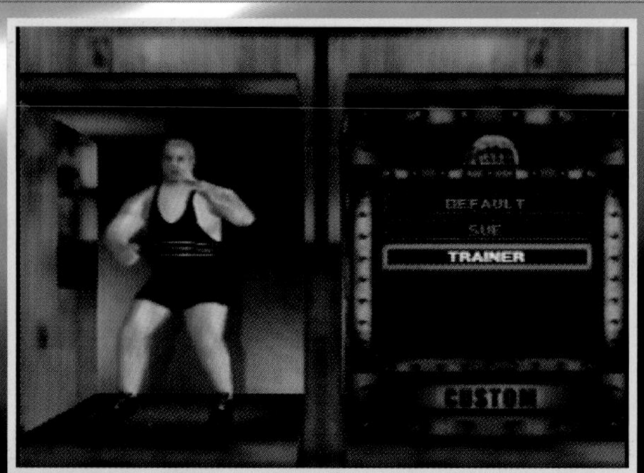

## INVERTED ATOMIC DROP

In an Inverted Atomic Drop, the two wrestlers face one another and the wrestler executing the throw hoists his opponent into the air from a Bearhug-like position, then brings his victim slamming down, crotch-first, onto his braced knee. (See Atomic Drop)

**DAMAGE: 4**

## INSIDE FOREARM

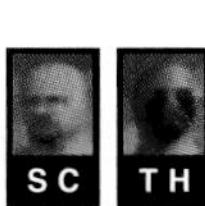

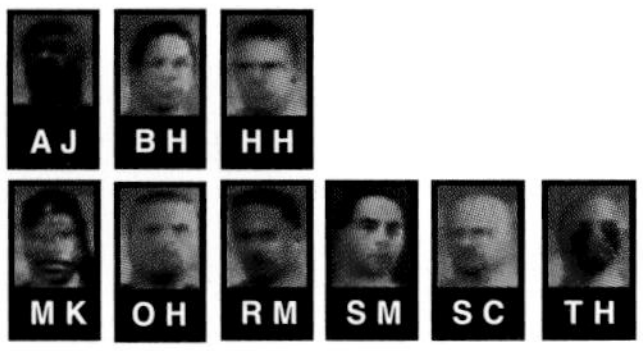

A European-style Forearm Smash, it is thrown from underneath the victim's chin, often following nearly 360 degrees of rotation on the part of the attacker's arm, thereby rocking the opponent upward with a strong blow to the jaw.

**DAMAGE: 2**

## INVERTED STF

An STF (see STF) applied in reverse, with the attacking wrestler lying back-to-back against his prone victim, instead of belly-to-back.

**DAMAGE: 4**

## JAPANESE ARM DRAG

With both wrestlers charging toward one another, the wrestler on offense loops his arm around his opponent's and flips him forward and back-first to the mat.

**DAMAGE: 2**

## KAMIKAZE HEADBUTT

A flying Headbutt off the top rope (imagine a Falling Headbutt with a lot more momentum).

**DAMAGE: 5**

## KICK OPPONENT FROM STOMACH TO BACK

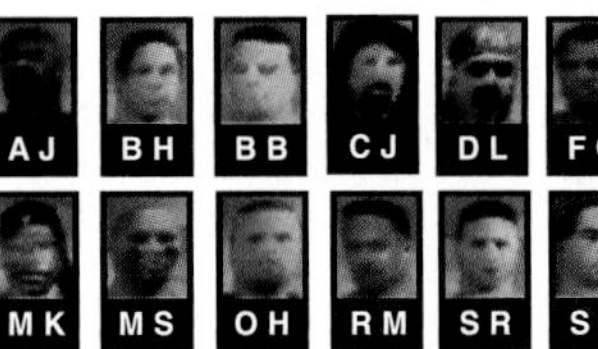

If your opponent is lying prone face-first on the mat, stunned, you might want to roll him over so he can see you execute the next crippling move!

**DAMAGE: N/**

## KNEE DROP

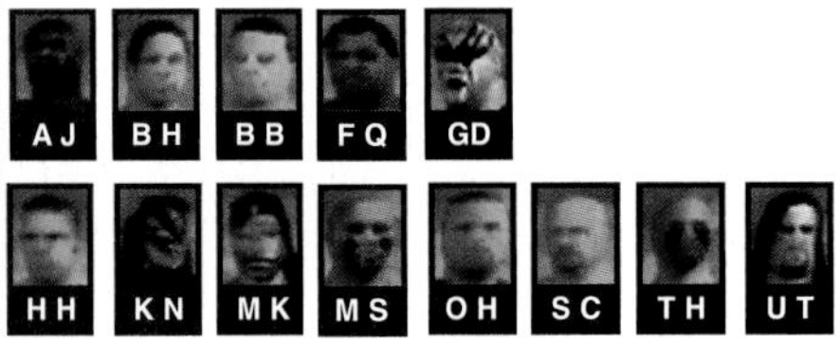

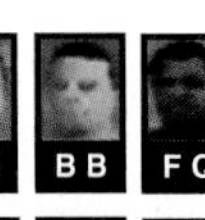

With the victim flat on the mat, the wrestler attempting the maneuver goes to the top rope, then leaps toward his opponent, landing with a knee against the victim's throat. Some wrestlers can only do this move from the standing position, some can execute it with a running start.

**DAMAGE: 4** (Standing or From Top Rope) **6** (Running)

## KNEE TO FACE

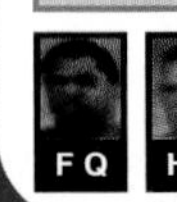

Knee, meet face. Face, this is knee.

**DAMAGE: 4**

## KNEEBREAKER

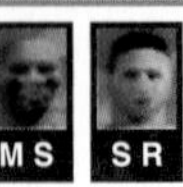



With the two wrestlers facing one another, one locks up the other and hoists him into the air, folding up one of the victim's legs behind him. The attacker then slams his opponent down onto the mat, jolting his knee.

**DAMAGE: 4**

## KNEE TO INSIDE LEG

A transition move in which the wrestler on offense moves from the victim's knee to an inside leg lock, which he then maintains.

**DAMAGE: 4**

## LAYING THE SMACK DOWN

RM

Also known as a Tornado DDT or Spinning DDT. The attacking wrestler ducks behind his opponent and climbs onto his back with a spinning kind of motion, which ends up with the attacker pulling the victim straight down to the mat for an extra-strong DDT.

**DAMAGE: 8**

## LEG DRAG

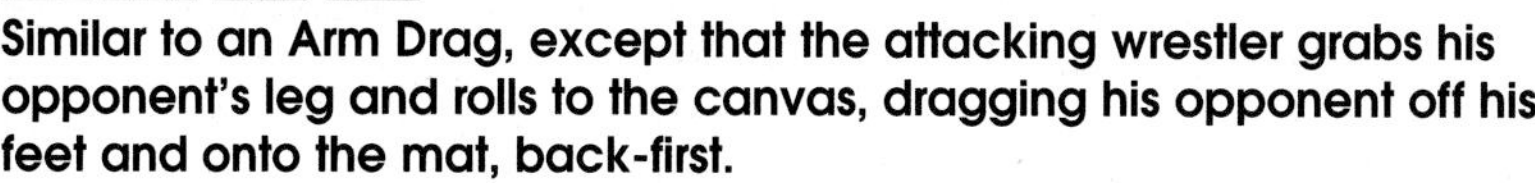

Similar to an Arm Drag, except that the attacking wrestler grabs his opponent's leg and rolls to the canvas, dragging his opponent off his feet and onto the mat, back-first.

**DAMAGE: 3**

## LEG LOCK

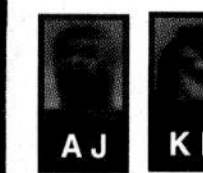

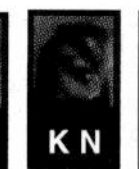

The attacking wrestler "grapevines" the leg of a victim on his back and applies knee-popping pressure.

**DAMAGE: 3**

## LEG DROP

With the victim flat on his back, the attacking wrestler jumps into the air and drops into a sitting position with the back of one leg slamming across the victim's chest or throat.

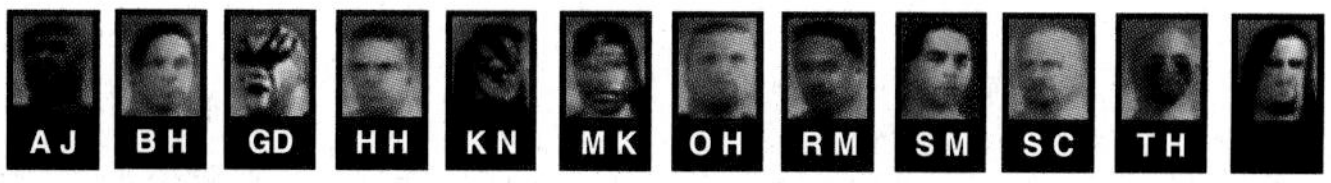

**DAMAGE: 4** (Standing or Running) **7** (From Top Turnbuckle)

## LEG GRAPEVINE

KN

OH

With the victim on his stomach, the attacking wrestler applies a move very similar to the Texas Cloverleaf (see Texas Cloverleaf), except instead of overlapping his victim's legs, he intertwines them before locking up.

**DAMAGE: 3**

## LEG LOCK CHOKEHOLD

OH

With the victim on his back, the attacking wrestler scissors his opponent's neck with his legs, locking his own ankles together and applying pressure on the victim's throat.

**DAMAGE: 4**

## MOONSAULT

With the opponent on his back or standing, the wrestler attempting the Moonsault climbs to the top rope, then flips backwards, landing Splash-style on his opponent. This move can also be performed from a standing position by certain wrestlers.

**DAMAGE: 7**

## MONKEY FLIP

SM

With his opponent in the corner, the attacking wrestler climbs onto his opponent's thighs, then falls back while keeping hold of the victim with his arms. The attacker rolls backwards to the mat while extending his legs, launching the victim into the air and onto his back.

**DAMAGE: 6**

## MAKE A WISH LEG SPLITTER

With the victim-to-be lying stunned on the mat, the attacking wrestler grabs each of his opponent's ankles with each hand, and pushes the legs in opposite directions.

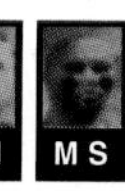

OH MS AJ

**DAMAGE: 5**

## NECK BREAKER

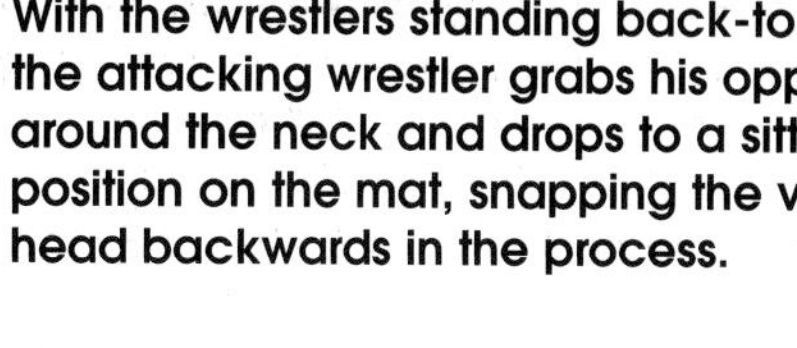

With the wrestlers standing back-to-back, the attacking wrestler grabs his opponent around the neck and drops to a sitting position on the mat, snapping the victim's head backwards in the process.

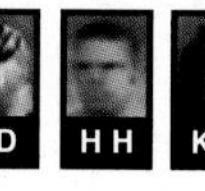

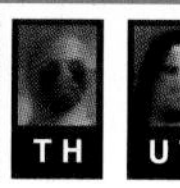

BH GD HH KN MK MS OH TH UT

**DAMAGE: 5** (from Starting position or from Behind) **2** (from a Tie-up)

## NERVE HOLD

The attacking wrestler clamps his dominant hand around the victim's trapezius muscle, between the neck and shoulder. This is a paralyzing hold which wears down an opponent very quickly. The wrestler applying the hold may brace the hand applying the hold with his other hand.

MK

**DAMAGE: 4**

## MANKIND

**FINISHER!**

## MANDIBLE CLAW

TOP SECRET

The softest tissue on the human body is found just beneath the tongue, and that is the target of Mankind's bizarre finisher. Clamping his right thumb under the victim's chin (bracing the victim's head with his other hand), he extends two fingers directly into his opponent's mouth and pushes down on that soft tissue, rendering the victim unconscious.

**DAMAGE: 9**

## MOSH — THE MOSH PIT

**TOP SECRET**

With the opponent standing in the ring facing him, Mosh climbs to the top rope, leaps onto his opponent's shoulders, as if to deliver a Hurricanrana, but instead rides his opponent onto the mat in a pinning position.

**FINISHER!**

**DAMAGE: 9**

## NORTHERN LIGHTS SUPLEX DAMAGE: 4

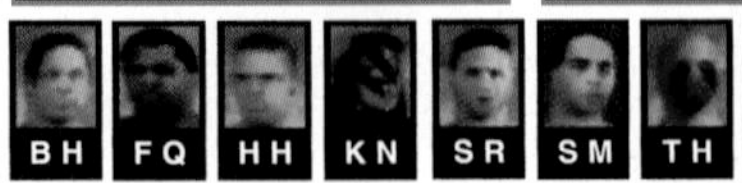


Very similar to a Fisherman's Suplex, except that the victim's leg is not hooked, allowing for a higher-impact landing (but less likelihood of a pin).

**Reversal:**

DDT

## OVERHEAD PRESS, DROP ONTO TURNBUCKLE

The wrestler on offense hoists the victim over his head as if pressing a barbell (see Gorilla Press Slam), but instead of executing into a Body Slam, the victim is dropped, chin-first, onto the top turnbuckle.

**DAMAGE: 7**

## OVERHEAD BELLY-BELLY SUPLEX

Just like a standard Belly-Belly Suplex, except the wrestler on offense throws his opponent straight overhead, rather than at an angle. This is also a "release" suplex in that the wrestler executing it releases his opponent once the throw is in progress, rather than riding him to the mat. It can also be used to throw a victim out of the ring.

**DAMAGE: 6** (from a Tie-Up or Start position) **8** (vs. Running Opponent)

## OKLAHOMA STAMPEDE

This is a Running or Charging Bodyslam, a variation of the Powerslam. The difference is that while the victim of a standard Powerslam is positioned over his opponent's shoulder, the victim of the Stampede is held in standard Bodyslam position.

**DAMAGE: 7**

## PAINKILLER

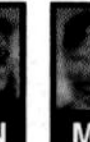

With the opponent on his stomach, the attacking wrestler locks up one of his opponent's arms in an armlock resembling the Cross Face Chicken Wing.

**DAMAGE: 4**

## POWER BOMB **DAMAGE: 9**

With the wrestlers face-to-face and the victim bent forward, the wrestler on offense locks up his opponent around the midsection, hoists him into an upside down position, then throws him, shoulders-first, into the mat.

**Reversal:**

**Hurricanranna**

## PILEDRIVER **DAMAGE: 9**

Many variations of this move have evolved over the years (see Pedigree, Tombstone Piledriver) but the current fashion calls for the wrestlers to face one another, the attacking wrestler bending his opponent toward him. The wrestler making the throw then locks his opponent's head, face-down, between the insides of his thighs, grabs the victim around the stomach and hoists him into the air, legs pointed upward. The wrestler executing the Piledriver then drops down into a sitting position, driving the opponent's head and neck into the mat with the weight of both men.

**Reversal:**

**Piledriver reversal (generic)**

## AHMED

# PEARL RIVER PLUNGE

Also known as a Tiger Driver, this move begins with the wrestlers face-to-face and the victim bent forward. Ahmed locks up his opponent around the midsection, hoists him into an upside-down position, as if for a Power Bomb (see Power Bomb). But instead of throwing him down, shoulders-first, Ahmed "rides" the victim's shoulders into the mat, while landing in a sitting position.

**FINISHER!**

**TOP SECRET**

**DAMAGE: 9**

## PUT OPPONENT ON TOP TURNBUCKLE

              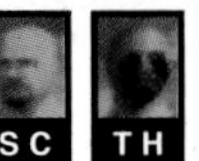

AJ BH BB CJ DL FQ GD HH KN MK MS OH RM SR SM SC TH UT

Placing a dazed opponent on the top turnbuckle can set him up for various high-flying maneuvers, such as a Top Rope Superplex.

**DAMAGE: N/A**

## POWERSLAM

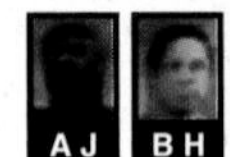   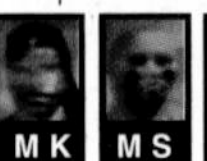 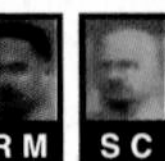

AJ BH BB FQ HH MK MS RM SC UT

The wrestler executing the move catches a charging opponent, then pivots and swivels on his planted legs as he twist his — and the victim's — body around for a strong Body Slam.

**DAMAGE: 7**

## PRESS SLAM

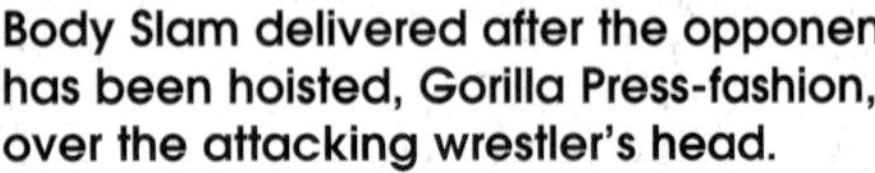

FQ

Body Slam delivered after the opponent has been hoisted, Gorilla Press-fashion, over the attacking wrestler's head.

**DAMAGE: 8**

## PUMP HANDLE SLAM

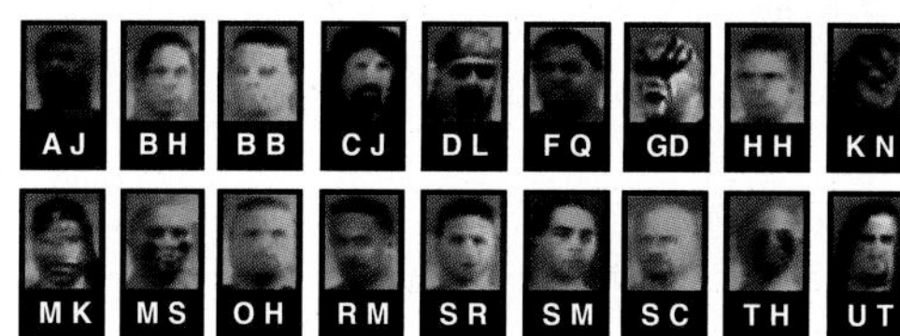


This move is executed from behind, in the corner. The move starts out almost like an Abdominal Stretch but is instead transformed into a hard slam.

**DAMAGE: 5**

## REAR CHIN LOCK

With the victim on his back, the attacking wrestler locks his arm around his opponent's chin and stretches him.

**DAMAGE: 4**

## REPEATED ELBOWS

GD SC

**DAMAGE: 3**

## REPEATED KICKS TO RIBS

OH SC

**DAMAGE: 3**

## TRIPLE H

# PEDIGREE

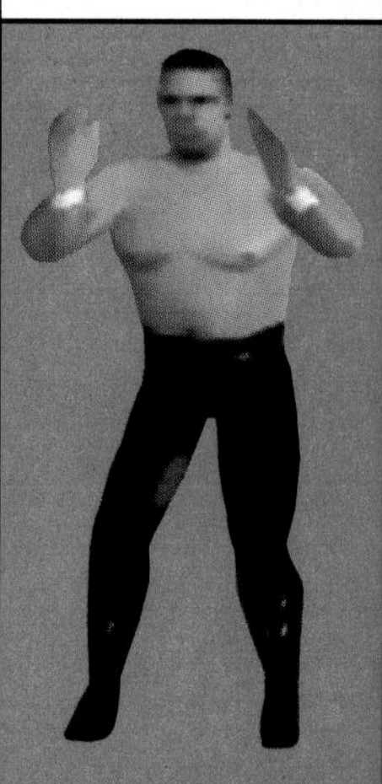

A variation on the Piledriver, in which Triple H locks his opponent's head between his knees and hoists him around the midsection. He then slams the victim, back-first, into the canvas.

TOP SECRET

**FINISHER!**

**DAMAGE: 9**

## REVERSE CHINLOCK

RM SR SM SC

The wrestler on offense attacks his prone opponent by wrapping his dominant arm around the victim's neck, in a reversed headlock.

**DAMAGE: 4**

## REVERSE DDT

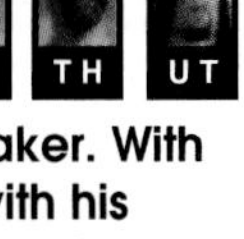

GD KN MK MS RM SR SC TH UT

A combination DDT and Neckbreaker. With the wrestler on offense standing with his belly to his opponent's back, he overlaps his arm around the victim's neck and drops him, DDT-style, to the mat. Also known as a Deathdrop.

**DAMAGE: 6**

## SUPER SECRETS

### EXTRA GOLDUST MIRROR MATCHES

Beat the Challenge with Goldust on Normal Difficulty, and you'll get access to 2 more of his outrageous costumes, for use in "Mirror Matches" (Goldust and Goldust vs. Goldust and Goldust, for example).

## REVERSE INDIAN DEATHLOCK

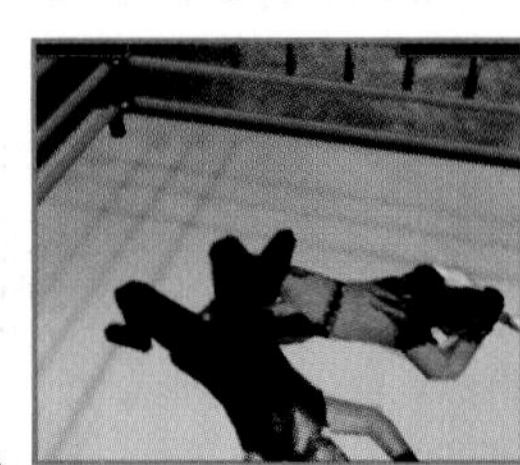

MK OH TH

This is an Indian Deathlock (see Indian Deathlock) delivered to an opponent laying face-down on the mat.

**DAMAGE: 6**

## REVERSE FUJI LEG BAR

SR

This is a Fuji Leg Bar (see Fuji Leg Bar) delivered with the victim on his stomach.

**DAMAGE: 3**

## REVERSE PAINKILLER

BH MS SR TH

This is a submission-style arm lock (see Painkiller) delivered while the victim is laying face-down on the mat.

**DAMAGE: 5**

## RUSSIAN LEG SWEEP

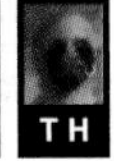

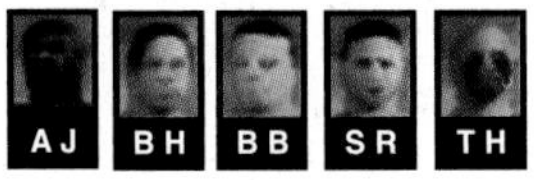

AJ BH BB SR TH

With the wrestlers standing side-by-side, the wrestler on offense hooks his near leg around his victim's and uses his near arm to obtain control over his opponent, throwing them both backwards to the mat.

**DAMAGE: 4**

## ROCKY

## ROCK BOTTOM

This move is a form of throw in which the wrestlers face one another in a standing position. Rocky then locks up his victim around the neck in a variation on the Cobra Clutch (see Cobra Clutch), hoists him, then throws him onto his back.

TOP SECRET

**DAMAGE: 9**

## SHORT-ARM SCISSORS

BH RM SR TH

With the victim on the mat, the attacking wrestler pulls his opponent's arm taut, then scissors his legs around the victim's arm.

**DAMAGE: 4**

## SAMOAN DROP

**DAMAGE: 4** (from a Tie-Up) **6** (from Starting Position)

BH BB FQ GD MK MS OH RM SR SM SC

The wrestler on offense lifts his opponent across his shoulders, as if in a standing Fireman's Carry, then slams backwards, driving his own head into the victim's ribs when they crash to the mat.

**Reversal:**

**Crucifix**

## SHAMROCK — SHAMROCK ANKLE LOCK

FINISHER!

TOP SECRET

A simple but brutally effective move in which the victim is laying, stomach-down, on the mat. The attacking wrestler then grabs the victim's foot, twists the ankle, and begins to bend it to the snapping point. A classic submission move.

**DAMAGE: 9**

## SHOOTING STAR PRESS

MS OH RM SR SM TH

One of the most visually impressive of all flying maneuvers. The victim is on his back, staring at the ceiling lights while the attacking wrestler scales the ropes, soars into the air and executes a backward flip, landing chest-first on the victim.

**DAMAGE: 8**

## SHORT-ARM CLOTHESLINE

The wrestler on offense winds up as if to whip his opponent into the ropes or turnbuckle. Just as the victim builds momentum, however, and an instant before the attacking wrestler releases the Whip, the attacker catches the victim with a quick Clothesline (see Clothesline).

**DAMAGE: 5**

## SHARP SHOOTER

**BRET HART**

**FINISHER!**

**OWEN HART**

**FINISHER!**

**TOP SECRET**

The wrestler applying this finisher begins with the same conditions as the Figure Four (see Figure Four Leglock). The opponent is on his back and the attacking wrestler begins to apply what looks like a Figure Four, but instead of sitting down, the attacking wrestler turns his opponent over onto his stomach, then leans backwards, as if in a Half Crab (see Half Crab). The pressure is enormous and, because the victim is on his stomach, this submission hold is among the most difficult to escape.

**DAMAGE: 9**

## SHOULDER TACKLE

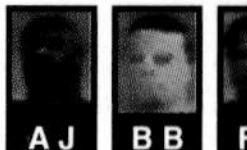

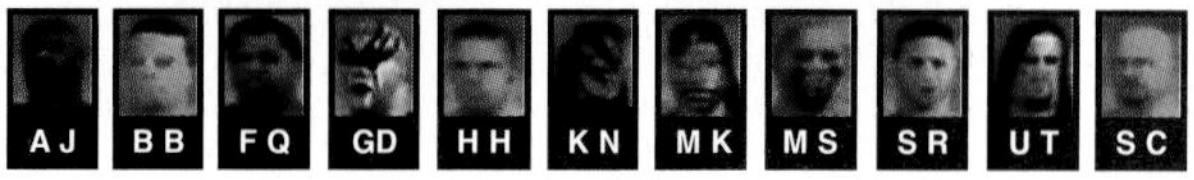

The attacking wrestler delivers a football-style shoulder block from the top rope onto a dazed opponent's chest and shoulder.

**DAMAGE: 6**

## SIDE SLAM

Similar to a Side Back Breaker, only instead of dropping the opponent onto a braced knee, the attacking wrestler drops the victim straight down, back-first, onto the mat.

**DAMAGE: 3**

## SINGLE-ARM DDT

With the wrestlers facing one another, the attacking grappler bends his opponent forward and hooks him around the neck in a form of reverse headlock, before slamming backwards, driving his opponent's head into the mat.

**DAMAGE: 6**

## SHOULDER BREAKER

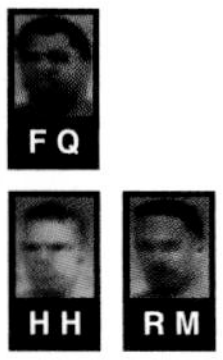

The wrestler making the throw hoists his opponent over his shoulder as if to deliver a Powerslam. Instead, however, the victim is driven straight down, with his shoulder slamming into the dominant wrestler's braced knee.

**DAMAGE: 6** (from Standing position) **2** (from a Tie-Up)

## SIDE BACK BREAKER

The wrestler on offense grabs his opponent around the waist and hoists him in the air, pivoting around to bring the victim parallel to the mat, facing up. The attacker then drops to one knee, dropping the victim onto his braced knee, catching him near the floating ribs.

**DAMAGE: 9**

## SIDE BELLY-BELLY SUPLEX

**DAMAGE: 6** (from Standing Position) **2** (from a Tie-Up)

This is a traditional Belly-to-Belly Suplex in which the wrestlers face one another and the wrestler executing the move locks his opponent's midsection, then lifts and throws his victim sideways to the mat.

Reversal:

**Side Belly-Belly Suplex**

## SIDEWALK SLAM

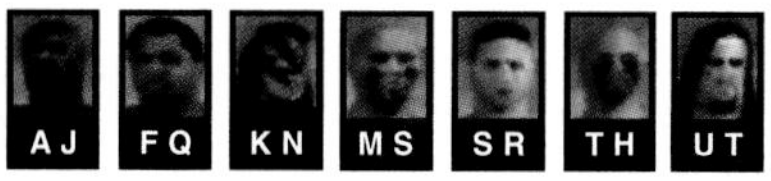

The wrestler executing this move whips his opponent into the ropes, then catches him coming off as if in a Bearhug (see Bearhug). With his opponent's momentum now totally stopped, the wrestler executing the move hooks his foe behind the knees and pushes forward, slamming his victim, back-first, onto the canvas. Some wrestlers can execute this maneuver from the Starting Position or from a Tie-Up.

**DAMAGE: 7** (from Starting Position or vs. Running Opponent) **3** (from a Tie-Up)

## SMALL PACKAGE **DAMAGE: 1**

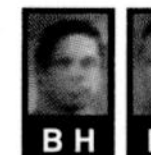

A pinning move, the wrestler on offense takes his opponent to the mat and "wraps up" his arms and legs into a "small package" which the attacking wrestler will attempt to hold for a three-count.

**Reversal:**

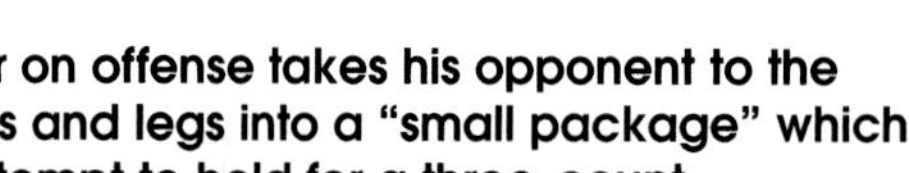

Small Package

## SLEEPER

A submission hold. The wrestler sidesteps his opponent, gets behind him and wraps his left arm tightly around his opponent's chin, bracing it with a vertically positioned right arm against the victim's right ear. The left hand then clamps onto the opponent's carotid artery, briefly cutting off the blood supply to the brain and, eventually, rendering the victim unconscious.

**DAMAGE: 3**

## SNAP MARE

Two wrestlers stand back-to-front. The wrestler in front grasps his opponent around the neck and flips him forward in a snap-like motion, throwing him back-first to the mat.

**DAMAGE: 5**

## SMASH HEAD INTO TURNBUCKLE

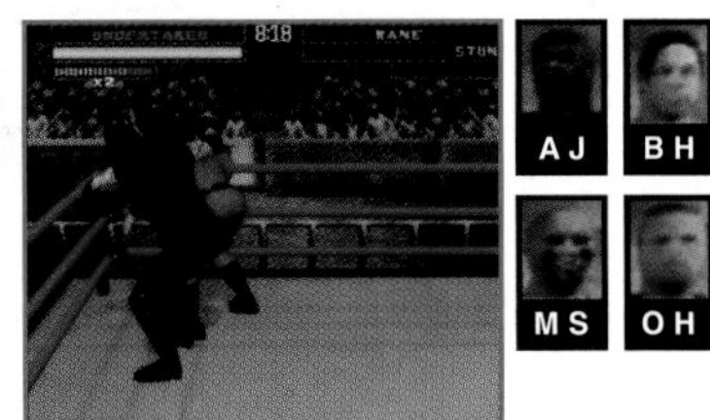

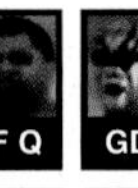

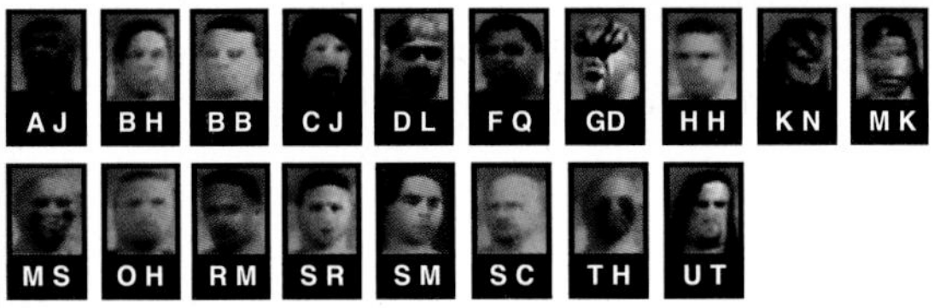

AJ BH BB CJ DL FQ GD HH KN MK

MS OH RM SR SM SC TH UT

**DAMAGE: 3**

## SOMERSAULT SENTON SPLASH

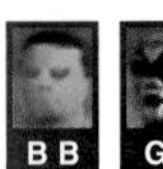
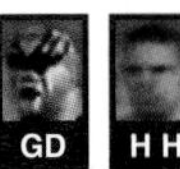

BB GD HH MK MS OH TH

With one wrestler outside the ring, the wrestler executing the move charges toward the ropes, forward somersaults over them and lands, back-first, on his opponent.

**DAMAGE: 8**

## STANDING JUMP KICK

AJ RM

Delivered from a standing position, the wrestler on offense leaps into the air and delivers a stiff kick to his opponent.

**DAMAGE: 4**

## SPINNING TOE HOLD

BB GD RM

With the opponent on his back, the attacking wrestler takes a leg, plants his own foot in between his opponent's legs, and bends his opponent's leg inward, using his own planted leg as a lever. The attacking wrestler continues to pivot, reapplying the hold several times or until the victim submits.

**DAMAGE: 3**

## THRASHER — SOMERSAULT LEG DROP

FINISHER!

TOP SECRET

Also known as the 360-Degree Legdrop. With his victim lying on the mat, Thrasher climbs to the top turnbuckle, leaps and somersaults forward, landing with a Legdrop across the victim's throat.

**DAMAGE: 9**

## SUPER SECRETS

### EXTRA STONE COLD MIRROR MATCHES

Beat the Challenge with Steve Austin on Hard Difficulty, and you'll get access to 2 more of his costumes, for use in Mirror Matches.

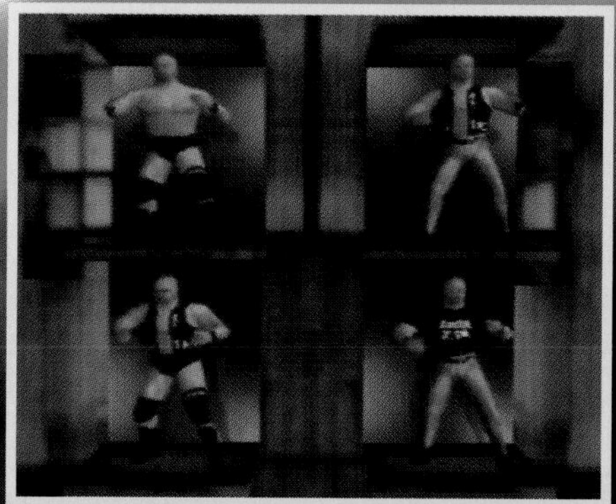

## SPINEBUSTER

8:46
KANE

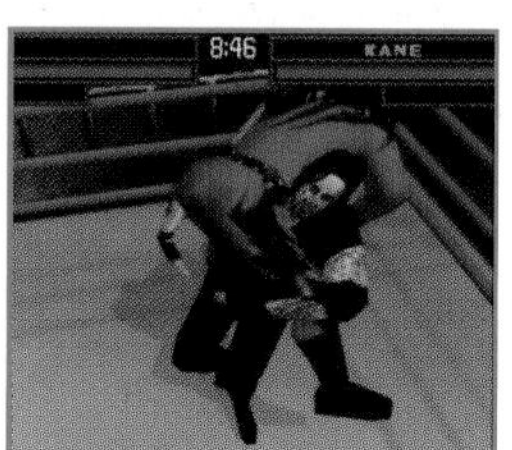

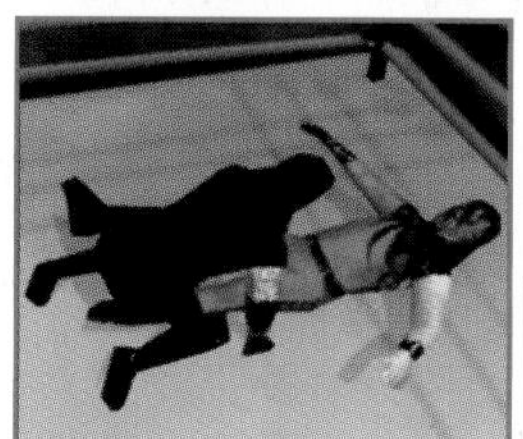

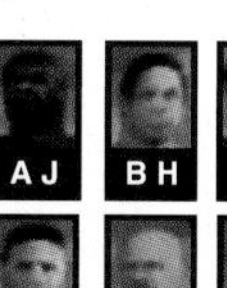

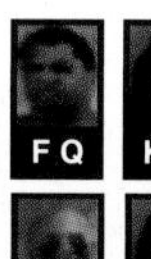

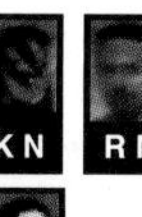

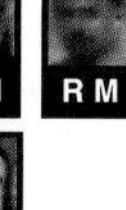

AJ
BH
FQ
KN
RM
SR
SC
TH
UT

From a Starting position or against a running opponent, the wrestler catches his opponent in a hold resembling a Bearhug (see Bearhug). From this position, the wrestler in command spins on his feet and slams his opponent down, spine-first, onto the mat.

**DAMAGE: 6** (from Starting Position) **7** (vs. Running Opponent)

## SPINNING HEEL KICK

OWEN HART
14:04
KANE

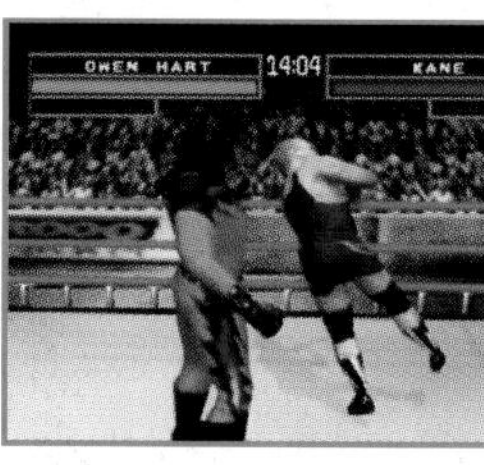

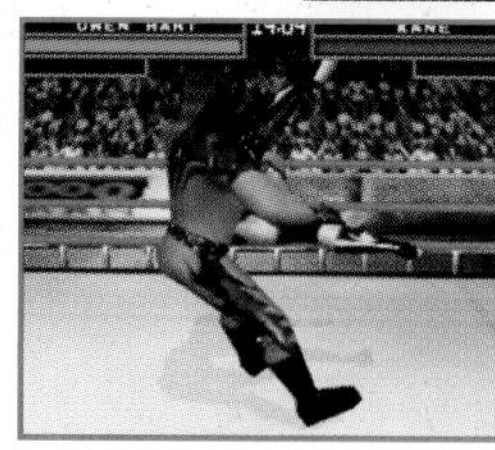

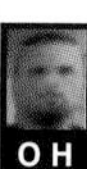

OH

The attacking wrestler charges his opponent, building momentum until he is several steps away from the victim. The wrestler executing the move then leaves his feet, spinning backwards and delivering a roundhouse kick in the process.

**DAMAGE: 4**

## STOMP

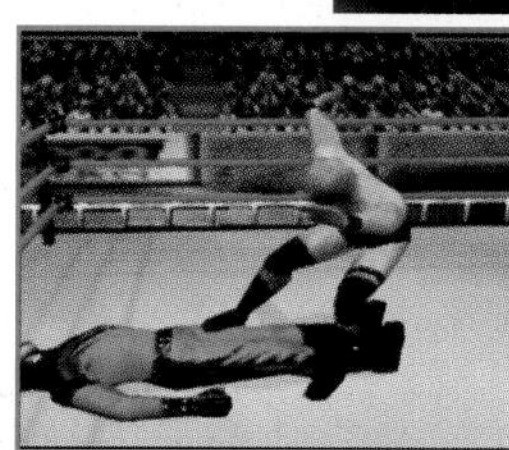

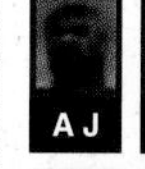

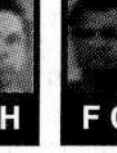

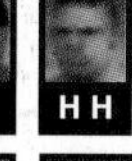

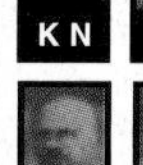

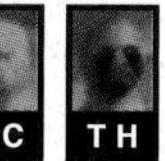

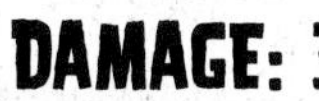

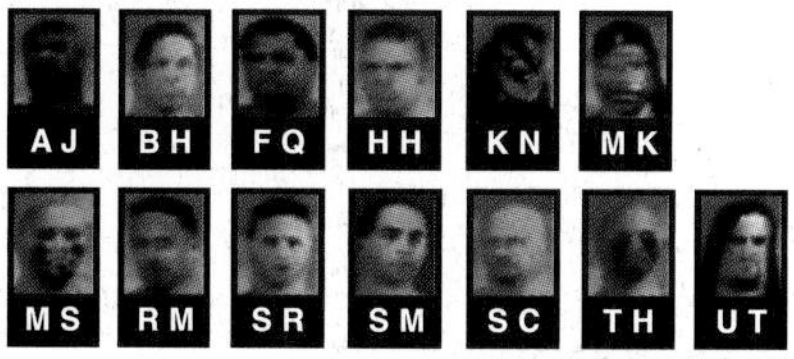

AJ
BH
FQ
HH
KN
MK
MS
RM
SR
SM
SC
TH
UT

**DAMAGE: 3**

A Splash is basically a spread-eagled dive onto an opponent. The victim can be either on his feet, back or stomach, and various wrestlers can initiate this maneuver from a standing position, from a running start, from the top turnbuckle or apron, or even over the top rope to a victim outside the ring.

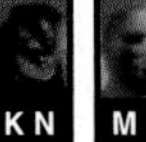

AJ BH BB KN MS OH RM SR SM SC TH UT

**DAMAGE: 3** (Opponent in Corner) **7** (Ground Hits, Standing) **8** (From Top Turnbuckle or Apron)

## SQUEEZE HEAD

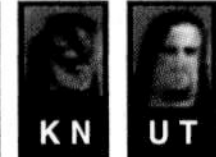

AJ KN UT

**DAMAGE: 3**

## STEP-OVER TOEHOLD

HH SM SC

With the victim on his back, the wrestler in command "steps over" his opponent's leg and grabs his foot, bending it backwards around his own pivot leg, putting pressure on the victim's ankle.

**DAMAGE: 3**

## STF

RM SR SC TH

With the opponent on his stomach, the wrestler applying the STF steps into a Toehold, then drops to the mat, maintaining the hold, and bars an arm across the victim's face in a Chinlock-type maneuver. The STF gets its name from the fact that it combines a Stepover Toehold with a Facelock, literally bending the victim's head backwards toward his feet while his legs are being bowed in the opposite direction.

**DAMAGE: 4**

## STEP IN BACK ELBOW

HH SM SC

This is a variation on the traditional Elbow Smash, delivered abruptly after stepping behind the victim.

**DAMAGE: 4**

## STONE COLD STUNNER

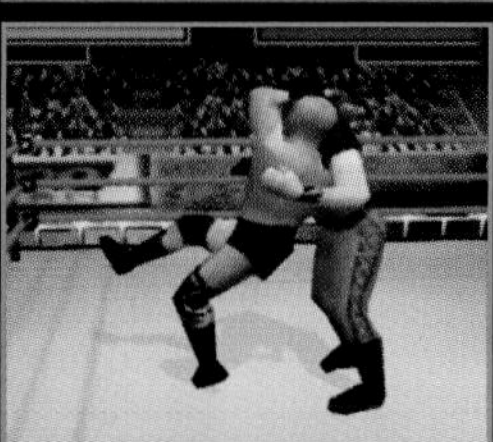

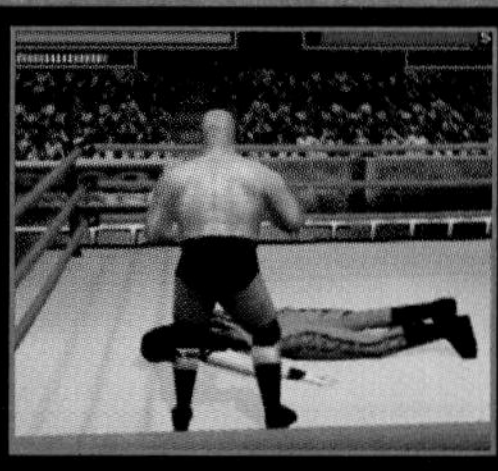

Austin's finisher is actually a two-part move. The first portion of the attack comes when Stone Cold unleashes a sudden, savage kick to his opponent's midsection. Then, with the victim bent over forward, Austin turns his body, positioning himself back-to-belly with his opponent. He then places his victim's head on his shoulder, locks it down by wrapping an arm around the victim's neck, then drops into a sitting position, jamming the victim's jaw into Austin's Stone Cold shoulder.

FINISHER!

TOP SECRET

**DAMAGE: 9**

## STUMP PULLER

BB GD

With the opponent seated helplessly on the mat, the attacking wrestler stands behind him and pulls up, submission-style, on the victim's legs.

**DAMAGE: 4**

## SUNSET FLIP

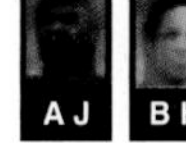

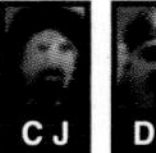

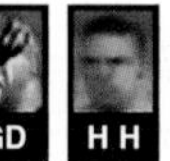

AJ BH BB CJ DL FQ GD HH KN MK MS OH RM SR SM SC TH UT

With the victim standing stunned in the middle of the ring, the attacking wrestler leaps off the top turnbuckle and flies over the victim's head and toward the mat. Before landing headfirst behind his opponent, however, the wrestler on offense grabs his opponent around the waist and pulls his own head up between his opponent's legs. The momentum flips the victim backwards with the controlling wrestler rolling into a pinning combination. NOTE: This maneuver can be executed by only a few wrestlers from the top turnbuckle, but all wrestlers in the game can attempt this move against an opponent who's outside the ring.

**DAMAGE: 2**

## SUPERPLEX

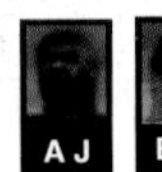

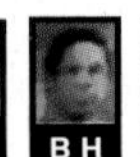

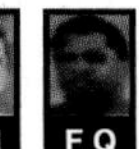

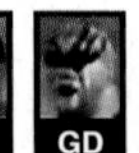

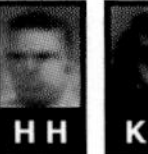

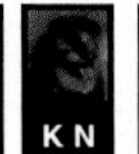

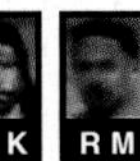

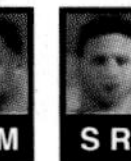

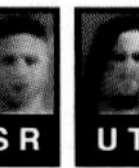

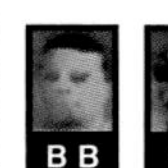

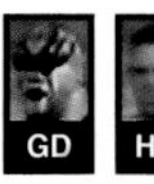

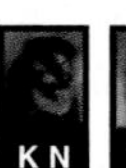

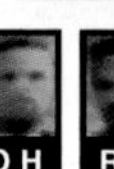

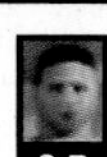

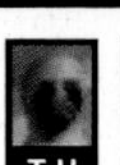

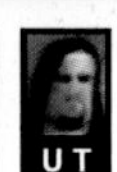

BB
GD
HH
KN
OH
RM
SR
TH
UT

A Suplex (see Vertical Suplex) delivered with the attacking wrestler's feet planted on the second rope while the opponent sits helplessly on the top rope.

**DAMAGE: 5-8**

## SUPLEX OFF APRON

AJ
BH
FQ
GD
HH
KN
MK
RM
SR
UT

This is a Vertical Suplex delivered by a wrestler standing outside the ropes, on the ring apron, to a wrestler standing inside the ring. This is a "release"-style suplex, as no one would want to ride an opponent backwards off the apron!

**DAMAGE: 6**

## SWINGING DDT

SHAWN MICHAELS
14:18
KANE

SHAWN MICHAELS
14:17
KANE

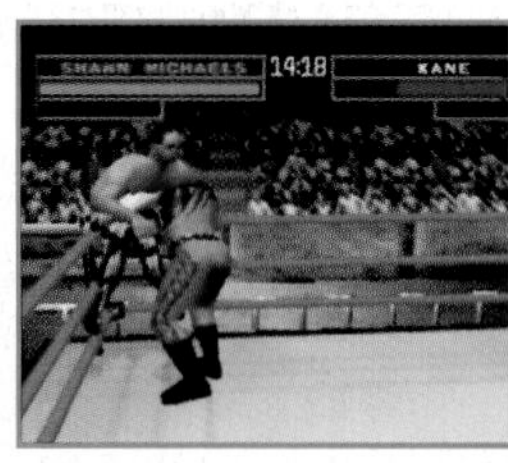

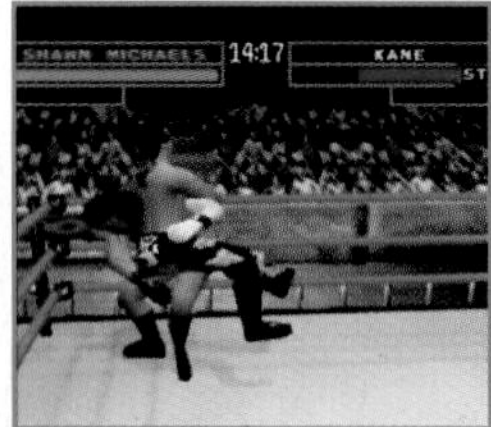

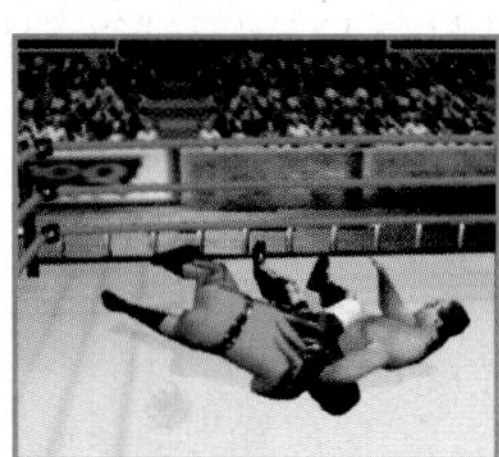

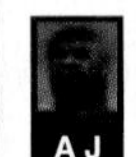

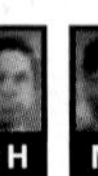

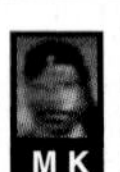

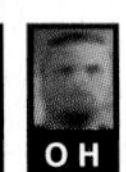

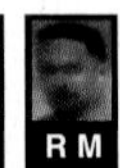

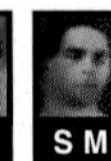

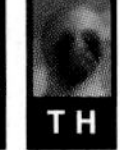

AJ
BH
MK
OH
RM
SM
TH

The wrestler on offense rotates around his opponent while locking him into a Front Facelock, gaining momentum in the process. In a single, fluid motion, while maintaining the Facelock, the wrestler executing the move jerks backwards to the mat with the top of the victim's head taking the brunt of the bump upon landing.

**DAMAGE: 7**

## TACKLE WITH PUNCHES

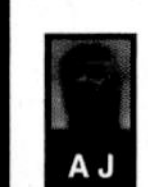

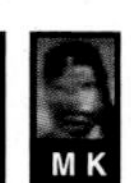

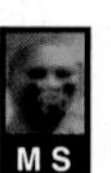

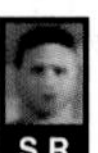

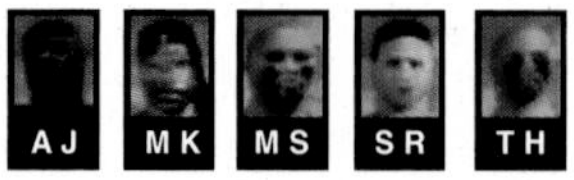

AJ
MK
MS
SR
TH

The attacking wrestler tackles his opponent, football-style, and immediately follows the impact with a barrage of punches to the head.

**DAMAGE: 5**

## TEXAS CLOVERLEAF

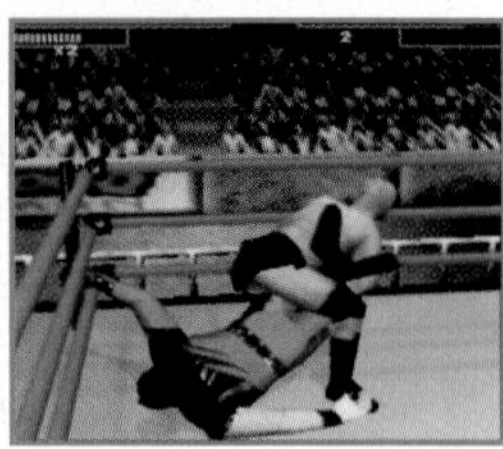

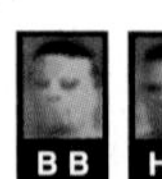

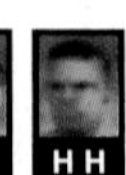

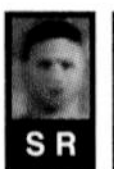

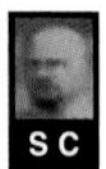

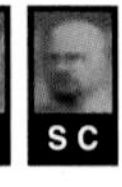

BB
HH
SR
SC

With the victim on his stomach, the attacking wrestler overlaps his opponent's legs, reaches down to establish his arm as a vertical base, and locks in. Similar to an Indian Deathlock (see Indian Deathlock), except it's being executed entirely with the attacking wrestler's arms, thereby allowing his legs to apply leverage.

**DAMAGE: 4**

## SURFBOARD

FQ HH KN MK OH UT

With the victim on his belly, the wrestler on offense plants a leg in the small of his opponent's back. He then wraps up his victims' arms and/or legs, pulling the legs toward the head and the arms toward the rump. The move gets its name from the fact that the wrestler applying the move appears to be standing on a surfboard.

**DAMAGE: 5**

## SHAWN

## SWEET CHIN MUSIC

TOP SECRET

This is Shawn's high-flying side kick delivered to the victim's chin.

**FINISHER!**

**DAMAGE: 9**

## PRESS WITH PUNCHES

SC

This maneuver has the attacker charging his opponent, then leaping into the air and slamming into the victim, chest-on-chest. The momentum carries the attacker forward and knocks the victim backwards into a pinning situation. The attacking wrestler then presses his advantage with a flurry of punches.

**DAMAGE: 7**

## THRUST TO THROAT

With his fingers clamped together, the wrestler delivering this blow drives his stiffened fingertips directly into the victim's throat.

**DAMAGE: 6**

## TREE OF WOE

MK

The attacking wrestler ties up his opponent's legs in the top turnbuckle, causing him to hang helplessly from the top rope (i.e., tied to the Tree of Woe). This is followed by the attacker charging diagonally across the ring into his helpless opponent's midsection.

**DAMAGE: 7**

## TOP WRISTLOCK

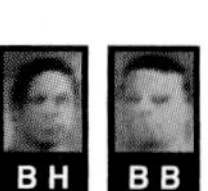

This is your basic overhand Wristlock.

**DAMAGE: 2**

## THROAT TOSS

Similar to a Choke Slam, except the victim is lifted in a choke hold and is thrown rather than slammed.

**DAMAGE: 6**

## TOP ROPE SUPERPLEX

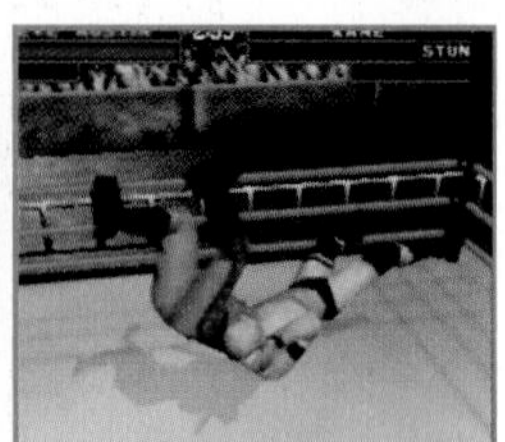

In the standard Superplex, the victim is seated on the top rope and the wrestler on offense is standing on the first or, more commonly, the middle rope when the Suplex is executed. In the Top Rope Superplex, both wrestlers are standing on the top rope when a Vertical Suplex (see Vertical Suplex) is delivered.

**DAMAGE: 9**

ANE

UNDERTAKER

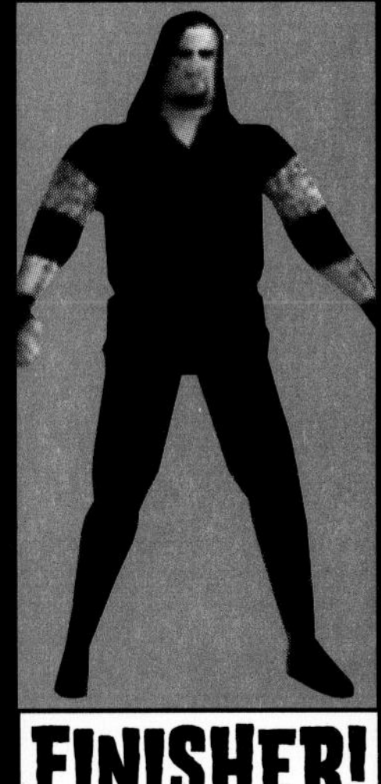

ISHER!

FINISHER!

## TOMBSTONE PILEDRIVER

The Tombstone Piledriver (see Piledriver) is delivered belly-to-belly, with the victim held inverted against the body of the wrestler executing the driver, his head locked between his opponent's legs. The wrestler in command then drops to his knees, slamming the victim into the mat, head-first.

TOP SECRET

**DAMAGE: 9**

## TORPEDO DROP KICK

BB OH RM

A Drop Kick (see Drop Kick) delivered off the top rope where the attacking wrestler leaps high into the air and hits his victim while descending at an almost vertical angle.

**DAMAGE: 8**

## SUPER SECRETS

### REFLECTIONS (N64 ONLY)

Beat the Challenge with any wrestler on any difficulty, and you'll be able to change the wrestlers' shadows into full-color reflections instead! Ever wonder what it'd be like to wrestle on a mirror? Now's your chance to find out!

## TORTURE RACK

With the victim clamped in a sort of standing Fireman's Carry and stretched across the attacking wrestler's shoulders, the wrestler executing the maneuver grabs the victim around the neck with one hand and around the legs with the other. He then pushes both head and legs forward, which forces the victim's spine to arch painfully backwards against the back of the attacking wrestler's neck.

**DAMAGE: 6**

## UNDERHOOK SUPLEX

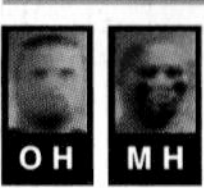


Also known as a Full Eagle Suplex, the wrestler making the throw stands facing his opponent, then bends him forward, as if for a Piledriver. Instead, however, he underhooks the victim's arms (as in the Pedigree) in an inverted Full Nelson, locks his fingers together, then hoists the victim straight into the air and releases the move as the opponent sails overhead toward a back-first meeting with the canvas.

**DAMAGE: 9**

## VERTICAL SUPLEX

**DAMAGE: 7**

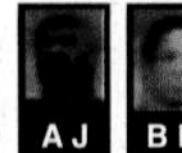

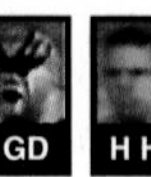

The throw begins with a Front Facelock maintained by the attacking wrestler's non-dominant arm, while the dominant arm reaches down and grabs a handful of the victim's tights. The victim is then lifted straight up and into the air, feet pointing to the sky, at which point the wrestler executing the throw "rides" it backwards, maintaining the Suplex, thereby adding his own weight to the impact of the opponent's landing.

**Reversal:**

**Vertical Suplex Reversal (Generic)**

## VICTORY ROLL

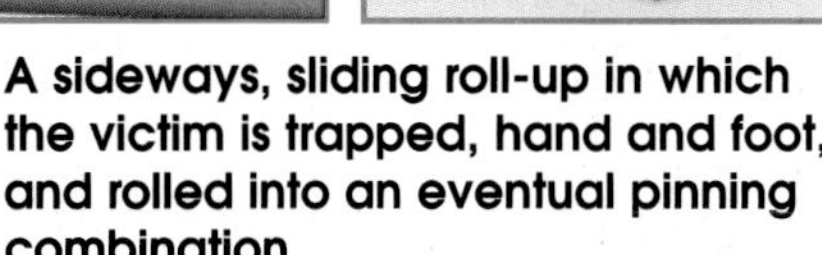


A sideways, sliding roll-up in which the victim is trapped, hand and foot, and rolled into an eventual pinning combination.

**DAMAGE: 3**

*SPECIAL NOTE*

Since this book was created before the War Zone games were released, there may have been last-minute changes that we were unable to include herein. For corrections, additions and extra strategy tips, visit our companion web site, at http://www.acclaim.net/games/wwf-warzone/strategyGuide.html

## WHEEL KICK

This move is very similar to the Spinning Heel Kick, but delivered from the top rope.

**DAMAGE: 9**

## WHIP

**DAMAGE: 3** (from a Tie-Up) **5** (from Starting position) **5** (into side of apron, cage, or barricades)

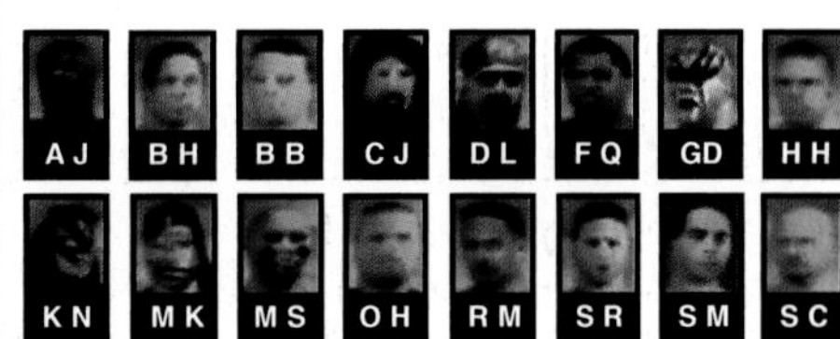


The opponent is thrown or "whipped"by the attacking wrestler. Damage only occurs if the victim runs into the corner turnbuckles, the ring apron, the barricades or the side of the cage (in a cage match).

**Reversal:**

| Whip reversal (generic) |
|---|

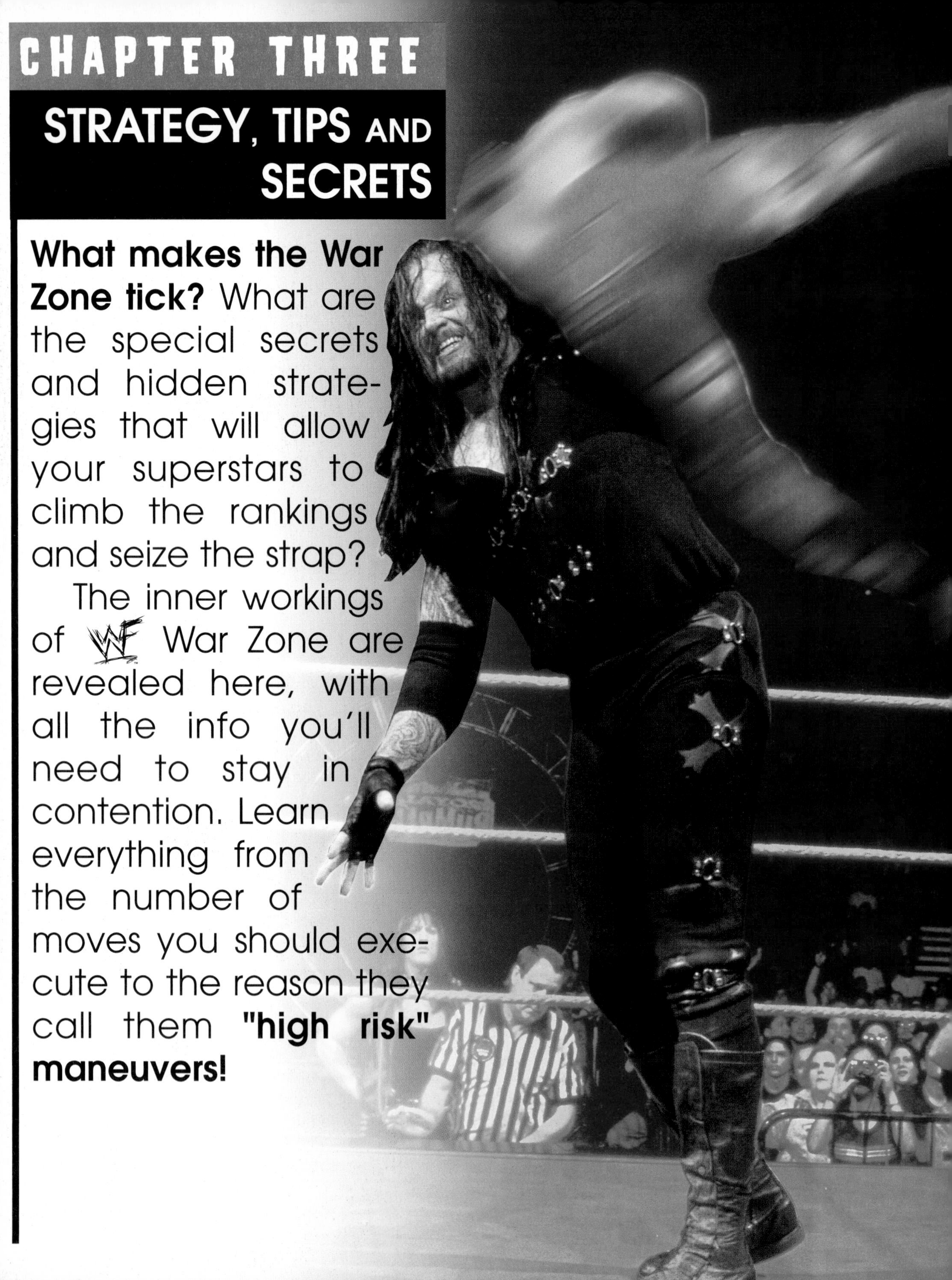

# CHAPTER THREE

## STRATEGY, TIPS AND SECRETS

**What makes the War Zone tick?** What are the special secrets and hidden strategies that will allow your superstars to climb the rankings and seize the strap?

The inner workings of WWF War Zone are revealed here, with all the info you'll need to stay in contention. Learn everything from the number of moves you should execute to the reason they call them **"high risk" maneuvers!**

Most wrestling games suffer from two significant, frustrating problems: a limited number of moves, and an unsatisfactory set of conditions for determining success out of the original tie-up position.

WWF War Zone has obviously solved the first problem by giving each wrestler dozens and dozens of moves from a variety of positions. The solution to the second problem, however, while equally elegant, requires a bit more explanation.

**In War Zone, the results of a tie-up are determined through an increasingly sophisticated series of filters.**

## THE TIE-UP

In all previous wrestling games, once the gamer's wrestler went into the lock-up (also known as the tie-up or the referee's position) the determination of which grappler would get off that all-important first move was a virtually random issue. One or both players would begin bashing away at buttons in a mad frenzy and one or the other would succeed while the other nursed a sore thumb.

In WWF War Zone, the results of a tie-up are determined through an increasingly sophisticated series of filters. Every wrestler has nine possible moves they can execute out of the initial tie-up. Some wrestlers are even able to execute their finishing maneuvers out of the tie-up (though such finishing moves can only be delivered when the opponent's damage has reached the red zone).

You have three basic button commands: kick, punch, or tie-up. Now let's say you initiate the tie-up. At this point, a window of time opens up during which you can initiate a move. Let's say you select a kick — which is a "1" damage move, or the lowest level of damage you can inflict (with 9 being the highest). Now your opponent has a certain amount of time to input his or her own move. If your opponent also selects a kick, then you've both called for "1" damage moves, in which case — assuming all else is equal, which is a big assumption, as you'll read below — the game will randomly determine who will succeed. But if your opponent calls for a punch — which is a "2" damage move — your kick will always succeed because, all other things being equal, the lower damage move will always win.

But once that initial move is executed, everything changes. This is where the modifiers, or filters, kick in. If you look up at your wrestler's name, for example, you'll see that it starts out white. But as you inflict damage on your opponent, that white turns first light blue, then medium blue, and then a darker blue. This represents the availability of securing a bonus through a tie-up — the darker the blue, the more of a tie-up advantage you get. In other words, if I've just gotten in a few good shots, I want to tie you up immediately because the dark blue indicates I'm going to enjoy at least a 7 point bonus in a tie-up. Light blue gives you a 1 - 3 point advantage; medium blue a 4 - 6 point advantage, and dark blue indicates a bonus of 7 or more points. Now when we tie up, even if he goes for a wimpy kick, I still stand an excellent chance of pulling off a high damage maneuver because of that bonus.

It's always advantageous to go for a tie-up when you know you're likely to win. You get a 3-point risk bonus to any move you pull off out of the tie-up — unless your opponent is stunned.

The logic for determining low and medium moves are the same. The kick-punch tie-ups are the 1-2-3 moves. Any direction press followed by kick, punch or tie-up are 4-5-6 moves. But the 7-8-9 moves are dual-directional combos which tend to be specific to individual wrestlers. The Bulldog's Hanging Vertical Suplex, for example, is his highest damage move out of a tie-up. And, as discussed elsewhere, a few finishers are delivered from the tie-up as well.

**Wimp Warning:** Some players, used to older wrestling games that let them master a few simple moves and still win matches, will find themselves in a whole world of trouble if they employ that strategy in this game.

Let's say you keep doing a hip toss out of the tie-up. It's just a 1 point damage move, after all, but it'll always succeed, right?

Wrong.

If a player continues to enter low-risk moves from the tie-up, there's a chart the game consults in which low-risk moves are able to always be beaten by certain higher-risk moves — regardless of any other bonuses.

So remember:

If your opponent picks a "1" damage move, a "6" or "9" damage move will always beat it.

If your opponent picks a "2" damage move, a "5" or "8" will always beat it.

If your opponent picks a "3" damage move, a "4" or "7" will always beat it.

It's a little bit of rock, paper, scissors, but it works. If a guy is going with the cheesy, low-risk stuff and you know he's going to keep doing it, you can pull off a corresponding high-damage move on him and discourage that type of wrestling in the future.

**Many of the more powerful moves in War Zone are REVERSIBLE.**

## REVERSALS

Many of the more powerful moves in War Zone are reversible. The process to reverse one of these moves is quite simple: Press "Block" at the right time and you'll get the reversal. If you press Block too early, you miss your chance. Too late? Obviously. One item to note: the more damaging a move, the less chance there is to reverse the move.

There is another hitch to reversing a move here; your wrestler has to have the counter-move in his moveset. For example, your opponent has a Hurricanranna that he keeps popping you with and you're a bit sick of it by now. The reversal to the Hurricanranna is the Power Bomb — but if your wrestler doesn't have the Power Bomb as one of his moves, you can't reverse the Hurricanranna. And so on.

## OFFENSIVE GET-UPS:

If your Opponent keeps knocking you down, then crowding your space, the offensive get-up will help make a little space for you. Simply press "Punch" when your wrestler is getting to his feet and you will smack your opponent, either knocking him down or at least pushing him away from you, giving you some time to get organized.

## IN AND OUT OF THE RING

There are some situations that will never come up in a conventional fighting game that can happen quite often in WF War Zone. Here are a few:

1) If you're outside the ring and your opponent is in the ring near you, push any button (Punch, Kick or Tie-up) to try to pull him out of the ring.

2) If you're up on the ring apron and you're near an opponent who's in the ring, hit Punch or Kick to try and punch him over the ropes. Or hit Tie-up — if your opponent's back is to the ropes, you'll catch him in a Headlock, and if he's facing the ropes, you'll give him a Hiptoss right out of the ring!

3) If one of your opponents is on the apron and you're in the ring, you've got a few options. You can run against the ropes and into your opponent, knocking him to the concrete floor. (However, if he hits Block in time, he can grip the ropes and not fall!) Or you can punch or kick him off the apron. Finally, you can hit "Tie-up" and go for a Vertical Suplex into the ring.

4) Want to toss your opponent out of the ring, over the top rope? Get his back up against the ropes, then hit the combo for Whip from Starting Position (direction, direction, Block). You'll pick him up and dump him onto the floor!

## STUNNING INFO

When your opponent is stunned, there's an evolution of strategy as the match continues.

Early in the match, your opponent isn't going to stay stunned long — you're not going to have time to get too fancy. So your best bet is to force him into a tie-up and pull off a high-damage move. You don't get the tie-up bonus (because he's stunned), but you get a sureshot 9-pointer if you want it, with a double-damage bonus because he's stunned.

A bit later in the match, your weakened opponent will stay stunned for a while longer — long enough for you to get behind him and hit him with a "From Behind" move for triple damage.

Finally, late in the match, when you've softened him up so that he's stunned for a nice, long time, climb to that top turnbuckle and nail him with a quadruple-damage aerial move. Now that's gonna hurt!

## CROWD RESPONSES

The World Wrestling Federation refers to its product regularly as "sports entertainment." WF War Zone takes this philosophy literally. With a huge list of audience catcalls and a game-related crowd response meter, you have to show some range and take some risks in order to get over with the fans — which actually increases the damage you inflict on your opponent!

Along with their ratings for Strength, Striking Ability, etc., each wrestler has a Charisma rating. The higher a wrestler's charisma rating, the more patience the audience will have with him; the lower the rating, well ... let's just say that wrestler is going to have to work his butt off in order to win the crowd over. So, while a wrestler with "10" charisma can get away with a fairly ordinary, workmanlike match, a wrestler with a "1" charisma had better be a ball of fire in that ring.

The charisma ratings are not related to the wrestler's status as a fan favorite or rulebreaker. A wrestler gets the crowd on his side by performing high risk, high impact maneuvers and by mixing up his selection of maneuvers. The crowd gets restless when a wrestler is boring — fighting too defensively or working the same few moves to death.

Take some chances, execute a few big damage moves successfully, and the crowd will start chanting your wrestler's name, allowing you to pick up a damage bonus during the period the crowd is chanting. Your attacks now have a better chance of success, giving you a period during which you can really put the smack down on your opponent with the crowd's lusty, full-throated support. This allows you to set up some big-time moves — any successful attack off the turnbuckle at this point, for example, generates damage a full magnitude higher.

Previous wrestling games were largely governed by something known as the "Rule of Threes." This law, basically put, said that you can execute the same move twice in a row with a good chance of success, but you stand almost no chance of executing it a third time. The crowd in War Zone, however, eliminates the need for this artificial device. A really skilled, high charisma wrestler might get off the same move five times in a row — but he still risks getting on the crowds' nerves.

Of course, you can attempt any move at any time. However, the more different moves you execute, the better off you are. Crowds likes diversity and wrestlers with a limited repertoire will suffer from those crowd reaction bonuses which will be awarded to their opponent. War Zone forces players to expand their number of moves and keep from falling into a comfort zone which ultimately limits your enjoyment of the game.

In one of the game's most unique effects, individual fans will call out to your wrestler. These taunts were generated in stereo, so if you listen closely, you'll actually be able to tell where the remark is coming from within the virtual arena.

If you hear encouraging catcalls, you can tell who's currently more likely to get the crowd chanting his name. Conversely, when somebody at ringside tells you that you stink, it's a pretty good cue to start mixing up those moves and taking the offense before you get buried.

## FLEXES & TAUNTS

Wrestlers have the ability to flex their muscles or taunt their opponent in the right situation. A flex or taunt can produce double damage on the next move, if executed successfully. In fact, once you get really skilled at "working" a crowd, you can get a chant going. Then, while the crowd calls your wrestler's name, you flex, then scale the top rope and execute a move with four times the normal damage! So let's say you have a big strong guy doing a 7 point move — he would get another 2 points in damage for his strength, with the whole thing multiplied by 4! It becomes possible, under this scenario, to take out one-sixth of an opponent's total damage in a single maneuver!

Warning: The damage bonus after a flex or taunt applies to whoever executes the next crowd-pleasing move — including your opponent. So if you get the crowd fired up, you'd better make sure you're the one pulling the next move off. Talk about your double-edged swords...!

## PLAY-BY-PLAY

Make sure you listen very closely to the play-by-play generated by Vince McMahon and J.R., because they will cue you in some very important ways. For example, if your style is about to start boring the crowd, the announcers will make a remark to that effect ("The crowd's starting to get restless, Vince!").

If you pull of a hot move ("What a clothesline by Mankind!") you will be similarly alerted by the play-by-play and color team. So keep your ears open — as with the real thing, in WWF War Zone Vince and good old J.R. have a lot to tell you.

## RING GENERALSHIP

When a wrestler is described as a "Ring General", it refers to his ability to make use of the ring to his benefit. A true ring general first determines what kind of opponent he's facing. If he's up against a speedy opponent who likes to fly, he will "cut down" the size of the ring. This is done by forcing the action into a

**High-flying tag teams present a constant threat from all directions.**

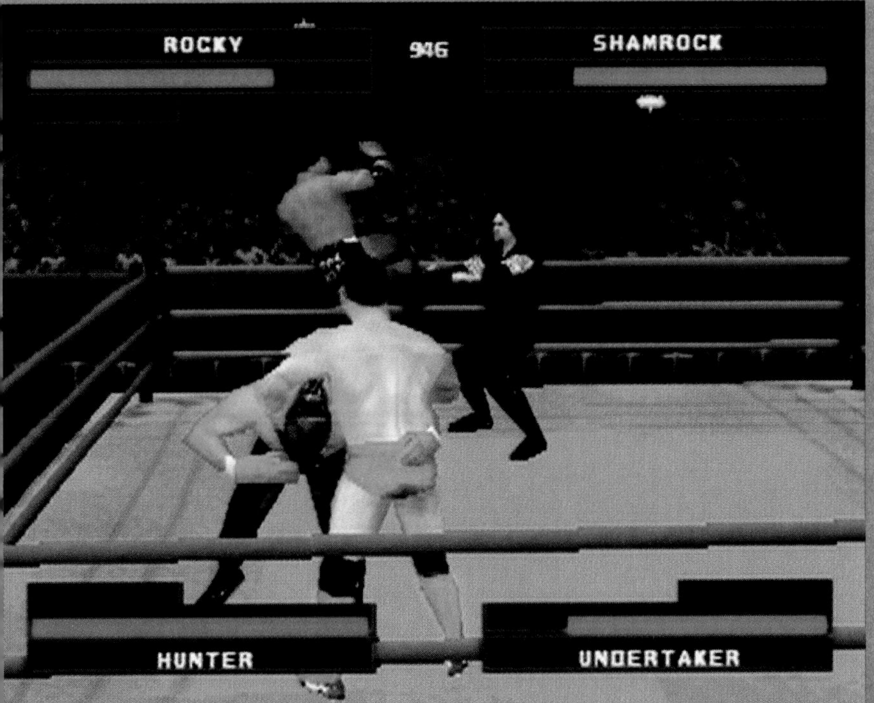


corner, and by constantly pushing the action toward the ropes. This has the effect of "shrinking" the ring and keeps the faster wrestler from gaining the momentum he requires to work at maximum efficiency.

Large wrestlers should all be experts at cutting down a ring. They should also attempt to maintain a vertical base — i.e. remain standing — during their exchanges. There's a saying in wrestling: "Everybody's the same size on their back." In other words, once you've knocked a big man off his feet, he isn't in a position to use his power. If you can keep him trapped on the canvas, you can weaken him with holds and other attacks to the point where he becomes vulnerable to a pin or submission. If handled correctly, the bigger the are, the harder they can be made to fall.

Speedy wrestlers must attempt to dictate the pace of a match. If they run into a ring general who will attempt to cut down the ring, they can counter this by simply going into overdrive and leading the match. If their opponent is constantly recovering from attacks or attempting to block or reverse moves, then they aren't likely to be concentrating on their ring position.

## TAG TEAMS

The alchemy involved in creating a perfect pro wrestling tag team has been practiced for approximately half a century. There are several prototypical tag teams, however, and we'll list each of them along with their strengths and weaknesses.

**1) THE FLYER AND THE BRUTE**

This tandem consists of one very speedy, acrobatic wrestler and one very powerful, stationary-type wrestler. Shawn Michaels and Kane would make a good example of this type of team.

**STRENGTH:** If everything works right, the smaller wrestler isolates one opponent, peppers him with damage, then tags in the big man to finish him off.

**WEAKNESSES:** If things don't go according to plan, the smaller wrestler may get isolated and taken apart before his larger partner can rescue him.

**2) THE GEMINI**

This tag team consists of two wrestlers who are very much the same size and who wrestle similar styles. The traditional brother tag teams such as the Briscos and the Funks exemplified this type of team, though wrestlers don't have to be brothers to work this type of team. The Headbangers are a perfect example of the Gemini type of team.

**STRENGTH:** Balance is the key to the Gemini in all things. With both wrestlers possessing similar skills, the opponent feels as if he is being attacked by a single wrestler who never gets tired. This type of team lives or dies by frequent tags.

**WEAKNESSES:** If one member gets isolated and

double-teamed, the Gemini-style tandem find their resources cut in half. Again, they have to continue tagging in and out so that the wrestler in the ring is always in peak condition. Anything that interrupts that exchange cripples the effectiveness of this type of team.

**3) FLYERS**

High-flying tag teams have been popular since the '50s. They present a constant threat from all directions, and their high-risk attack can generate big dividends even against larger teams. A good example of a flying team in War Zone would be Shawn Michaels and Thrasher.

**STRENGTH:** Flyers are usually in excellent cardiovascular condition and, unlike the larger wrestlers — whose huge muscles require constant infusions of oxygen, and generally lack endurance — they can usually outlast the big men. If they keep tagging off and don't let themselves get caught, flyers can upset even the biggest tandems.

**WEAKNESS:** If a smaller wrestler falls into the clutches of a larger wrestler after a failed high risk maneuver, he will get hurt. He is then apt to be isolated and destroyed.

**4) POWER FLYERS**

This type of team was popularized by the British Bulldogs and the Legion of Doom. These were power wrestlers capable of flying. Usually one member of the team did more flying while the other executed most of the power moves. Nonetheless, both wrestlers are able to handle either end when necessary. Any combination of Owen Hart, Ken Shamrock and Ahmed Johnson would probably make a good team of this type.

**STRENGTH:** This kind of team offers a more complete package, able to use superior strength in conjunction with a high impact aerial attack to dominate almost any type of team.

**WEAKNESSES:** When this type of team gets beaten, it's generally because they have been lured into fighting a match that is either all power or all flying. A power team will attempt to draw them into a power match, thereby negating the Power Flyers' all-important edge — their flying ability. In a test of pure power versus power, the Power Flyers will not match up as well. A similar scenario can be set up by pure flyers, who entice the team to take to the air where they lose the advantage of their strength.

## A Few More WWF War Zone Tag Team Tips:

- When wrestlers tag off to their partner, they have 5 referee counts (about 15 seconds) in which they can double-team an opponent, after which the wrestler tagging out is forced outside the ring by the computer.
- The wrestler standing on the apron should *not* wander around. Every 2 counts (each count represents about three seconds) a wrestler spends standing in the correct neutral spot earns them 1 count of what is called Ring Time. Ring Time can be used to get in the ring and double-team an opponent, or it can be used to break up a pinning or otherwise dangerous situation facing your partner. Ring Time is very valuable, so don't squander it.

• Always have your wrestler tag out before he gets into trouble. Of course, there are times when you might want to disregard this advice. Let's say your health status is still acceptable but it's getting close to the point of concern. Ordinarily, if the opportunity presented itself at this point to tag out to a healthy partner, you'd take it. But let's say you've just knocked your opponent to the mat and you're in a position to Flex/Taunt and deliver a heavy duty plus-damage move. Because of the cumulative nature of damage bonuses, when the opportunity arises to set up a double- or triple-bonus move, you want to think very seriously about taking it — even if a tag-out seems like the safer thing to do.

## WEAPONS

In Weapons Matches, the various objects are used to enhance the base weapon damage of 9. Here's how they stack up:

**Bell = +1**
**Closed Chair = +3**
**Open Chair = +3**
**TV = +4**
**Video Camera = +0**

The Bell can be used for a maximum of 3 hits, the chairs and video camera twice and the TV once (though items will reappear). It is also possible to slam someone through the Chairs, the TV or even the Table, causing double damage in the process.

## WRESTLER ATTRIBUTES

**Building A Better Wrestler**

Beyond the wide range of body, head and costume types available to you through the Custom Wrestler feature, it is important to understand the qualities that make up each of these superstars. The following is a list and explanation of the qualities which make up our virtual wrestlers.

**1) STRENGTH**

This factor determines how much damage a wrestler can do with a given move. As with all ratings, they range from 0-10. Average Strength is 5, so a wrestler with a "0" Strength will execute 70% of the damage possible on a move while a grappler with a "10" will do 130% of that damage.

**2) TOUGHNESS**

Sort of the counter-move to Strength. If a wrestler with a Strength of 5 meets a wrestler with a Toughness of 5, he will execute all the base damage. An opponent with a higher Toughness rating, meanwhile, will suffer less than the 5 damage, whereas a wrestler with a lower Toughness rating will suffer more.

**3) SPEED**

This rating determines everything from how fast a wrestler moves around the ring to how quickly they climb the turnbuckle. It also determines how swiftly a wrestler can dodge an attack or how quickly he recovers (the amount of time it takes for him to return to the Ready stance) after executing a Block or missing a grapple attempt.

**4) RECOVERY**

First, you must understand how the health meters work in this game. When a wrestler's health meter hits zero, it is automatically replaced by the Stun meter. There is also a Hold meter, a Submission meter and a Pin meter. The Recovery rating determines how quickly the health meter fills back up after suffering damage and how long that wrestler tends to remain stunned.

**5) CHARISMA**

Perhaps the most important and unique component of War Zone. Every wrestler is rated in this category from 0 to 10, which indicates a Charisma bonus of anywhere from zero to 200%. The easiest way to understand how Charisma works is to understand that in wrestling — as in life! — a charismatic wrestler can get away with murder. Whereas an average or low Charisma wrestler will have to show off plenty of move variety and take lots of heavy duty offensive risks to keep the crowd happy, a high Charisma wrestler is so adored by the fans that he can execute half as many moves, wrestle defensively and still hear the cheers of the crowd!

But wait, there's more. Every wrestler is given from 1 to 10 seconds of defense time per 30 seconds of game time, which can be used blocking or dodging your opponent. If you use more defense time than you have allocated, the crowd will boo you. The number of defense time seconds is directly correlated to the wrestler's Charisma rating.

SPECIAL TIP: **If you have a high Charisma wrestler and you're facing a low Charisma wrestler, it's smart to play a defensive game. Keep blocking; your Charisma differential should more than compensate for your lack of wrestling pyrotechnics. Remember, the crowd loves ya!**

Wimp Warning: **However, if you have a low charisma wrestler, you'd better not play it too safe, or the crowd will hate ya!**

## TWITCHING

While War Zone offers players a lot of strategy and options, occasionally it still helps to be really good at manipulating a game controller. The meters, for example — Health, Stun, Hold, Pain, and Pin — can be brought back up faster on defense by bashing the buttons as fast as you can.

From the other side, slamming buttons will suppress recovery of the Hold and Pain meters, and keep a hold locked on just a little longer, for example.

Another situation where button-slamming comes when your wrestler is dazed; hitting the buttons rapidly will bring him back around more quickly.

## GENERAL TIPS

• Don't be afraid to leave the ring. If your opponent is starting to hit you with high-impact moves, get the hell out of there. If nothing else, it gives your wrestler a chance to recover and it may even disrupt your opponent's timing. Momentum is a big part of any game, and if the other gamer gets into a groove, shutting down the action may disrupt him.

• Determine your attack, based on your wrestler's strengths and his opponent's weaknesses, before the bell rings. Have a battle plan. If everything starts to unravel, of course, it helps to have a Plan B ready. But inside the ring, he who hesitates is lost. When you're hitting the stroke, don't second-guess yourself. Know how you're going to deal with any potential situation before it happens and then do it.

• There's at least one exception to every rule.

• And, in the words of a great wrestler and world-class thinker: "Win if you can. Lose if you must. But always cheat!"

# Damage Bonus Levels

| Situation | Bonus Level |
|---|---|
| Any Move | 1 |
| Against Corner | 1 |
| Behind Opponent | 1 |
| Using Weapon | 1 |
| Opponent Stunned | 1 |
| Taunt in Effect | 1 |
| Crowd Chanting | 1 |
| Finishing Move | 1 |
| Turnbuckle to Inside of Ring | 2 |
| Apron to Outside of Ring | 2 |
| From Top of Cage | 3 |
| Turnbuckle to Outside of Ring | 3 |

NOTES:

• Bonus Levels are additive. For any and all situations that are true when executing a move, add up the corresponding bonus levels and multiply that number by the move damage to get your total damage.

(Example: Hitting a stunned opponent from behind with a weapon while the crowd is chanting for you would work out to: 1 for the move, 1 for being behind the opponent, 1 for using a weapon, 1 for the opponent being stunned, and 1 for the crowd bonus equals 5, which means your move will hit him for 5x damage!)

• If you bounce off the ropes before doing a Running move, you get a 50% damage bonus.

• Reversals double your Crowd bonus.

## More Tips From the Game Designers and Playtesters at Acclaim!

### Jeff Robinson

Lead, Quality Assurance: Iguana West

• Learn the reversals. It is important to know who can do what to whom. The same move does not work for everyone.

• Experiment with ranges and priorities of ready moves. Vertical suplexes can be done farther away and with a higher priority than a fireman's carry, for example.

• Take advantage of misses. When a wrestler misses a tie-up or a move from the start position, he will be exposed for a split second. This window varies with speed, but make him pay for his misses!

• Study and test the different attributes. A person who puts max strength and toughness for his custom wrestler is going to be missing out. Each attribute has been balanced and affects game play in different ways.

• Mix up the moves. This will keep the crowd on your side, and your opponent guessing.

• Learn the tie-up system. This is the most important part in the game. The system is simple to pick up, but complicated enough for the

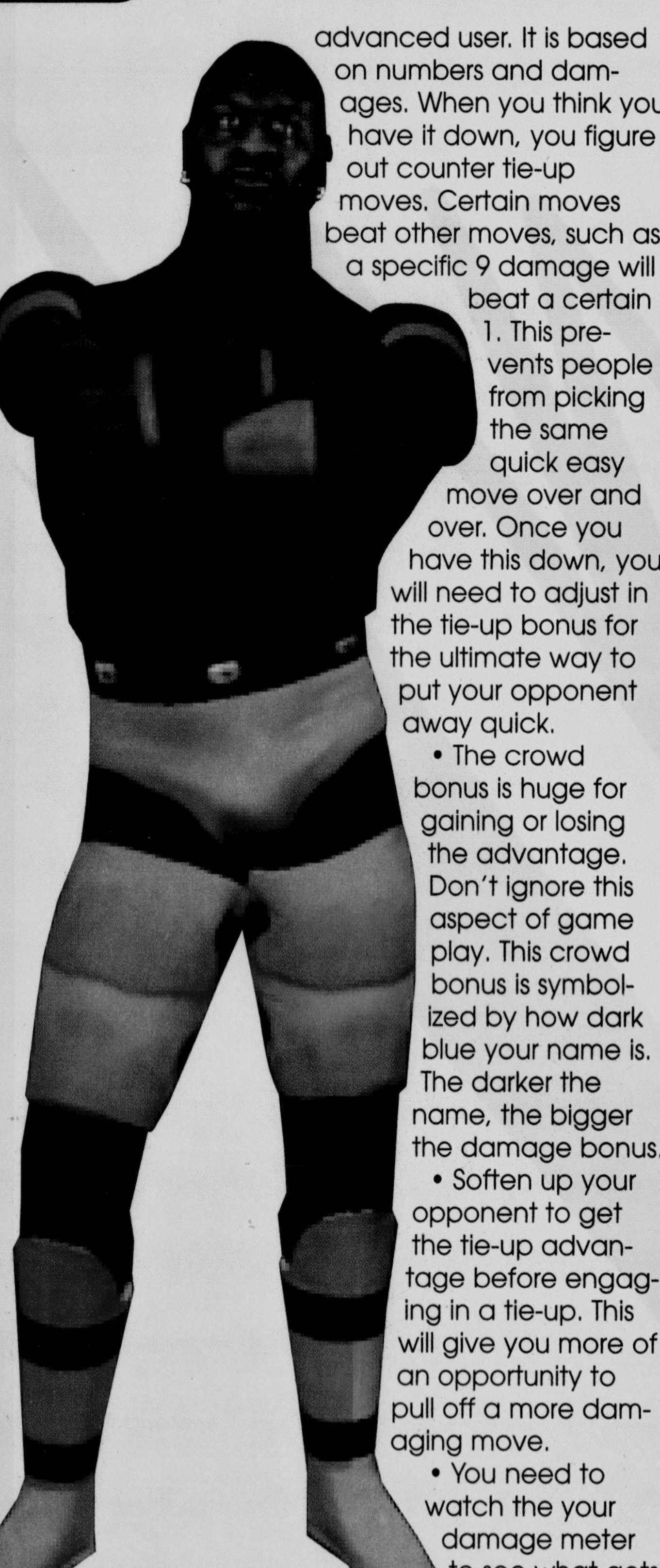

advanced user. It is based on numbers and damages. When you think you have it down, you figure out counter tie-up moves. Certain moves beat other moves, such as a specific 9 damage will beat a certain 1. This prevents people from picking the same quick easy move over and over. Once you have this down, you will need to adjust in the tie-up bonus for the ultimate way to put your opponent away quick.

• The crowd bonus is huge for gaining or losing the advantage. Don't ignore this aspect of game play. This crowd bonus is symbolized by how dark blue your name is. The darker the name, the bigger the damage bonus.

• Soften up your opponent to get the tie-up advantage before engaging in a tie-up. This will give you more of an opportunity to pull off a more damaging move.

• You need to watch the your damage meter to see what gets bonuses. Bouncing off the ropes does more damage that a normal running attack. Once your learn what does what, you can go for max damage. Leap from the turnbuckle with the crowd bonus onto a stunned opponent for 4X damage. That is going to leave a mark!

• Follow up kicks, punches and blocks with a quick move from the Start position. Some slower wrestlers are quick to react, so go in for the kill.

## T.L. Shelton

Quality Assurance

• Memorize your moves, ranges, and reversals. They vary for each wrestler.

• Practice tapping your block button so that you can react after your opponent has failed to grab or hit you in any way.

• Don't be afraid to be dodge crazy. Remember, you can't grab what you can't catch!

• Learn to use any type of advantage that you may have. Don't be afraid to use the light blue "crowd" advantage. This will save you from being pummeled a lot. Always working for the dark blue advantage will most likely get you in trouble instead of helping you. (Don't get me wrong, definitely go for a tie-up. You have the advantage, use it!)

• Adjust to your opponent's style while constantly switching your game up. This will keep him guessing.

• Use many different moves. The crowd likes this and will get on your side quicker. With this technique, you will be inflicting serious damage in no time at all.

• Don't forget about the turnbuckle and rope moves. The cause enough damage to be worth the risk involved.

• Taunts/Poses should be saved for the more advanced user. They double the damage for the next move, but this applies for both wrestlers. They can be very risky with the amount of time the taunting/ posing wrestler is exposed. Remember, taunts do not affect a stunned opponent.

## Preston Whitney

Quality Assurance

- Reversals, turnbuckle, and moves from the Starting Position are the thing to go for when you are a quick wrestler.
- Punch, dodge, then perform a Start Position move or try to dodge behind the opponent.
- Try for the crowd bonus and tie-up bonus for a HUGE damaging move!
- Try not to do many of the same moves. You don't want the crowd bonus on your opponent's side.
- Choose Ahmed. Throw a quick Punch followed by a Gutwrench. When your opponent gets up, knock him down with a High Jump Kick. You will have the deep blue advantage, so go for the tie-up. Polish him off with the big Powerbomb. They should not be stunned.
- Undertaker/Kane: Both of these wrestlers have a larger body frame, so they have great range when it comes to Start Position moves. Use this to your advantage!

**TIP: For even more strategy tips, check out the interviews in the "Behind the Scenes" chapter!**

**SPECIAL NOTE**

Since this book was created before the War Zone games were released, there may have been last-minute changes that we were unable to include herein. For corrections, additions and extra strategy tips, visit our companion web site, at http://www.acclaim.net/games/wwf-warzone/strategyGuide.html

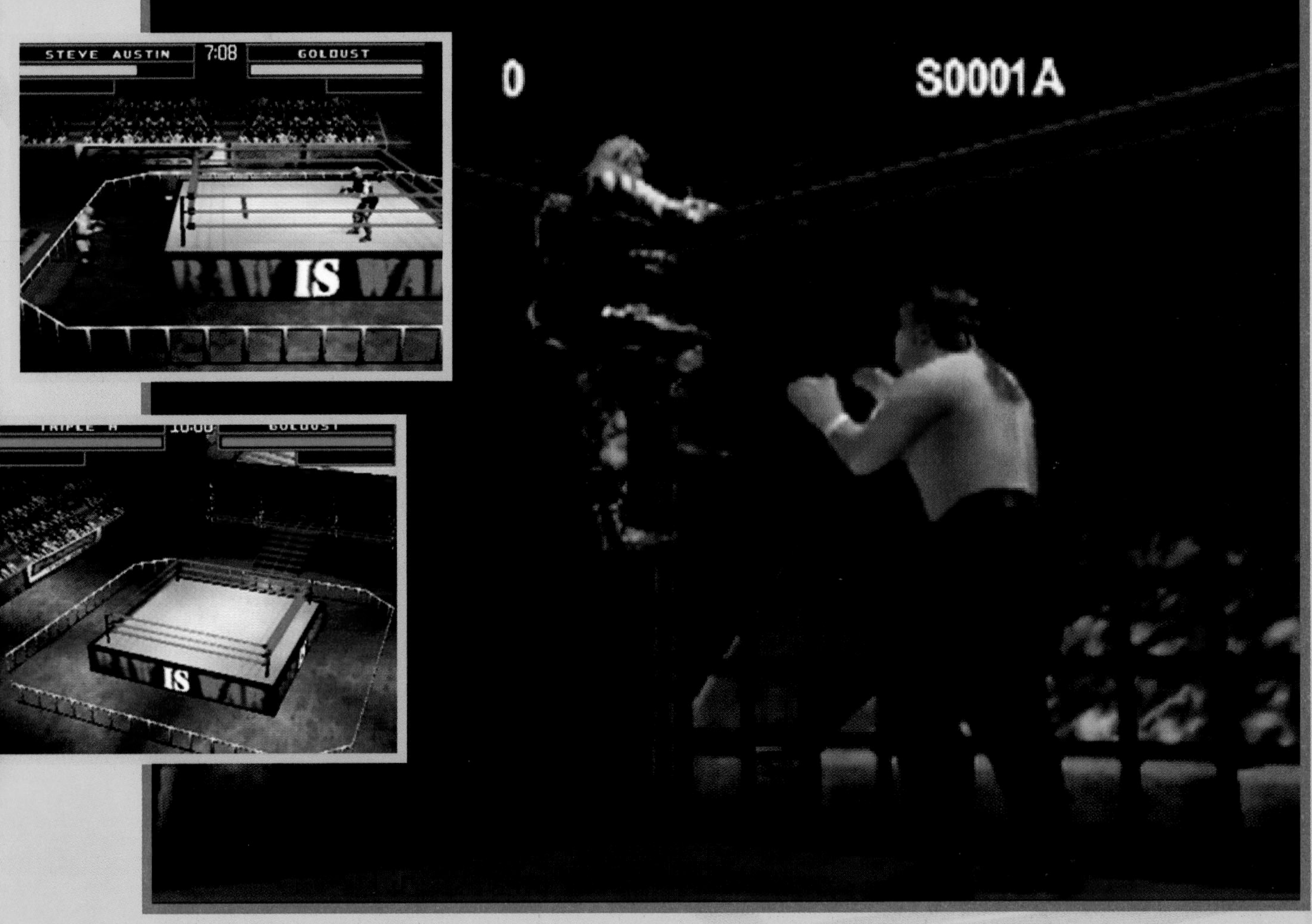

# CHAPTER FOUR

# HOW TO RUN YOUR OWN PROMOTION

Interested in entering even more deeply into the wildly entertaining World Wrestling Federation universe? Well, there is a way to get there, and it's called a Virtual Promotion. Check it out — you may find yourself running a rousing wrestling promotion that even Vince McMahon would be proud to call his own!

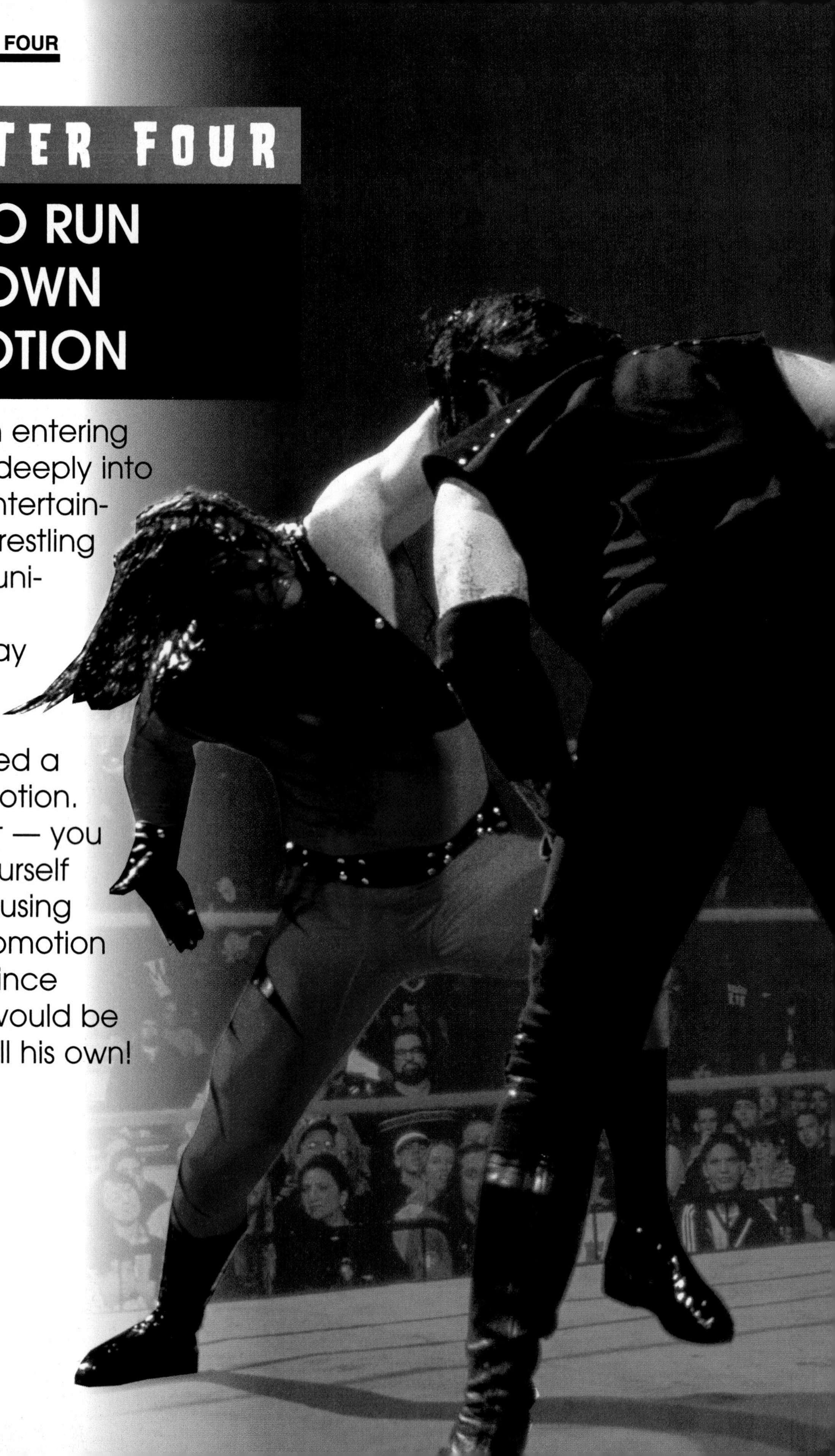

**As we've seen, the Challenge scenario allows a single player to take a wrestler and guide him through the ranks to the top of the World Wrestling Federation ladder. There is, however, yet another way to simulate this sense of being part of a wrestling promotion, and that is through the formation of a "Virtual Promotion".**

**This is a setup whereby a group of gamers get together and form their own version of the World Wrestling Federation. Up to a dozen or more players can participate, live and in person, on a weekly basis. If you have many potential members, each player would get to control a single wrestler. If there are only half a dozen or so gamers in your promotion, then each gamer can control two wrestlers.**

**Here's an easy, step-by-step guide to setting up your own promotion.**

## 1) DRAFTING

The first thing that must be done is the dispersal of talent. Using some random format (rolling dice works well), the gamers each draw a draft position. The player with the number one pick gets the first choice of which wrestler he wants to guide to the top. The player with the next pick takes their choice and so on, until all the wrestlers have been assigned.

Remember, great care was taken in the making of WF War Zone to ensure that any wrestler can beat any wrestler, so no one will be at a disadvantage.

## 2) SEEDING

To start a campaign, it will be necessary to establish random seedings (rankings which determine who the champions are and who must fight who to move up in the rankings). Fortunately, the game already contains the required tools to establish random seedings. Simply access the Challenge option, select a wrestler, then copy down the seedings as they appear on screen. These will serve as the rankings for your Virtual Promotion.

Of course, using this system means that one wrestler will simply be arbitrarily crowned Champion without winning a single match. Live with it. If the lucky player isn't worthy, he will soon be bounced from that lofty position. We also recommend ignoring the Intercontinental Championship when playing in this mode for reasons explained below ("Crowning a Kingpin").

## 3) MATCH MAKING

The key to any league or promotion such as this is regular competition. Ideally, all the members of the promotion should show up at least once a week for a major card. This will be just like an actual wrestling event, with superstars who finished lower in the seedings battling one another in the preliminaries (undercard) to move up, while the top wrestlers go at it to determine championships and top contenders (main events).

See the charts on the following pages for an example of how to match your wrestlers up.

## 4) THE PROMOTER

While it is possible using basic democratic principles (i.e. majority rules) for everyone in the promotion to run a wrestler or two, there is an alternative method in which one of the gamers assumes the role of Promoter. This role is similar to the Game Master in a non-electronic fantasy role-playing game. While the Promoter doesn't actually get to participate in the quest/campaign by running a character/wrestler,he is, in this case, a Virtual

Vince McMahon. He sets up the cards, determine the contenders (all other rankings being equal) and track the win/loss ratings as wrestlers move up or down in the pecking order. The Promoter can also dictate specialty matches.

And maybe even provide running commentary during the matches, if he really wants to "get into it"!

## 5) MOVING UP/MOVING DOWN

While the actual number can be determined by the members of the promotion, we recommend that once two wrestlers are matched up, they are automatically locked into a feud. A feud is settled when one wrestler wins a majority of the matches, establishing dominance. The number can be as little as best two out of three (but not recommended since luck would be too big a factor) or as many as best seven out of 13 (after that point, the interest would begin to fade). The wrestler who wins, advances (unless he was fighting a wrestler ranked lower than him, in which case he simply maintains his position). The wrestler who lost would drop back a slot (unless all the wrestlers rated below him also lost their feuds in this round, in which case he would stay where he was).

**A FEUD is settled when one wrestler wins a majority of the matches, establishing DOMINANCE.**

## 6) CROWNING A KINGPIN

We recommend when playing this game in Virtual Promotion format that the Intercontinental belt be ignored and the wrestlers fight exclusively for the World Heavyweight Championship strap. The existence of two belts creates a lot of problems in this type of environment. For example, the Intercontinental Champion is, in theory, always the Number One challenger for the World title, and that would leave a situation where whoever was World Champ would also be Intercontinental Champion, thereby confusing the process needlessly. Besides, eliminating the IC strap gives the big belt all the more significance!

## 7) WELCOME TO THE WAR ZONE!

You now have a fully functioning promotion, a virtual clone of the World Wrestling Federation and, if you let the group play at your place, you can probably get to be the Promoter as well. So take it to the limit. Have a weekly party with guests over to watch the matches (in fact, if you ran your events on Mondays, you could finish the evening by watching *Raw/WarZone* together). Do interviews promoting your wrestler(s). **Have fun.** And watch as the various gamers spend the rest of the week practicing relentlessly with their wrestlers, just so they can spring that surprise maneuver at the next week's event!

# HOW TO START A PROMOTION WITH 10 WRESTLERS

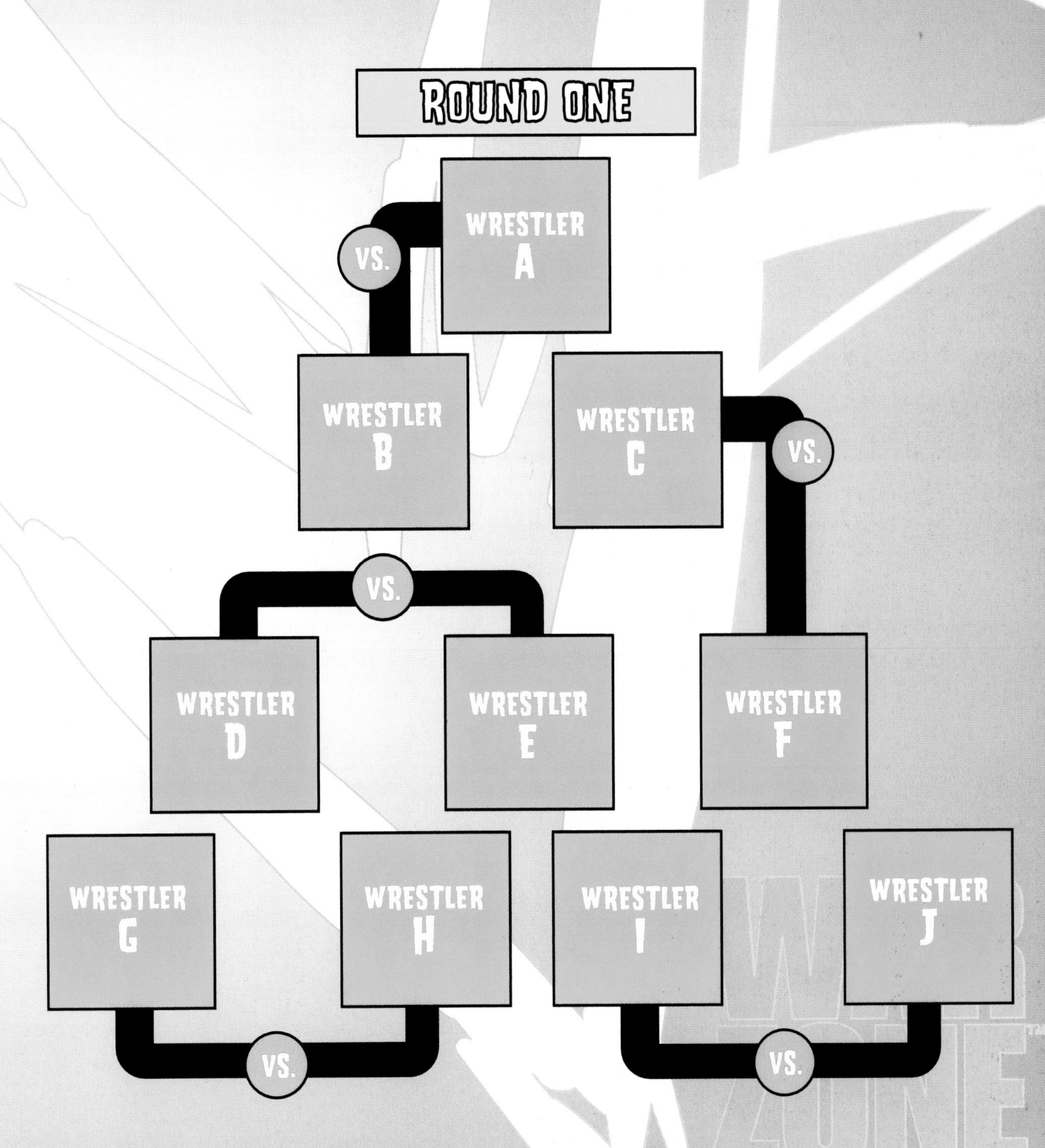

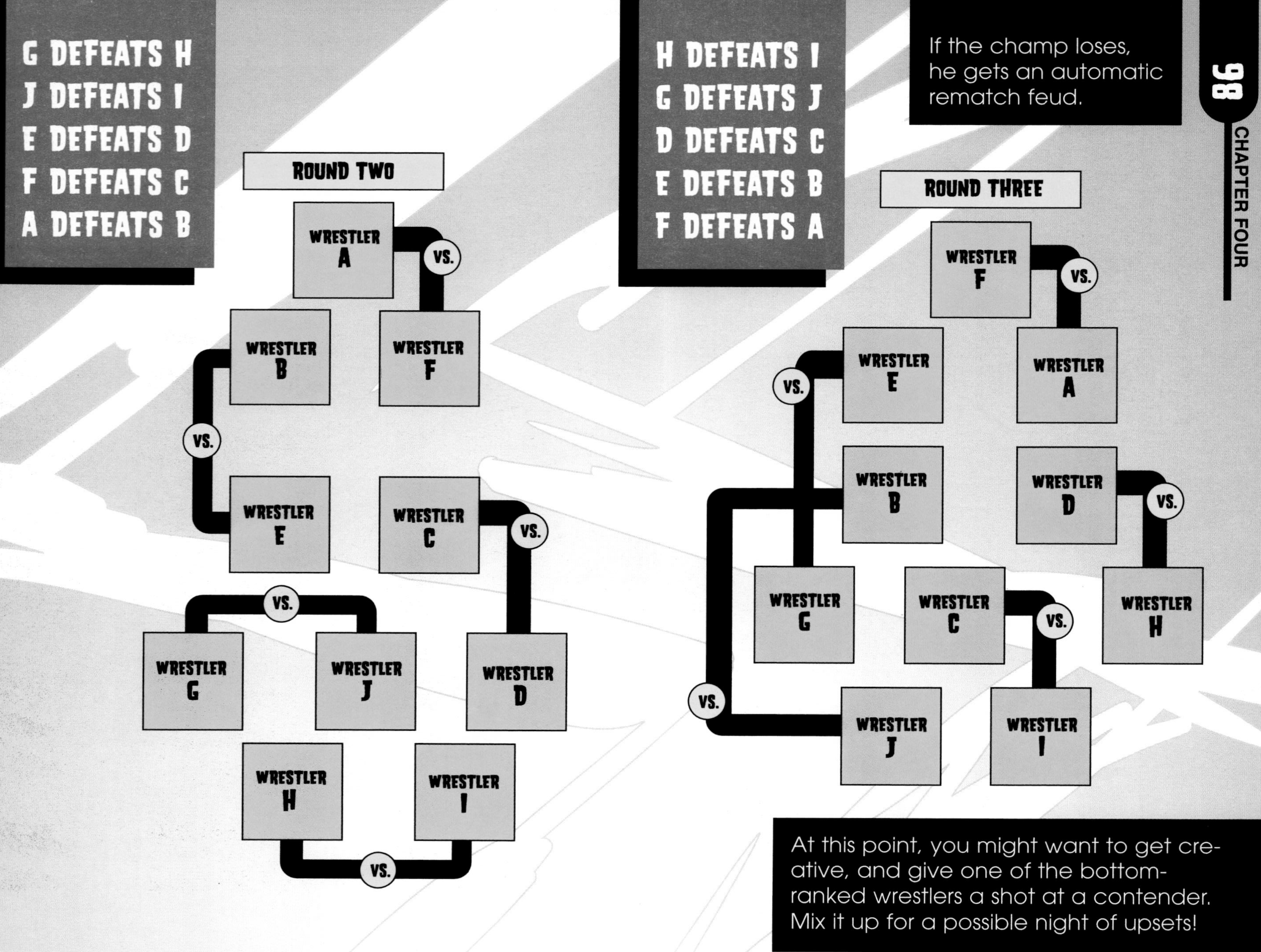


If the champ loses, he gets an automatic rematch feud.

At this point, you might want to get creative, and give one of the bottom-ranked wrestlers a shot at a contender. Mix it up for a possible night of upsets!

# CHAPTER FIVE

## BEHIND THE SCENES

Step behind the curtain, ladies and gentlemen, and get the "insider" lowdown on how this revolutionary wrestling simulation was constructed. Learn how images of the wrestlers were digitally mapped at Acclaim's world famous motion capture installation, and how changes in the dynamic World Wrestling Federation threatened to alter the game itself. It's all here ... behind the scenes.

Creating a realistic electronic wrestling simulation is one of the toughest tasks that any development group can face.

Producing a wrestling game with literally hundreds of moves is an assignment most members of the software community would consider totally unrealistic. Nonetheless, that's just what the Iguana Salt Lake (formerly Sculptured Software) crew and Acclaim producer Mike Archer set out to do with WWF War Zone, the latest entry in the long and successful World Wrestling Federation game franchise.

None of the game's planned innovations would work, however, unless the game were set in a 3D environment. "When we first decided to go to 3D, we met with some resistance," admits Archer. "They felt it would be tough to do grapples and lock-ups and holds, the twining of the bodies. But Iguana Salt Lake has been able to iron out all those problems. It was a natural progression: the next generation of technology and the new wave of wrestling. It was a natural — they were made for each other!"

The new wave of wrestling that Archer refers to has been led by Vince McMahon's World Wrestling Federation. McMahon revolutionized pro wrestling in the mid-'80s and now, in the fading years of the 20th Century, he is reinventing it all over again. The cutting-edge ring entrances and overall production values that the promotion pioneered a decade ago have been reconceptualized. Shows like *Raw* and *WarZone*, with their battlefield pyrotechnics and perfectly layered dramatic presentation, represent the leading edge in what McMahon has always called "sports entertainment."

Archer has been with Acclaim's wrestling franchise for several years now. "I came in right after Royal Rumble and took over Raw. I've been the producer on every World Wrestling Federation release since then." Before that, he was a game tester at Acclaim and before that, Mike had actually trained to be a pro wrestler. So why did he make the transition from vertical suplexes to video games? "Wrestling was too tough a way to make a living," he admits. "I had a girlfriend and I was thinking about getting married when I saw an ad in the paper for a job at Acclaim as a game tester. I was 26 years old (most playtesters are younger than that), so I was basically taking two steps backwards in order to move ahead. But when I got to Acclaim, they were doing wrestling games and I was able to offer a lot of input and I moved on from there."

The Iguana Salt Lake team

working with Archer was headed up by designer Tim Huntsman, who counted Mike Archer among his main assets in getting this incredible job completed to everyone's satisfaction. "Mike really knows his stuff. He's got a very good concept of the wrestling industry and he was able to fight certain powers-that-be to make sure we got some of the new, evolving moves into the game. On our end, we've jumped through technological hoops to create the space to hold all these images and animations. These wrestlers have a lot of moves. We have a list of around 500 moves, but no one wrestler can execute them all. It's never been done on this scope before, but based on the fact that our graphic technology is so good and our wrestlers are so lifelike, we had to make an effort to get as many of the actual moves into the game as possible. People see this stuff on television and they say, 'Dang, that's really cool!' And when the player can actually pull off a Hurricanrana or execute a Moonsault, that's a great payoff!"

The research and development for this game involved some extensive research. "I got together with some guys and we literally went over wrestling tapes from everywhere in the world," says Archer. The team then recruited veteran wrestler Dr. Tom Pritchard and the athletic young P.J. Walker (Aldo Montoya) to actually execute the moves at the famous Acclaim motion capture facility on Long Island. A one-quarter sized wrestling ring was constructed and the two wrestlers, clad in full motion capture suits, spent weeks executing some of the most dangerous moves in pro wrestling.

"We went through every single one of these moves," Archer explained. "We had the guys in for about a week-and-a-half first time, and then we did a pick-up shoot. We had Dr. Tom — who's still got a lot of life left in him — doing Asai Moonsaults while P.J. did the Hurricanrannas and stuff like that. And while our mats were softer than an actual ring, you're not bumping for eight hours straight in a real ring. These guys came in at nine in the morning and we suited them up. First off, it's a pain in the neck to wear that motion capture rig. Then we had them bumping all day long. We had them falling off boxes to give the move a bigger drop, and we had them going over hard wood

**"When you see a high definition model of these guys it looks like a photograph, it's so good."**

**— Tim Huntsman, Game Designer**

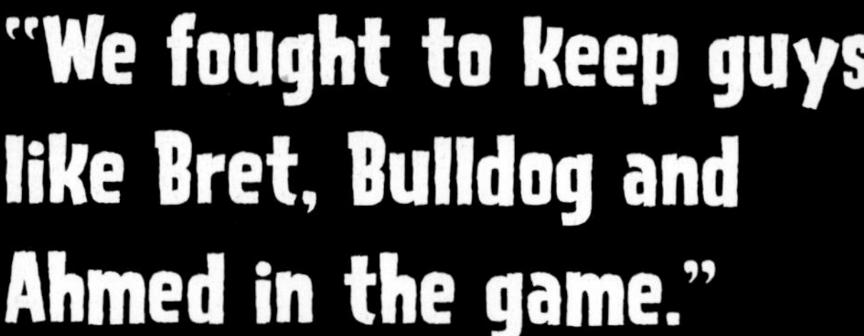

for the clothesline out of the ring. They both took their share of lumps, but it came out great."

Much of the success is laid at Iguana Salt Lake's collective feet. Archer was especially happy with the team's ability to improvise. "At one point," he recalls, "Doc (Pritchard) hurt his neck, so we tried to stay away from a lot of the neck-related moves. But Iguana Salt Lake was able to create many of the moves based on reference material."

The motion capture shoot took place in three stages. "A lot of times after a shoot you realize you forgot something so you have to go back and do a pick-up," says Archer. "But it was actually a lot of fun. The wrestlers were great and other than them getting beat up a little, they seemed to have fun. The Salt Lake guys were also great and so was the stunt coordinator — who came in to make sure nobody got killed."

Rather than capture the moves of individual wrestlers, then piece them together, most of the motion capture was done with both grapplers. "A punch or a kick is a one-man capture," explains Archer. "But any time they overlapped, it was a two-man capture — which made life miserable for Iguana, but it made the game that much better."

"Capturing two men at a time is technically more difficult because you've got to decode it so that the program knows that this sensor belongs to that guy's shoulder and that sensor belongs to the other guy's leg," Huntsman explains. "So on that end it's harder. There were also problems linking one kind of motion to another type of motion. For example, going from the middle of a walk animation to an attack — there's a transition there, and it's really hard to get everything lined up. We had to go through each move and make sure their vertices were aligned and everything was set to zero and was pointing at each other. Then you've got to tweak with ranges, how you're letting the collision happen between the two wrestlers."

Speaking of collisions, high impact figures prominently into

**SUPER SECRETS**

## HERO MODE

**If you beat the Challenge with a custom wrestler who has 40 of the possible 50 points, you'll get access to a special Hero wrestler caled Rattlesnake, who has all 50! Now there's a guy who can sit wherever he wants!**

the game program. "The more dynamic a move, the higher the wrestler bounces off the mat, the more damage it's going to produce. Of course, you've got to wear an opponent down and get him dazed before you can pull off a major move. We're also going for signature moves with each wrestler. Goldust, for example, is the only wrestler with the Butt Drop. It isn't a finisher, but it's his move exclusively."

Huntsman also believes in the importance of making all the wrestlers in the game equal, eliminating the possibility of mismatches. This is not accomplished by simply giving every wrestler the same basic set of moves, but through some extensive technological fine-tuning. "Part of my biggest problem was making Wrestler One equal Wrestler Two, so the difference was always zero," Huntsman recalls. "Not just in terms of their number of moves, but in the types of moves. Certain maneuvers lead to pinning combinations, for example, but you don't have to knock the guy down and pin him the way you do in every other wrestling game. You can put your opponent into a Small Package or go for a Victory Roll.

"The stronger guys will tend to be a little slower. The faster guys who aren't necessarily doing as much damage can still get off one-and-a-half shots whereas the larger guys may get off only one. Every fighting game or wrestling game that's ever come out has always had a couple of characters where everybody knows, play this guy if you want to win, or stay away from that character. We're all very conscious of that situation and we're making certain there are no weak characters. Anybody can take any wrestler and, based on the abilities of the person holding the controller, defeat any other wrestler."

The game, which has been in development for nearly two years, has seen a lot of changes occur in the World Wrestling Federation since start-up. "Shawn (Michaels) was a fan favorite when we began the project," Archer recalls. "And his interviews were very friendly." Of course, things have changed a bit since then. "So what can we update? It was too late to update his Grudge FMVs (full-motion video sequences). But we felt they were generic enough to work. So, Iguana spent their time updating the costumes. So Rocky's now wearing his black trunks. But changing speech is tough." The team even had to deal with one wrestler altering his finishing maneuver. Two years ago, Rocky Maivia used a rugged Shoulderbreaker to polish off opponents, but has now changed over to the Rock Bottom, a head-and-arm slam. "We had the foresight to shoot Rock Bottom, because he was using that move all along. But after he injured his knee, he stopped doing the Shoulderbreaker and went to Rock Bottom. So all the guys at Iguana had to do was clean it up a bit and now it looks just like Rocky's move."

**"Hunter Hearst Helmsley gave me a "Power Bomb" on the mats where we were doing the motion capture, and all of a sudden I had much greater respect for what the wrestlers go through."**
**— Jonathan Dansie, Motion Editor**

Bigger problems were created when three of the game's wrestlers — Bret Hart, British Bulldog, and Ahmed Johnson — left the World Wrestling Federation. "We fought to keep guys like Bret, Bulldog and Ahmed in the game for several reasons," Archer says. "If we had had the time, we might have taken them out, because we do want to look current. But you don't want to pull three wrestlers out and drop the number of wrestlers in the game. We wanted to have as many wrestlers as we could. Also, Bret Hart is still a big name, so let WCW help market our game. The World Wrestling Federation understands about deadlines and they were

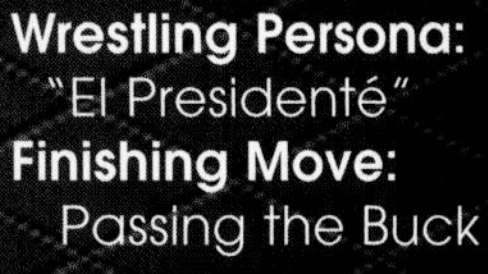

**Paul Boyle** — Artist

**Wrestling Persona:**
"El Presidenté"
**Finishing Move:**
Passing the Buck

**"There was a difficulty (the inability to run high poly count scenes) the N64 presented that did not allow us to have the Reward sequences that are in the PSX version. Other than that, the main part of the game is killer."**

cool with it. We can make our changes — alter the color of a wrestler's trunks — but to pull guys out at that late a date would have really hurt us."

Adds Huntsman: "It takes a lot of time to create each wrestler model — each digital representation is done by hand. Other wrestling games basically have one or two body styles, but each of our wrestlers has a very unique body style. When you see a high definition model of these guys it looks like a photograph, it's so good. So everything has to be complete and that takes a lot of time, and we didn't have the time to replace that many models."

There's also a human factor involved when a wrestler departs the franchise. "I never thought I'd be working on a World Wrestling Federation game without Bret Hart," Archer admits with some sadness. "He is a terrific guy, a true gentleman. It's going to be tough doing the next one without him. He wouldn't talk about it, but Bret was supposed to come in on a Monday for some scanning, but they told us he couldn't make it. He was all apologetic, but he's Bret Hart, right? Then I found out what happened. He had visited a kid in hospital years earlier and the kid was telling him how he was going to graduate from high school. And Bret promised him that, on that day, he would be there. And it turned out that that Monday was the day the kid was graduating."

Among the game's most revolutionary features are its Challenge scenario and the Custom Wrestler options. The Challenge feature allows the player to control a single wrestler and work their way up through the randomly-seeded rankings, while the amazing Custom option allows players to assemble their own grapplers out

## Sean Igo

PSX Development, Sound

**Wrestling Persona:**
"Professor Evil" (A Snidely Whiplash sort of melodrama villain with the opera hat, cloak, green skin and curly moustache)
**Finishing Move:**
Tie Opponent to Railroad Tracks, nyaah-hah-hah!!!

**"Adding [new features] to code that has been stable for months is like pulling out and sticking in bits of a house of cards, because anything new may break something the whole game depends on."**

of a wide inventory of body and head types. "It's really hard to set up the foundation for something like that," concedes Huntsman. "We generated so much artwork, you can do just about anything you can conceive of with that Custom feature."

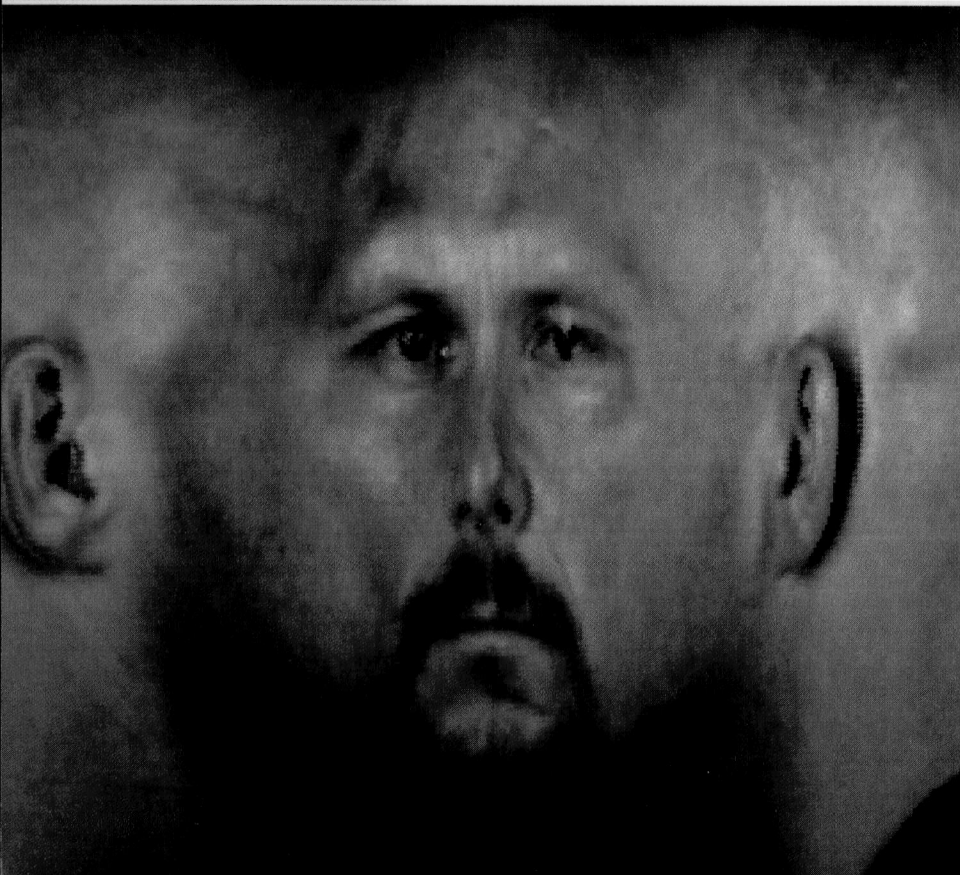

The entire team is high on this project. "We have worked really hard at making our wrestlers look spectacular. We have worked really hard at making our motion run at a really high speed. A lot of praise really belongs with the Iguana guys," Archer insists. "I can sit and draw up move lists from now to kingdom come, but if you can't get it into the game, you can't get the button combos and you can't edit it correctly, what good am I?"

"A lot of guys on the Iguana Salt Lake team are really into wrestling," Huntsman notes, "so it's been a lot of fun. It gives us that extra level of enthusiasm, the inspiration to try a little harder to get that cool move in there."

Archer has been astounded by some of the game's development as it nears conclusion. "It's an aggressive game. It was an aggressive concept. But when you see what Iguana is doing, it's incredible. The last time I visited Salt Lake City, they were working on a Moonsault. This time out, they've got the Moonsault and a Shooting Star Press" — one of the most eye-popping moves in pro wrestling — "and a Senton Splash. I'm even toying with the idea of giving the Moonsault to Mankind — just because I think everybody would love to see him do a Moonsault."

Archer acknowledges that Acclaim is no longer the only wrestling franchise on the block. "This is the first year that we really have competition," he says frankly, "which is healthy. If we didn't have that competition, we might've cut corners. There's some good stuff out there, but I'll tell you what..." At this point, one can almost hear the pro wrestler in Mike Archer as he proclaims: "...this game is going to stomp the crap out of all of them!"

## Backstage Info, Plus More Secrets and Tips Direct from the Game Designers and Playtesters

### Mike Engberg

Original Project Manager

**Q: What was your role in the development of this game? What were your day-to-day responsibilities on the project?**

I was the original project manager on the project but now I am the Director of Product Development at the Iguana, SLC studio. Originally, I helped create the game design and worked with the team to develop a plan on the look of the game and what we wanted to accomplish. I created the original schedule for the game and worked with everyone on the team to help them complete their tasks on time. Currently I work closely with the Project Manager and the other directors to monitor the game's progress and review all aspects of the game, and make suggestions for improvement. We are trying to set a very high standard for quality throughout.

### Jonathan Dansie

Art Motion Editor

**Wrestling Persona:** "The Paladin"
**Finishing Move:** The Wheels of Justice

"I actually dreaded going onto a wrestling project, especially after WrestleMania's format. I really thought it was hokey. Now I have huge respect for the stuntmen who are the best in the World Wrestling Federation. They put themselves through tremendous punishment and keep going with injuries that would stop most athletes cold, all because of loyalty to their fans. I really admire the coordination and talent that it takes to pull all these moves off."

**Tip:** Some moves do huge amounts of damage — pulling off these moves can tip the scales very quickly. A good example is the drop kick (not the most powerful, but easy to pull off). Just make sure not to repeat the same move too many times without doing some other move in between or the crowd will "boo" you and your opponent will have an advantage. If you can time it right you can tie a couple of moves together like drop kick and as your opponent gets up follow it up with a crucifix — these combinations are deadly.

**Q: How tough was the decision to go 3-D with this game? Were there times when you thought maybe you'd bitten off more than you could chew? What difficulties arose, and how were they surmounted?**

It wasn't difficult to decide to go 3D at all. The last two WWF games we did were Wrestlemania and In

**"We had originally planned on having a ladder match in the game, which we ended up dropping."**
**— Mike Engberg, Project Manager**

Your House. We knew that the 2D game had run its course and we were really excited about moving into 3D. We had finished JAM Extreme and were working on Fastbreak so we had a good amount of 3D sports experience and knew that we could do the game. One of our biggest challenges was in creating as realistic wrestlers as possible, and at the same time being able to keep the frame rate up with four of them on the screen at once. We didn't want to sacrifice gameplay and speed or look, which was a huge challenge.

**Q: What would you say are the main differences between the N64 and PSX versions of the game? Which platform posed which challenges in terms of game development?**

The most noticeable difference between the two games is the lack of grudge match FMVs (full-motion videos) on the N64. They don't add a lot to gameplay, but for true WWF fans they are a real kick in the pants. The N64, because of its graphics hardware, certainly has an edge in look over the Playstation, although we are using virtually the same art on both platforms. We have added two different game modes to the N64 which were possible because of the lack of load times using the cart(ridge).

Originally, we knew we were going to have a ton of announcer speech for the game and we worried about how much we would be able to fit onto the N64. However, we were able to develop some amazing compression code that is allowing us to put almost all of the announcer audio onto the N64 so that it will be very difficult to tell the difference between the two games.

**Q: How is War Zone different from a standard fighting game? How did the developmental mindset differ?**

We really like the popular fighting games here such as Tekken and SoulBlade and wanted to try and be a crossover game between current wrestling games and fighting games. We didn't like the overly simplistic button combinations of most of the popular wrestling games, and felt that we could add more depth to the game by making it easy to pick up but hard to master. We feel as though we've come pretty close to accomplishing that, with lots of little strategies that the experienced player will learn.

At the same time, the game is definitely a wrestling game. It's different from a fighting game in that the majority of moves that you perform are linked moves, where you grab the opponent and throw him or try and make him submit. You can do moves from so many different positions, behind him, at his feet or head when he's on the ground, from the turnbuckle, off the apron, etc. There are just a lot more situations that you have to plan for than in a traditional fighting game.

**Q: What surprised you most during the making of this game?**

The difficulty of taking motion capture and applying it effectively into the game. It was much more time-consuming and required much more editing to give it the punch that we wanted than I had expected that it would be. However, I do feel as though we ended up with some of the best looking motion in a wrestling game to date.

**Q: What part of your work on this project are you most proud of?**

I'm really proud of the level that we took the look of the game to. If you compare our wrestlers with any other wrestling games' wrestlers out there you will see what I am talking about. Most other games' wrestlers look like cartoon characters with bodies made of marsh-

# MOTION CAPTURE TECHNIQUES

P.J. Walker and Dr. Tom Pritchard, in full Motion Capture gear, record one of hundreds of wrestling moves for the game. First P.J. sets Dr. Tom up for a Backbreaker...

... then he hits game producer (and former pro wrestler) Mike Archer with a Leg Drop...

...but in the end, Mike and Dr. Tom get their revenge!

together. We went to an enormous amount of work to make our wrestlers instantly recognizable to any WWF fan. I am also extremely proud of our Custom Wrestler feature. You can make so many wrestlers with this feature and it just makes it so that the game allows for thousands of different, very cool wrestlers.

**Q: Were there aspects of the game that didn't quite work out, or that couldn't be finished in time? If so, are they planned for a future Acclaim wrestling game?**

We had originally planned on having a ladder match in the game, which we ended up dropping. Originally, the ladder would be stuck to the center of the ring and the first wrestler to climb to the top and get the belt would win. You wouldn't be able to actually move the ladder around or use what we really wanted to do was drop this game mode and do it right in the next game so that it would be like a true WWF ladder match. So our hope is that in the next game we will have a really cool ladder match where the wrestlers can do all sorts of things with the ladder.

**Q: Were you a wrestling fan at all before this project? If not, have you become one? If so, has it changed your perception?**

This is my second wrestling game and I've come to really appreciate the athleticism and entertainment value of the wrestling. I've met several of the wrestlers who are in the game, plus Vince McMahon and Jim Ross. I really respect their work ethic and what they put themselves through for their sport. Once when I was out to record Vince and JR, we were capturing sound effects on a practice ring and the wrestling trainer taught me how to fall to my back on the ring mat, which I tried. Man! Talk about ringing your bell. I don't know how those guys' bodies stand up to the punishment they must take!

**Q: Name one specific**

It was a challenge to make it work like I wanted because of the way we texture the 3D characters. There were a lot of pallette issues, load time issues, etc. that made it difficult. But I'm really happy with how it turned out and feel like it ended up being very close to what I originally envisioned. That's really a testament to the team, because they are the ones who made it happen.

**Q: If you were a pro wrestler, what would your persona be called? And what would your finishing move be?**

After taking that one bump I know better than to ever try to be a pro wrestler.

**Q: Any special tips for players of the game?**

Keep an eye on your name's color changes!

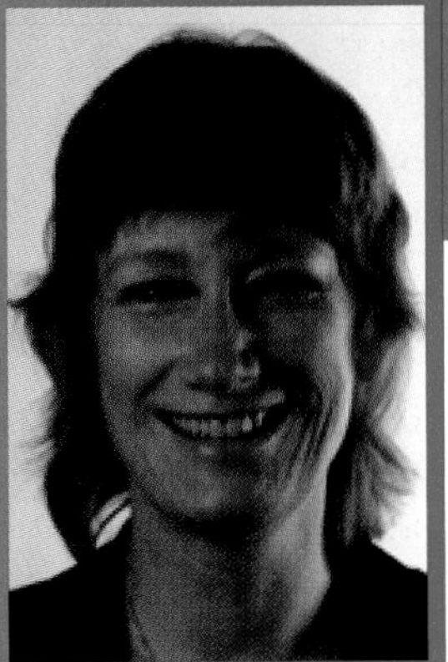

## Jane Bradley — Lead Artist

**Wrestling Persona:** "Big Red"
**Finishing Move:** Right Kick to the Solar Plexus

**Q: What was your role in the development of War Zone? What are your day-to-day responsibilities on the project?**

I was lead artist on the War Zone game. I was responsible

al stage to finish. I was also responsible for modeling, texturing and implementing the soft-point information we used in creating the characters. Paul Boyle and Dan Whittington also worked with me in this area.

**Q: Was this an N64-friendly game or was it a battle to get all those 3D animations working on the N64?**

All that we have done here has required a great deal of hard work. However, I believe the result was definitely N64-friendly in the end. It all looks great on the N64.

**Q: What was the hardest part for you?**

The hardest part is probably the conceptual stage. This is where the major decisions about how the game will look are made. It is also the most enjoyable part, because there is a great deal of creativity involved on all of the artists' part.

## Dan Whittington

Artist

"Through this game, I had a chance to make people and the wrestling environment look as real as possible. Creating realistic artwork is what I live for. The mix couldn't have been better for me if they had tried."

## MOTION CAPTURE

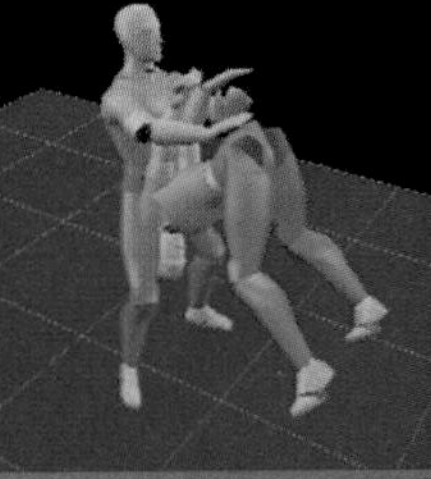

Once the moves have been captured, it's time to use simplified digital wrestlers (with only minimal texture-mapping) to test them and work out the bugs.

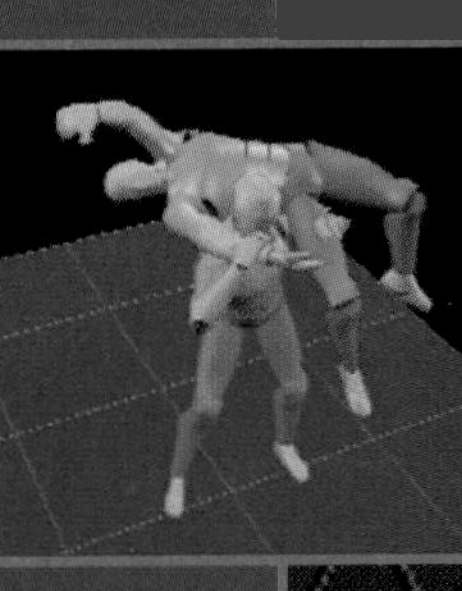

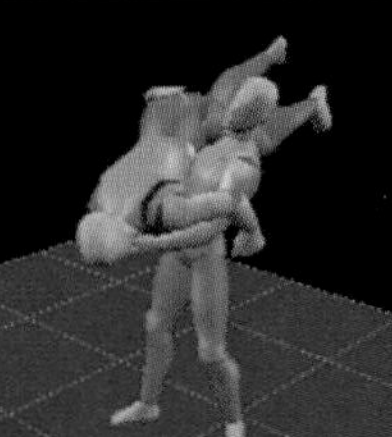

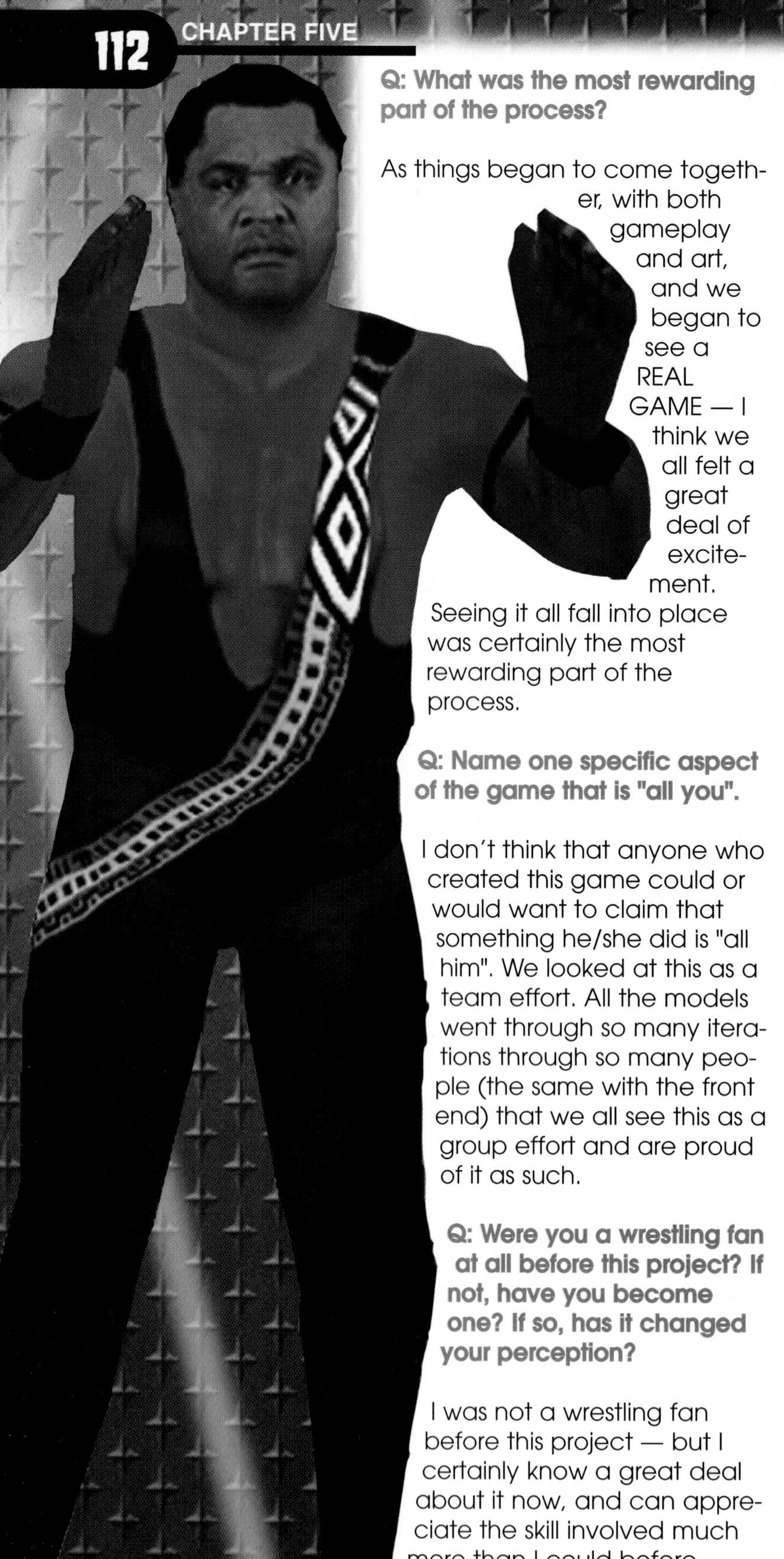

**Q: What was the most rewarding part of the process?**

As things began to come together, with both gameplay and art, and we began to see a REAL GAME — I think we all felt a great deal of excitement. Seeing it all fall into place was certainly the most rewarding part of the process.

**Q: Name one specific aspect of the game that is "all you".**

I don't think that anyone who created this game could or would want to claim that something he/she did is "all him". We looked at this as a team effort. All the models went through so many iterations through so many people (the same with the front end) that we all see this as a group effort and are proud of it as such.

**Q: Were you a wrestling fan at all before this project? If not, have you become one? If so, has it changed your perception?**

I was not a wrestling fan before this project — but I certainly know a great deal about it now, and can appreciate the skill involved much more than I could before.

## Mark Ganus

— Audio Manager

**Wrestling Persona:** "The Dark Viper"
**Finishing Move:** The deadly and feared Triple Ankle Gnaw

**Q: What was your role in the development of War Zone? What were your day-to-day responsibilities on the project?**

As manager over audio, I'm responsible for all the sound issues (quality and content) that involve this development house. My daily tasks generally range from keeping the sound team focused and productive (easy, as they are self-motivated and professional animals, er, people) to engineering audio for both platforms and converting War Zone's data for the N64.

**Q: What would you say are the main differences between the N64 and PSX versions of the game? Which platform posed which challenges in terms of game development?**

For sound, it's PSX's huge storage (the CD), CD quality audio, but limited RAM, versus the N64's speed for compression, lesser RAM issues, but limited ROM. For the PSX, there were two big challenges: (1) Dealing with the massive amounts of audio to be developed, processed, scripted, and programmed, and (2) Managing the PSX's sound RAM to have the appropriate sounds either resident, buffered, or streaming off the CD. For the N64, it was the challenge of compressing unheard of amounts of commentary and sound effects onto our cart(ridge), allowing us to reduce much of the repetitiveness found on most cartridge-based sports titles.

**Q: What surprised you most during the making of this game?**

The really aggressive sound requirements of the game. I believe I can say that of the forty or so titles that I've developed sound for, this is the most audio intensive game I've worked on!

**Q: What part of your work on this project are you most proud of?**

Managing the fine balancing act between quantity and quality.

**Q: Were there aspects of the game that didn't quite work out, or that couldn't be finished in time? If so, are they planned for a future Acclaim wrestling game?**

There's never enough time or opportunities for getting in the final-final-final recording session with the talent. We're planning more 'field trips' to catch the wrestlers while they work — should be fun!

**Q: Were you a wrestling fan at all before this project? If not, have you become one? If so, has it changed your perception?**

I've been a part of several of the WWF series games, so to me, "WWF" often means Working Weekends until Finished — so it's hard to separate my involvement. But actually, I've gotten to learn more about the characters and their stories — which makes the sport much more interesting. I think the true fans of wrestling will be in for a treat with War Zone.

**Q: Name one specific aspect of the game that is "all you".**

I think when Mankind taunts: "I'd love to put you out of your own misery ... but I'm having too much fun!" really says it all for me.

**Q: Any funny stories during the development of this game?**

None that are legal. But I do remember the team stripping the Project Manager naked and throwing him out into the parking lot with bells around his neck and a bullseye painted on his ... oh wait ... that was during my previous project.

**Q: Any special tips for players of the game?**

Sound is tied into the play mechanics, so get the crowd onto your side. But I really hope there's not any odd button combos that evoke weird sounds ...

## Dean Morrell

— Lead Sound Designer/Technician

**Wrestling Persona:** "The Flaming Garbage Disposal"
**Finishing Move:** Top Rope Overhead Hanging Reverse Weiner Lock (a brutal submission hold)

**Q: What was your role in the development of War Zone? What were your day-to-day responsibilities on the project?**

I'm the lead sound designer/technician for this project. It's been my job to gather, edit and prepare sounds to go in the game. From there, I'd convert the sound for the Sony and/or hand it over to Mark Ganus to be converted for the N64.

**Q: What would you say are the main differences between the N64 and PSX versions of the game? Which platform posed which challenges in terms of game development?**

From the audio perspective, the biggest difference is obviously the amount of storage on the CD versus the cart(ridge), but there are also some other issues that go along with that. Any sound in the cart can be played instantly with no delays, but when you deal with sound on CD-based game, you have to plan things out more carefully. If you don't plan it well, then things like seek times and sound memory restraints will play havoc with you.

**Q: How is War Zone different from a standard fighting game? How did the developmental mindset differ?**

Again, from the audio point of view, this is the biggest game we've ever done. With over 4,000 sounds on the PSX and right around 1,000 on the N64, it's taken a lot more time for us to do them right.

**Q: What surprised you most during the making of this game?**

Learning how much fun it is to record and direct the wrestlers. It was pretty nervous about it, and didn't really know what to expect. I found out that they really are professional, easy to work with, and a lot of fun.

It was also really surprising to learn how loud some of my co-workers could yell when we recorded the catcalls and crowd chants.

**Q: What part of your work on this project are you most proud of?**

That would probably be the

---

**SUPER SECRETS**

## BELCHES

**Beat the Challenge with Mosh or Thrasher on any difficulty level, and you'll hear belches and burps instead of grunts during the wrestling matches! That'll teach those guys to tank up on root beer before stepping into the ring...**

---

## Dave Christenson

Artist

**"For me (the biggest challenge) was creating the custom wrestlers. Each wrestler consists of 18 different textures (head, chest, back, upper arm, lower arm, hand, thumb, etc.) So when we had to create 6 different races, both male and female, with 3 different body textures (muscular, hairy and normal) we ended up creating hundreds and hundreds of textures. We also created 5 unique heads for every race for a total of 50 different faces. I also created unique color palettes for each texture so that the player can even adjust the lightness or darkness of the skin tone."**

**Tip:** There are some really cool cheats for the custom wrestler. You can make yourself into about anything from a skeleton to a 400-pound woman in a bikini!

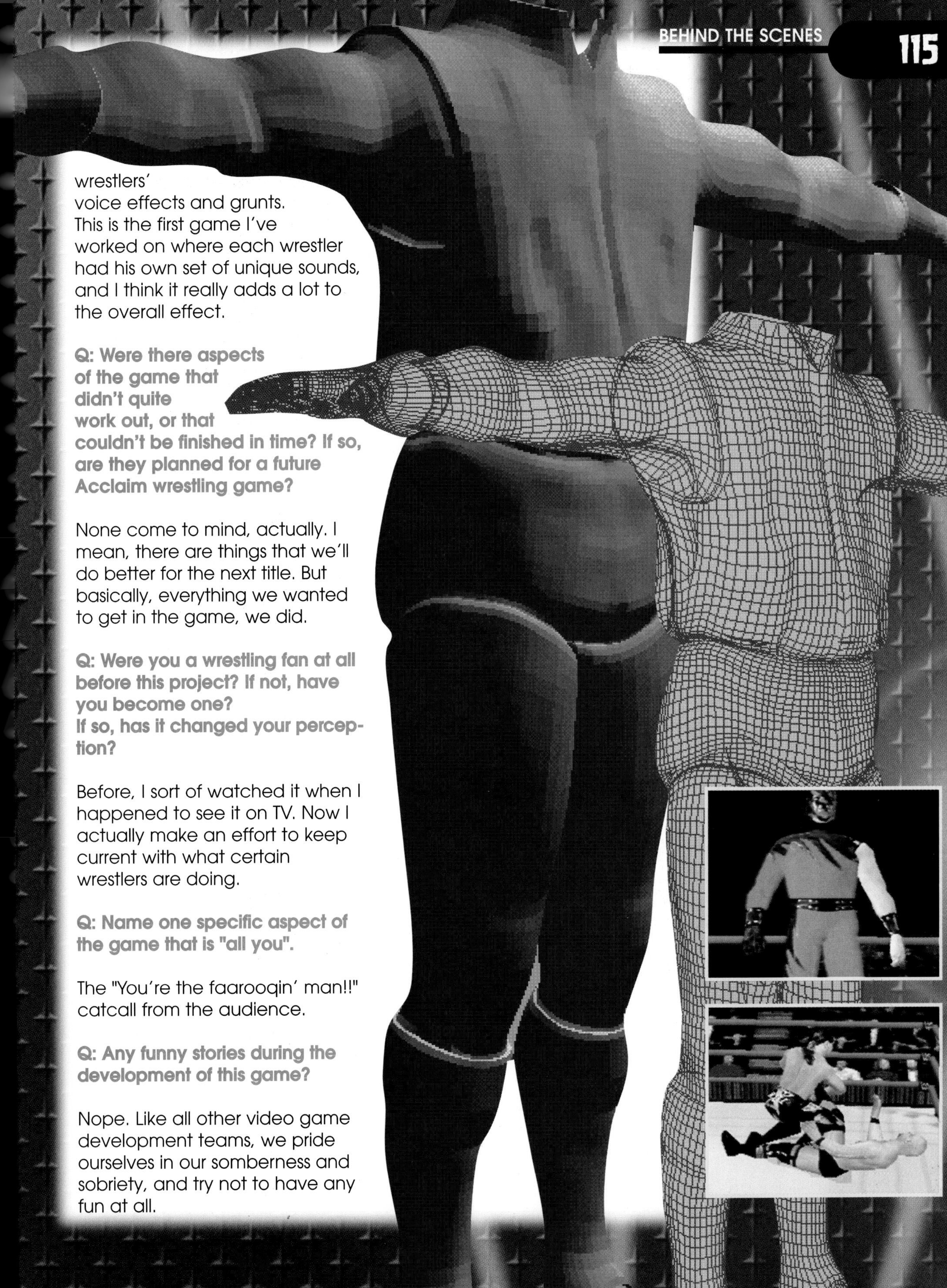

wrestlers' voice effects and grunts. This is the first game I've worked on where each wrestler had his own set of unique sounds, and I think it really adds a lot to the overall effect.

**Q: Were there aspects of the game that didn't quite work out, or that couldn't be finished in time? If so, are they planned for a future Acclaim wrestling game?**

None come to mind, actually. I mean, there are things that we'll do better for the next title. But basically, everything we wanted to get in the game, we did.

**Q: Were you a wrestling fan at all before this project? If not, have you become one? If so, has it changed your perception?**

Before, I sort of watched it when I happened to see it on TV. Now I actually make an effort to keep current with what certain wrestlers are doing.

**Q: Name one specific aspect of the game that is "all you".**

The "You're the faarooqin' man!!" catcall from the audience.

**Q: Any funny stories during the development of this game?**

Nope. Like all other video game development teams, we pride ourselves in our somberness and sobriety, and try not to have any fun at all.

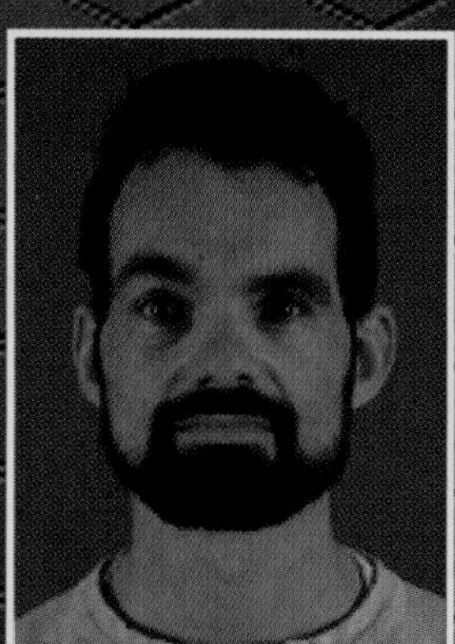

## Scott Pugh

N64 Development

**Wrestling Persona:**
"The Mallard" (The outfit would be full body tights, shiny black and green, so that its color would resemble a mallard duck)

**Finishing Move:**
The Flying Splash

**"The soap opera part of wrestling is interesting, but it's the awesome athletic moves that get my attention."**

**Tip:** Beware of Goldust as a tag team partner.

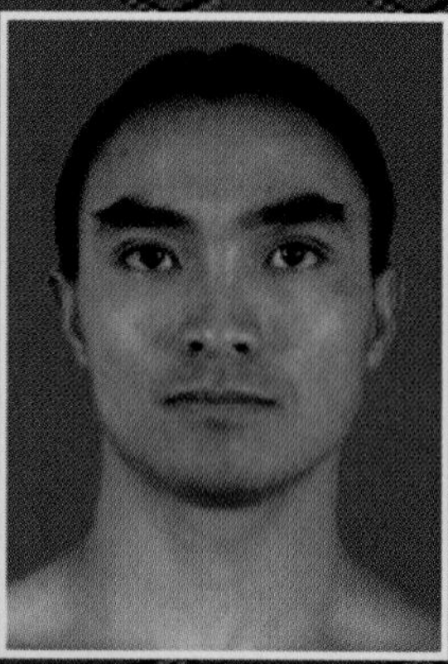

## Lee Phung — Artist

**Wrestling Persona:**
"Kubla"
**Finishing Move:** DDT

**"I had to work closely with the artists and programers to make sure my textures fit correctly with their 3d models."**

Except for maybe the time we plugged in the belching and farting noises in place of the grunts.

**Q: Any special tips for players of the game?**

Do your homework first, and for heaven's sake, change your shirt.

ACCLAIM PRESENTS THE OFFICIAL

TUROK

# ENTERTAINMENT MAGAZINES

**Only $4.95 each!**

**Available in Comic Book specialty shops and wherever Magazines are sold**

TUROK
OFFICIAL COMIC BOOK MAGAZINE

EXCLUSIVE!!
·COMIC!
·INTERVIEWS!
·TIPS, TRICKS AND TOYS!

September '98

ADON
OFFICIAL COMIC BOOK MAGAZINE

MACK

October '98

**Each 64 Page Official Turok Magazine features EXCLUSIVE Game Tips and Hints for Acclaim's Turok 2: Seeds of Evil video game and also:**

- **All new comic stories featuring Turok and Adon**
- **Interviews with Turok 2: Seeds of Evil video game developers and testers**
- **Previews of the Turok toy line from Playmates Toys**

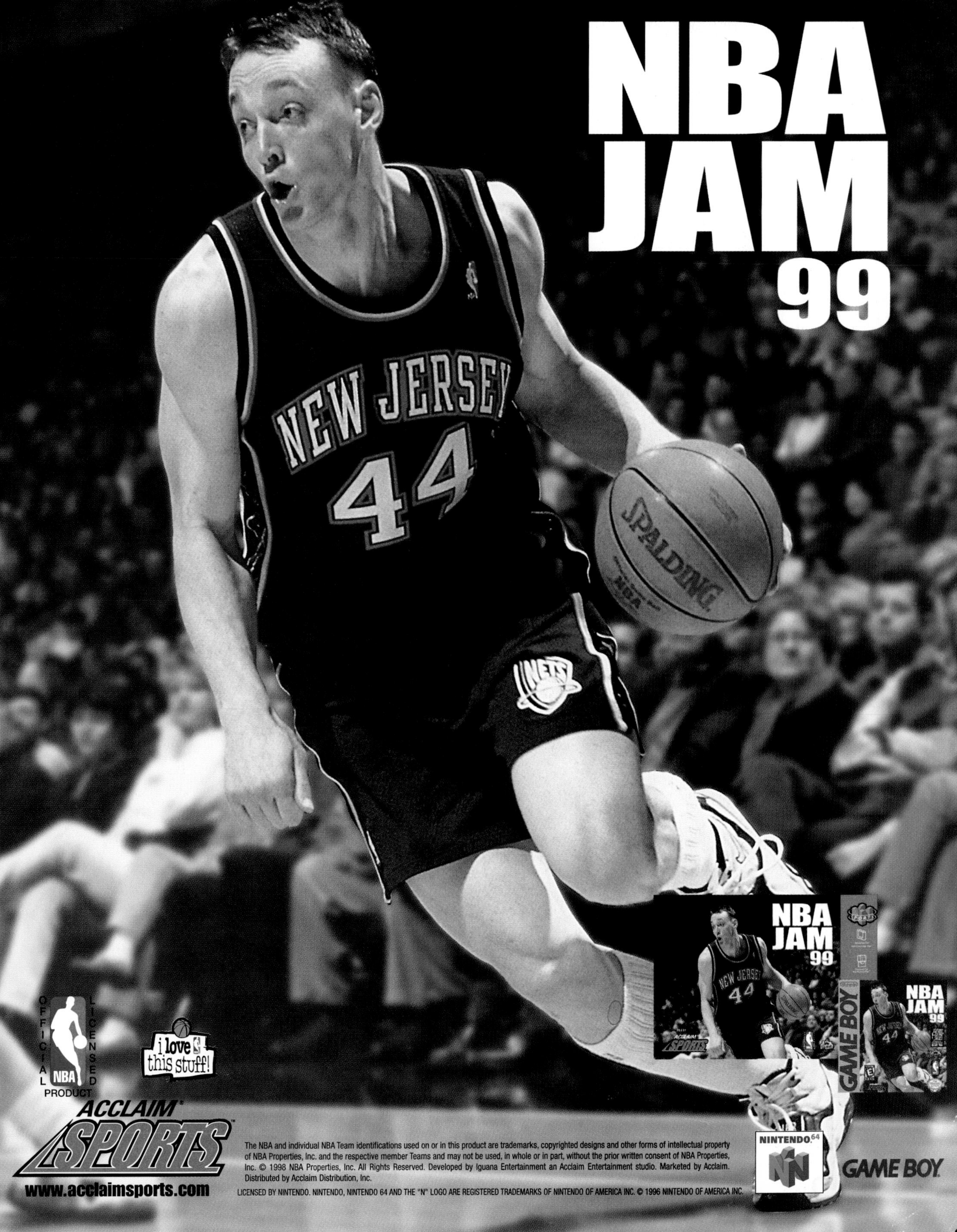
NBA
JAM
99
NEW JERSEY
44
SPALDING
NBA
NETS
NBA
JAM
99
NEW JERSEY
44
GAME BOY
NBA
JAM
99
OFFICIAL LICENSED NBA PRODUCT
i love this stuff!
ACCLAIM
SPORTS
www.acclaimsports.com
The NBA and individual NBA Team identifications used on or in this product are trademarks, copyrighted designs and other forms of intellectual property of NBA Properties, Inc. and the respective member Teams and may not be used, in whole or in part, without the prior written consent of NBA Properties, Inc. © 1998 NBA Properties, Inc. All Rights Reserved. Developed by Iguana Entertainment an Acclaim Entertainment studio. Marketed by Acclaim. Distributed by Acclaim Distribution, Inc.
LICENSED BY NINTENDO. NINTENDO, NINTENDO 64 AND THE "N" LOGO ARE REGISTERED TRADEMARKS OF NINTENDO OF AMERICA INC. © 1996 NINTENDO OF AMERICA INC.
NINTENDO 64
GAME BOY

TUROK®